A Lasting Gift

Sandra L. Cronk at her home in Princeton, NJ,
August, 1977

A Lasting Gift

The Journal and Selected Writings of Sandra L. Cronk

edited by
Martha Paxson Grundy

foreword by
Parker J. Palmer

Quaker Press of Friends General Conference
Philadelphia, Pennsylvania
with
The School of the Spirit

Composition and design by David Botwinik
Cover photography by David Botwinik

ISBN: 978-1-888305-84-5

Library of Congress Cataloging-in-Publication Data
Cronk, Sandra Lee, 1942–
   [Selections. 2009]
   A lasting gift : the journal and selected writings of Sandra L. Cronk / edited by
Martha Paxson Grundy ; foreword by Parker J. Palmer.
      p. cm.
   Includes bibliographical references.
   ISBN 978-1-888305-84-5 (alk. paper)
   1. Cronk, Sandra Lee, 1942—Diaries. 2. Christian life—Quaker authors. I. Grundy,
Martha Paxson. II. Title.

BX7795.C825A25 2009
289.60973'09045—dc22

                              2009032020

To order more copies of this publication or other Quaker titles call
1-800-966-4556 or on the world wide web at www.quakerbooks.org

It is so easy to talk of all the grand theories of spirituality. Yet our lives often take us to another reality. That other reality shatters the idol we constantly rebuild of a life full of great experiences of God. Those experiences are sometimes given. But I sometimes think the opposite experiences are the most important because they bring us out of dependence on our mastery of the spiritual life and throw us in all our frailty toward growing dependence on God (not "growth" in the spiritual life).

— *letter from Sandra L. Cronk, December 26, 1985*

Contents

Foreword

I met Sandra Cronk in the spring of 1978 at Pendle Hill, the Quaker living-learning community near Philadelphia, where I was working as dean of studies. Sandra (or "Sonnie," rhymes with Bonnie, as everyone called her) had applied for a position on our teaching staff. Sonnie's scholarly résumé was impressive. Her work on the Old Order Amish and Mennonites, which had won her a Ph.D. in the history of religions from the University of Chicago, would be of real value to our program. But I knew that teaching at Pendle Hill required more than scholarship.

Pendle Hill is an adult study center that gives no grades, keeps no transcripts and awards no credentials, a school where teaching is all carrot and no stick. People come to Pendle Hill as students because they are on a quest for meaning, sometimes precipitated by a personal crisis. Our best teachers had knowledge and skill, to be sure, but they also had the knack of connecting with people, of "speaking to their condition" in ways that are not much valued in conventional academic culture. A Pendle Hill teacher who lacked a certain charisma—the strange attractor that kept students coming back for more—would soon be teaching to an empty classroom. Or so it seemed to me.

As I interviewed Sonnie, I wondered if she could fill the bill. She was formal, reserved and retiring in a way that reminded me of academics who were more at home in the library than the classroom. The ill-health that (as I later learned) had plagued her since her teenage years had also taken its toll: she was wan and gave the impression that she might tire easily.

I was a robust thirty-nine-year-old who had not yet been much tested by life. Headstrong in my opinions, and ignorant of how wrong first impressions can be, I had serious doubts whether Sonnie was a good match for us. But that decision was not mine alone to make. Because Pendle Hill took "life together" seriously, the hiring process involved a grueling series of individual and small group interviews with virtually every sector of the community.

In an essay called "Learning to Listen," Sonnie writes about how exhausting these interviews were for her and how she wished that our vocational discernment could have taken a quieter, more centered form. "The interview process," she wrote, "was an amazing feat of endurance." I, too, found the process vexing, but for quite a different reason. As a young dean of studies, over-full of myself, I wanted the power to make decisions like this all alone!

As grace would have it, the communal process served Sonnie and me and everyone concerned wonderfully well. A collective wisdom emerged that outweighed my reservations: wiser heads and hearts helped me understand that Sonnie's "retiring" nature had more to do with spiritual centeredness than academic awkwardness. A gentle, thoughtful and prayerful person, she was a classic example of still waters running deep.

So Sonnie was invited to join the Pendle Hill teaching staff, and my concerns about her quickly disappeared as she began impressing our students with the same qualities that had won her the job: authenticity, integrity, congruence, an intellectual and spiritual depth from which one benefits simply by being in its presence.

As I look back on Sonnie's decade of devoted work at Pendle Hill, I find that I do not have many stories about her, and that does not surprise me. Sonnie was not the kind of person whose life creates public stories. Her Pendle Hill years were spent in thoughtful teaching, confidential counseling, quiet colleagueship, and centered prayer. Sonnie was called to deep and meaningful service of other people's souls—a vocation that attracted scant attention in the public world but had life-changing personal consequences for those she served as a teacher and spiritual guide.

In her very person, Sonnie taught me much about the priority of being over doing. If that sounds like an abstract philosophical lesson, please know that, for me, it is not. As I near age seventy—having lived a life of active doing, of wanting to "make my mark"—I am acutely aware of an impending day when I might lose my sense of meaning because I can no longer "do" but only "be." So I think back on what I learned from Sonnie's personal witness, knowing that what she taught me is a lesson I need to relearn.

As I do so, I find myself deeply moved by her last words—at least, the last words in her journal—which I record here exactly as they were written:

> I do not feel a need to find more of me, meaning, insight, direction, purpose. I do not feel a need to share. Sharing is often on this level—insight demanded by friends. This is a great burden we put on ourselves—process of self growth[,] individuation. A chance to be. Sleep if tired,

Clearly, Sonnie was tired, as one is at the end of life. Clearly, she was claiming "a chance to be" over against all the energy we put into "finding ourselves," and I find it reassuring that even Sonnie needed to relearn that lesson. None of us needs to find "more of me," because we are already found by God. Sonnie helped me learn that truth, and I am very grateful for the fact that she reaffirms it with her final written words.

I am grateful as well for the remarkable fact that Sonnie's journal ends with a comma, a punctuation mark that signifies a pause between parts of a sentence, a signal that there is more to come. Whatever that "more" may be, Sonnie is now living into it—in the eternal now—as are we all. May she and we rest in the peace that passes all understanding.

— *Parker J. Palmer, author of* A Hidden Wholeness,
Let Your Life Speak, *and* The Courage to Teach

Preface

Sandra Lee Cronk was one of the most quietly influential Friends in the unprogrammed[1] branch of the Religious Society of Friends during the last decades of the twentieth century. Her ministry was to her friends, and also to the Religious Society of Friends. Sonnie, as she was known, was a remarkable teacher and a perceptive writer. She had an amazing gift for spiritual companioning, and a great ability to lovingly listen individuals into a greater state of awareness. She could hear how God was at work in their lives and could enable them to see it, too. She also clearly saw the charism and experience of early Friends and spoke prophetically to the Quakerism she saw around her that seemed to be unaware of its transforming power.

One of Sonnie's gifts was a brilliant intellect that she yoked with a deep spiritual life. She practiced and preached that careful study— of the Bible, monastic life, the traditions of various Old Order sects, Quakerism, Christian thought and life through the ages—can greatly inform and strengthen one's walk with God. She cared deeply about the Religious Society of Friends and understood its original unique vision or gift, and how liberal Friends in the last half of the twentieth century were in danger of discarding this treasure for current spiritual fads or individual syncretistic pastiches of interesting and comforting bits and pieces from the larger "market place" of spirituality. Much of Sonnie's writing, especially the pamphlet *Peace Be with You: the Spiritual Basis of the Friends Peace Testimony*, ministers to Friends hungry for a deeper spiritual understanding and life, and calls the entire Religious Society back to our faith-roots. Some of her pieces were published in relatively obscure journals, so it seems right to include them so that they might enrich a wider audience. Part Two of the book contains the text of six articles and papers that are now out of print or difficult to obtain.

While she lived, her family was not aware that Sonnie had kept a journal. After her death her sister Cindy, quite by accident, opened an ordinary, spiral-bound notebook to find a hand-written narrative. The writing ended almost mid-sentence on the last page of the notebook, leading to a determined and ultimately successful search for a second, and then finally a third notebook.

After soul-searching discussions between the sisters Cindy Cronk Nowina and Barbara Cronk Clayton, and the then clerk of the School of the Spirit board Linda B. Chidsey, a decision was made to explore the possibility of making Sonnie's journal available to others. There was some hesitation because in many ways Sonnie was a very private person. But because she was such a wise, dedicated, and gifted teacher it was decided to make available this one final offering to help others along the path towards full acceptance of the all-encompassing love of God. A small committee was gathered to shepherd the process. The work of the committee unexpectedly stretched out for seven years, thus providing time for deeper understanding and healing.

Linda Chidsey's recollection of a conversation with Sonnie helped crystallize the decision. Linda later wrote it down for us:

> I remember a time when I traveled to Sonnie's home in Princeton to share and speak with her about my Minute of Recording in the Ministry in New York Yearly Meeting. As our conversation was concluding, I found myself wondering what Sonnie had been like as a child, a teenager, a young woman; and how she came to Friends. I had always felt Sonnie to be much older than me, reserved in nature, and possessing such wisdom. I remember feeling some reluctance about asking these more "personal" questions, however, I decided to simply go ahead. Sonnie responded quietly and without hesitation and as she did, I recall wondering if speaking about herself was something she did not often do. I believe I must have asked if this was the case, for she replied that usually people came to her to speak the deepest longings of their heart, to share their spiritual journey, to reflect upon how God was at work in their lives. Only rarely did she have the opportunity to speak aloud the experience of God's movement in her own life. It is for this reason I feel it so important that her journal be published and read widely—not only by those who knew and loved her in her earthly life, but by all those who feel the workings of God in their innermost being. In the publishing of her journal not only will her teaching and nurturing ministry continue, now she herself will have the opportunity to be "listened to" in the way she so graciously listened to others during her lifetime.

Traditional Quaker journals give very little outward personal or family information. They are not autobiographies. Instead, because their purpose is to show how God has worked in the life of the Friend (usually an acknowledged minister), they emphasize inward personal experiences. Following in this tradition, Sonnie tells the story of her spiritual formation, and there are many gaps in information about outward events in her life.

Unlike a traditional journal prepared for publication, Sonnie's begins by explaining that it is for her own use rather than for a wider audience. There are intimations later that she also thought perhaps it might be of use to others, but it seems to move back and forth between the intensely personal in a psychological sense and the more broadly heuristic in a spiritual sense. Her father's death and her own illnesses had a huge impact on her life. The second segment of her journal traces the flow and ebb of great grief, compounded by her poorly-diagnosed and poorly-treated illnesses. The third segment is quite different as she struggled with her own declining health and strength. It is difficult to decipher and tends to have sentence fragments and phrases that no doubt referred to external or internal experiences in her life.

Readers will find British spellings and punctuation often in Sonnie's writings. Her sister Cindy Nowina, a Canadian citizen, adopted British spelling some years ago, and her Epilogue retains her style.

We gratefully acknowledge permission to reprint the following article by Sandra Cronk: "Renewal among Unprogrammed Friends in America," from *Friend's Quarterly* Vol. 24 #4 (Oct. 1986) 163–70. The copyright for *Festival Quarterly*, a Mennonite magazine that stopped publication in 1996, is held by Good Books (www.GoodBooks.com). We are grateful for permission to reprint five articles from *Festival Quarterly*: "Learning to Listen" (Winter 1987), "Learning to Listen," part 2 (Winter 1988), "Substituting Activities for Community?" (Summer 1988), "Discovering and Nurturing Gifts and Ministry" (Winter/Spring 1989), and "Finding A Useable Past" (Fall 1989). We thank the Tract Association for allowing us to reprint five quotations from *Peace Be with You*. We appreciate permission from the family of

Sandra L. Cronk to quote from Sonnie's book, *Dark Night Journey*. We acknowledge with gratitude permission from Woodbrooke to quote from its Logbook, 1985, entries by Annette Wallis and Peter Ivory. We are grateful to Kathryn Damiano not only for permission to quote from her early description of the School of the Spirit Ministry, but for her insights and reflections on Sonnie's ministry. Thanks, too, to these individuals who graciously gave us permission to reprint excerpts from Sonnie's letters to them: Larry J. Peacock, Methodist minister who had been a Pendle Hill student in 1984, the letter written by Sonnie to him and his wife Anne, dated 12/26/1985; Ronald T. Pinheiro for letters from Sonnie in September 1989, and Sr. Kathleen Flood, O.P., for Sonnie's letter to her dated Sept. 9, 1999. We are also grateful to the following people for permission to quote from their letters to Sonnie: Allison Randall, dated April 3, 2000; Kathryn Nowina, April 3, 2000; and Sally Palmer's condolence letter to Margaret Cronk, April 14, 2000.

— Linda B. Chidsey
Marty Paxson Grundy
Ellen Michaud
Cindy Cronk Nowina
Pamela Nowina
Frances Taber
Eastern USA and Ontario, Canada, April 2009

Introduction

Many lives have been touched by Sandra Cronk's writing, teaching, spiritual direction, and mentoring. Her life gives witness to a profound understanding of a life lived in Christ. It, along with her teaching and spiritual companioning, provides a model for individual lives and raises a prophetic voice to the corporate body of the Religious Society of Friends.

Her personal journey—and then the trajectory of her teaching and writing—moved from an emphasis on outward work to bring about God's Kingdom to the critical importance of inward transformation, and finally to a life simply resting in God. Not only is the example of her spiritual journey of use to others struggling along that same path, and not only are her published writings filled with intellectual power and spiritual insight and clarity, but the context of her ministry within the Religious Society of Friends is also important. She struggled against the "death of God" and the secularization of Friends' social and peace action, inviting Friends to reclaim our original charism. In her journal Sonnie recorded the anguish she felt as she began to know experientially the spiritual depth and richness of earlier Friends' faith and practice, and to see the gap between what she was finding and what others in her meeting held. They seemed so oblivious to the great banquet available, and so content with their few small crumbs.

Sonnie was born in Syracuse, New York, on November 29, 1942. Like most children, at an early age she had an innate sense of God. She tasted the early joy, the simple, pure experience that comes before it is crowded out by a need for "intellectual explanations for relationship with God."[2] That pure experience was strengthened by a loving and Spirit-infused Sunday School teacher at the local Presbyterian church that her family attended in DeWitt.

During junior high school, however, her religious education teachers were unable or unwilling to answer her probing questions, and she found the adult services disappointingly devoid of the immediate knowledge and presence of God she had known as a young child. Balanced between hope and disillusion, she set about to find a spiritual home.

In 1960 when Sonnie was seventeen, the family moved to Princeton, New Jersey. While in high school Sonnie suffered the first of several lengthy and debilitating illnesses. Her younger sister Cindy remembers Sonnie crying as she struggled to get ready for school in the morning. If Sonnie was finally able to make it, Cindy would sometimes see her sister crying by her locker because she felt so awful. Frequently, she had to leave school. Unfortunately, Sonnie's suffering—constant pain in her joints and back, extreme fatigue, nausea—was compounded by the unhelpful response of a medical establishment that only just now, a half century later, is beginning to pay attention to this particular constellation of symptoms.

Sonnie graduated from Princeton High School two years later, and was admitted to Western Reserve University in Cleveland, Ohio. Realizing that religion was a constant and compelling theme in her life, she chose it for her major. While in college she found a Quaker meeting and felt she had "come home."

The Years in Cleveland

Sonnie was accepted into membership in Cleveland Meeting on April 3, 1964.[3] Although she had joined the Religious Society of Friends and was majoring in religion, God increasingly became an intellectual concept for her rather than the living reality she had known as a child. She was moving into a well-recognized stage of spiritual growth characterized by Enlightenment rationalism.[4] College was a time of questioning, of clinging to that which could be logically understood and defended. She became skeptical of the meaning and purpose of Christian (or any religious) language, symbols, liturgies, and explanations. At the same time she demanded that any religion worthy of its name be deeply concerned with peace and justice.

Cleveland Meeting was caught up in the controversy over the Vietnam War. Sonnie's younger sister Cindy remembers Sonnie talking about her anti-war activities and draft counselling assistance to conscientious objectors. A group of younger Friends pushed to break the law by sending token medical supplies to North Vietnam, while older members of the meeting cautioned against it. Although Sonnie makes no mention in her journal, sometime in 1965 a group of mostly young families split off and formed a separate meeting that did send a package of medicines to North Vietnam.

The choice of yearly meeting with which to affiliate also engaged Cleveland Meeting at this time.[5] Ohio Yearly Meeting (Conservative) was overtly Christian, mostly rural, and seen as old-fashioned. Lake Erie Yearly Meeting and Association was a liberal group, made up of newer meetings mostly near college campuses. The latter would seem to have been more in tune with the stage of spirituality in which Sonnie found herself. But even then she resonated with Ohio Yearly Meeting Friends who "lived in a manner that honored faithful response to God's leadings. The ability to recognize and respond to these leadings grew out of a quiet center of listening and permeated the whole culture."[6] Again, Sonnie makes no mention of this issue in her journal, indicating, perhaps, that she was not deeply engaged with the decision.

A decade later when Sonnie reflected on her college years, she fell into the genre of Quaker journals by writing only about her spiritual life.[7] We learn nothing about her social life, extra-curricular activities, or non-religion courses. We hear nothing about her teaching in Vacation Bible School for the Vermont Church Council in the summer of 1963; nothing about the next academic year when she practice-taught and participated in a child development study under Dr. Benjamin Spock.

We do hear that Sonnie enrolled in a joint bachelor's-master's degree program. Sonnie graduated in June 1966 with a B.A. and M.A., *magna cum laude*, and Phi Beta Kappa. Yet something in her led her to write that "out of kindness they let me graduate."[8] There seemed to be a persistent disjunction between her interior image of academic inadequacy, and the way her professors and others experienced her. She greatly feared academic failure yet was highly successful.

Divinity School and 57th Street Meeting

That fall Sonnie entered Divinity School at the University of Chicago. Her skepticism of orthodox Christianity led her to major in the history of religions. Graduate school was a challenge, but also provided the setting for life-changing breakthroughs that moved her into another stage of spiritual life and understanding. In these years, 1966 to 1977, Sonnie moved beyond her rebellion against orthodoxy through a conversion experience, or series of experiences, that became the "the turning point and base line" for the rest of her life. Her path began to diverge from that of many other Friends, bringing to birth her prophetic message to Quakers.

The theology and religious symbolism that had been an opaque irrelevancy gradually began to reveal deeper layers of meaning. She summed this up later by describing her program as:

> . . . devoted to a study of what students in the field call religious symbolism and ritual, or what most people call religious imagery, language and life-style. I have studied all of the modern world religions including: Christianity, Judaism, Islam, Buddhism, and Hinduism. I have learned about primitive religious traditions whose rich use of symbolism has been especially helpful to many modern people in their search for renewed openness to the symbolism of their own religious traditions. I have also studied methodology, i.e. the helpfulness and hindrances of different ways of studying religion.[9]

As her understanding of religious symbolism and language increased, paradoxically so did her fear of academic failure. Only Sonnie's own journey through the soul's "dark night" brought her to a knowing that nothing—not even her greatest fear—could separate her from God's love. She easily passed her exams and earned a second M.A. in March, 1970, but by that time she had come to realize that the degree was secondary to the goal of her life with God.

Her emerging understanding of her relationship with God was strengthened one week when she was sick in bed and a friend from the Intervarsity Christian Fellowship visited her. Before she left, the young woman prayed that Sonnie "might have a more personal relationship with Christ." The barrier Sonnie had erected "against seeing

Christ as God was the last and greatest barrier that needed to be broken down" to overcome her years of "liberal" wandering and return to that close relationship with God she had had as a child. The prayer was answered very soon as Sonnie came to "the realization that it was Christ—Christ, the Word; Christ, the Jesus of History; and Christ, the Risen Lord" who was speaking to her now in her life.

The final element in what she described as her "conversion" came when she was asked to articulate what she had learned in the past five years. She realized that everything that was happening in her life was leading her somewhere. There were no random events. She experienced this understanding as "an exhilarating experience." It was no coincidence that in the last few weeks of life, she reflected with contentment and gratitude on the path God had created for her in the previous months. Her experience of divine purposefulness and guidance became a theme in her life.

Reflecting on graduate school, Sonnie wrote:

Education is a very important element in my understanding of my own ministry. It is very hard to grow in the religious life without some serious intellectual searching. Through my experiences in graduate school, I am particularly aware of how inadequate an exclusively competitive, academic approach is to religious learning. It neglects the reasons for intellectual work, i. e. the wish to glorify God and become more faithful, creative, and useful disciples. A competitive approach is also likely to create an atmosphere of fear and insecurity so that students are unable to learn and grow. However, my experiences have also taught me the significance of rigorous, in-depth education. Our secular culture often erects barriers to our religious understanding. We grow up ignorant of the Bible. Many of us have never heard the Good News of Christ's love and transforming power. In our culture symbolic language and ritual behavior no longer convey their transcendent meanings. Thus, we are cut off from opportunities for growth. We need to work hard to learn more open ways of perceiving religious symbols so that our religious traditions can speak to us again and so that we can understand the way God is leading us today".[10]

In order to have time to pay attention to God's presence and guidance, Sonnie cut back on her class work and took on responsibilities for religious education at Chicago's 57th Street Friends Meeting. She taught in First Day School,[11] as she had in Cleveland Meeting, and served as co-clerk[12] of the Religious Education Committee. There she bumped up against the human failings of Friends. It was "agonizing" to see Friends' clay feet: committee dysfunction, parental indifference, undisciplined children, rebellion against orthodoxy, and lack of commitment. Her earlier idolization of Friends came crashing down.

But the most difficult and painful discovery was "the astonishing departure from the traditional Quaker message by meeting members." Addressing this became a major theme of her life's ministry.

At first the hostile climate of opinion among most of the Friends she met made her very cautious about raising these issues. Liberal Friends had absorbed "God is dead" attitudes from the wider world of religious thought. (*Time* magazine published an article with that title on October 22, 1965.) As a group, these Friends were happily ensconced in the rational-social action stage of spiritual development. Sonnie realized she had started there but had now moved on. She had changed while many in the General Conference branch of Friends had not.

Sonnie served on 57th Street Meeting's Worship and Ministry Committee from 1972 to 1974. She was only able to serve as clerk, however, for a few months. The pain, fatigue, and nausea that had plagued her earlier in high school reappeared, exacerbated by an adverse reaction to medication. When the medical doctors from whom she sought assistance told Sonnie her symptoms could not exist, she felt demeaned and dismissed. Her physical condition deteriorated to the point that she had to drop out of graduate school for a while. These blows came on the heels of the newly awakened awareness of the gulf between her passionate concern for a deeper Quaker life and the contentment with the rather superficial congeniality that was so widespread among Friends she met. She experienced feelings of worthlessness that threatened to engulf her.

She felt stripped of everything that mattered to her: "meeting, school, friends, a sense of accomplishment. With all taken away there was nothing left to depend on but God."[13] She was forced to reevaluate her idea that a person's worth was bound up in what he or she did or produced, to "stop using the measuring rod which assumes that our self-worth is rooted in our achievement."[14] She came to see that even if she could do nothing to help further God's kingdom, Christ did not withhold his love.

Just as God's love was constant, so was her family's. She had never thought it wouldn't be, but perhaps had taken it for granted. Now it became clear that her family was modeling God's unconditional love. Feeling held in both these bonds of love she was able to acknowledge that she needed to yield still more. She needed to give up her ideas of what she should be or do, and surrender to God's will. This was a recurring theme in her spiritual journey.

A Love of the 'Old Order'

Sonnie had finished her class work and exams at Chicago in the spring of 1974 and returned to Princeton to recover her health and work on her dissertation. The two aspects of religion most persistently appealing to her were community and mysticism. Her illness gave her time to read avidly about religious communities such as the Amish and Old Order Mennonites (known by outsiders as "Plain People"[15]), several Catholic orders, earlier Friends, General Conference Mennonites, Schwenkfelders, Moravians, Shakers, and various utopian groups.

What drew Sonnie to Old Order groups were those elements of communal life and piety that Friends used to have, but seemed to have largely lost. Here, among congregations of Amish, Old Order Mennonites, and River Brethren, as well as Schwenkfelders and Moravians—many of whom she was able to visit—Sonnie was able to touch that which was no longer a vital part of her own Religious Society of Friends. Among these folk she experienced "gentleness, humility, friendliness, warmth and hospitality." They were professing Christians who lived Christ-like lives. Sonnie valued them especially for "what they may have to teach us about the meaning of cooperation, simplicity, self-yielding, communal discipline, the strengths and weaknesses of tradition, the power of powerlessness, and the problems of acculturation."[16] She saw in them the communal aspects of accountability and discipline. Here were people resisting the siren call of individualism in favor of their own deep tradition of building a community that tried to be Christ's body, to model God's kingdom, to practice cooperative, self-giving, simple, Christ-like lives together.

In particular, Sonnie saw the Amish and Old Order Mennonites offering "a distinctive community life that attempts to incarnate the crucifixion experience in daily social life. Their community tries to surrender to God's will even though it brings suffering and pain. They wish to return love for hostility. They renounce the use of coercive and manipulative behavior."[17] She found of great value the Schwenkfelders offering "their grand story of pilgrimage in search of religious freedom and their even grander story of the struggle against the forces of acculturation once that religious freedom was found." The Moravians she saw as presenting "diverse forms of community life within one tradition showing how Christian faith may take different forms depending on the circumstances."[18]

Each of these themes, namely "a distinctive community life that attempts to incarnate crucifixion experience in daily life," "returning love for hostility," "renunciation of coercive and manipulative behavior," "search for religious freedom," "struggle against acculturation," "diverse forms of community life within one tradition," and "Christian faith taking on different forms to meet different circumstances," has resonances that contrasted with the late-twentieth-century reality of the Religious Society of Friends—as well as with many other religious groups. A careful study of these smaller faith communities provides an opportunity to learn something about practices that seem to be weak, fading, or less obviously adhered to among Friends and other church groups. Sonnie chose to study them in depth for her dissertation.

Her studies were helped by the fact that Sonnie was a sympathetic listener. She had studied German, and she knew enough about these groups to ask intelligent questions. But it was her own spiritual path paralleling theirs that cemented her bond with these folk. As one Amish pastor later said, "She told us things about ourselves we were unable to articulate for ourselves."[19] Mennonite Elder John Ruth pointed out what a great thing it is "to set aside one's own faith symbols and metaphors and to learn a whole new language." Sonnie had done this and was beloved for having done so.[20]

In order to "explore the meaning of religious community," Sonnie later explained, she studied "religious development in America with special concentration on the German communities from the radical Reformation tradition." As she wrote later:

> This stream of Christian history has much in common with our Quaker heritage. My dissertation was on the Old Order Amish and Old Order Mennonites. I have also explored other special religious communities in America's past and present including: two Catholic religious orders, the Harmony Society, Amana, Shakers, the Hasidim, and so forth. I have had the pleasure of visiting or living with many of these communities. Each of these groups has something significant to say to men and women who are searching today because they testify that faith is concerned with a transformed way of life not just a personal relationship with God (as extraordinarily important as that is). A transformed way of life means living in new relationships with others. Indeed, God's healing power often comes to us through the love of others. In this way the church-community is the body of Christ in the world continuing His work of redemption. Thus, a loving community is both an aid in our religious journey and an incarnation of the goal of that journey, i.e. God's Kingdom on earth.[21]

The realization that a "transformed way of life" was the hallmark of a committed religious life became a major theme in Sonnie's life and ministry.

Retreats

In addition to community, the other area of religious study that drew Sonnie was mysticism; she longed to experience a more contemplative life devoted to God. She pursued this by trying to take time for a retreat nearly every month of the 1974–75 year. Sonnie had some good experiences, and some that were not very helpful. They all informed her later work in spiritual direction and retreat facilitation. Eventually she developed her own format, which, in recent years, has become a model for Friends' retreats.

The impetus for beginning to write a journal may have arisen out of her retreat experiences in the spring of 1975. Over the Easter weekend she attended a retreat for neo-Conservative Friends at Powell House, the retreat and conference center of New York Yearly Meeting in Old Chatham, New York. Sonnie realized there that she was not called to join with such a separated group of Friends, as they had not separated themselves from the evils they decried. Instead she began to attend the Thursday evening group at Princeton Meeting, where she found Friends demonstrating a "sincere yielding to God's will, to be transformed from our selfish natures to God-centered creatures." In May she attended an individual retreat at Cenacle Retreat House in Highland Park, where she worked with a sensitive and skilled spiritual director. Sonnie went "to the retreat assuming my dissertation and its scheduled work would provide my greatest problem. Instead, I barely thought about it. I thought about where God was trying to lead me in the future." Several weeks after returning to Princeton, she began to write this journal.

When she finished recounting her past spiritual journey and retreat experiences in the journal (summer of 1975), she laid down her pen for over four months. When she picked it up again, the journal began to move forward with entries reflecting on her current interior state and what she was learning from God. She tended not to write in the midst of darkness and struggle, but to wait until there was some new glimmer of understanding to record. During this time she seemed to use the journal not as a therapeutic tool, but to record what God was teaching her so that she could remember, be grateful, and build on the lessons.

The dissertation work weighed oppressively on her. Her early search for possible employment to support herself after her degree was finished, was discouraging. The door to both teaching and retreat work seemed closed. She felt no support for her diagnosis of the ills of the Religious Society of Friends and saw no avenues to work toward healing them. Her desolation would later be purified and sifted to provide the personal experience informing her book on the *Dark Night Journey*.

Through the small details of family life—the little misunderstandings and inadvertent hurts as well as the joys—Sonnie felt she was learning to see herself more clearly, and to relax more confidently, or let go more willingly, into God's love. At this time, too, in the experiences of communal life in a reviving Princeton Meeting, she experienced the joy and blessing that God offers through the gathered body.

Once again she came to recognize the cause of her desolation was at least partly within herself: her own need for a sense of accomplishment. Once more God showed her that peace "comes with the cessation of striving for self-fulfillment." She saw the trap of working in a way that could lead her to dependence on human approval, and devastation at its lack. She needed to learn at a deeper level the irrelevance of social roles and social approbation.

She felt that God was leading her, and that she was being prepared for something, but was not yet privy to what it might be. So when she was asked to serve on several committees, she gladly accepted. In 1975 and 1976 she served as treasurer of the Princeton Interfaith Council Executive Committee. She served on Princeton Meeting's Worship and Ministry Committee from 1975 through 1978, and on Philadelphia Yearly Meeting's Worship and Ministry Committee from 1976 to 1982, serving as clerk of the latter from 1980 to 1982. These tended to be somewhat disappointing experiences, as the groups did not live up to their potential or her hopes for them. Opposition and criticism directed at her, especially when she was clerk, were very painful, and led to her stepping down at the end of her first term.[22]

Pendle Hill

Sonnie finally finished her dissertation[23] and was awarded a PhD in Religious History in December 1977. It was a tremendous relief to be done. Now the question of her employment took on real urgency. Teaching seemed to be the venue through which she could serve God, but she realized that both attentiveness to spiritual life and a rigorous scholarly approach were necessary. So it was with a sense of rightness that she accepted a job on the staff of Pendle Hill, a Quaker study center in Wallingford, outside of Philadelphia.

In her application to Pendle Hill Sonnie spelled out her vision of the ideal that Pendle Hill aspired to, and how it coincided with her own search:

Pendle Hill is devoted to disciplined study and searching in the areas of religious life and thought. The teachers and students live together in a worshipping and caring community. Thus, the study which takes place there is more than an intellectual exercise. It is a personal searching and growing out of the God-centered life and in the art of giving and receiving love. Pendle Hill recognizes that all spiritual searching (indeed, the religious life in general) is a communal activity. It takes place through practical work with others, through sharing one's deepest joys and fears, and, most important of all, through worshipping God together.

In the course of my own spiritual pilgrimage, I have come to share Pendle Hill's understanding of the religious life and its vision of the educational process. I also recognize the great need of Friends and other people of all religious backgrounds to have a place where they can pursue serious religious questions in the context of mutual help, prayer, worship, and in-depth intellectual study. Pendle Hill is unique in its ability to fulfill this many-sided need.[24]

Sonnie started in the fall of 1978 teaching courses on religious community, Old Order congregations, and prayer and contemplation. Later she added courses on Quakerism.

Part of Sonnie's work as a teacher at Pendle Hill was to provide spiritual guidance to a few "counselees" assigned to her. Although at first Sonnie felt terribly inadequate to the task, it became clear that her counselees felt otherwise. Soon other people began to seek her out. However, even before she had begun this work, she had acknowledged the experience and gifts that would in time make her such a gifted counselor:

I am deeply interested in the spiritual pilgrimages we each make in our lives. I feel led to a form of ministry which can help others in their journeys. I became a convinced Friend in my late teens. Today my life as a member of a community devoted to living in the presence of God and trying faithfully to follow His will is the core of my life. Paradoxically, some of the most significant steps in my own journey began after I found my new spiritual home among Friends. Christ's leadings since that time have brought me closer to Him, sometimes through sudden dramatic steps and sometimes through slow, painful steps. His openings have transformed my life. I know something of the pain of the journey as well as its joys. I know the personal crises which may portend death to all that is familiar and dear but which may be preludes to resurrection and new life. I have encouragement and insights to offer others who are also making this journey toward God.[25]

In January 1983 Sonnie transferred her membership from Princeton to Middletown Meeting in Media, Pennsylvania, close to Pendle Hill. She had begun serving on its Worship and Ministry Committee in 1980. Philadelphia Yearly Meeting also used her gifts, on the relatively minor Bequests Committee (1979–86), then as clerk of its Worship and Ministry Committee from 1980 to 1982 (with the painful criticism mentioned above). Being a teacher (1982–86) in the new Quaker Studies Program (QSP), seemed a more appropriate use of her gifts, as she saw it moving Friends toward their early spiritual center in Christ:

> This program has a year-long curriculum which includes study of the Bible, Christian Thought, and Quakerism. Along with these study components is a strong spiritual life emphasis. Each year includes several retreats on various spiritual disciplines (journaling, devotional reading, listening in prayer and worship, etc.). Participants have the opportunity to be part of a "spiritual friendship", i.e. an on-going relationship with another person in QSP which has as its focus the chance to talk together about some of the deeper questions of life and faith we often don't speak about in everyday conversations with friends and acquaintances.[26]

God's Peace

Sonnie's continuing ties with Mennonites had been strengthened by her research at Goshen College in Indiana during graduate school. In 1983 she furthered the relationship by teaching Quakerism and Spiritual Disciplines at Keystone Bible Institute, a Mennonite Church adult study program.[27]

Part of the appeal of Mennonites for Sonnie was that they, like Friends, were an historic peace church. Through her rigorous preparation to teach Quakerism, combined with her own spiritual experience of the reality of earlier Quaker understandings of the Christ Within, Sonnie was led to write about Friends' peace testimony. Perhaps this was an outgrowth of her earlier observation of the separation within Cleveland Meeting, and of knowing folks in four different meetings who had joined Friends during the Vietnam conflict because of the peace testimony. Too often these people were not very interested in a deeper, more committed relationship with God, nor did they understand the spiritual root of this testimony. They worked with passion and diligence for political solutions to war and violence while sometimes expressing impatience with interior personal transformation. This may have been the matrix out of which Sonnie wrote her pamphlet, *Peace Be With You: Spiritual Basis of the Friends Peace Testimony*, which was published by the Friends Tract Association in 1983. A quarter century later this little pamphlet remains the best modern statement of the basis of the peace testimony, firmly rooted in a Christian experience of God's unconditional love:

> Peace comes from God's gift of transforming love in Christ. Peace is both the result of this gift of love and its active expression at work in our lives. Thus, peace is both a goal and a process. Perhaps it is more accurate to say that the goal is in many respects the process. Peace is not just a vision of the perfected order of creation where all creatures live in harmony. Peace is the life-giving acts of love by which Christ expresses his caring for the whole world and by which we, in turn, express our caring for one another. Thus peace is possible not just at the end of time when Christ will be all in all. Peace is possible now in the midst of the tumult and strife, as we become part of the active love Christ showers on the world. This love is not extinguished by pain, bitterness, and violence. It continues in the midst of all our turning away from God. Thus, the peaceable kingdom is never threatened with extinction because of the hurts and wounds of this world. Its presence or lack of presence is never measured by the degree of violence which swirls around us. It is measured by Christ's boundless love which continues to be poured out on us, waiting only for our response.[28]

For those who thought peacemaking consisted only of vigils, letters to politicians, and protest marches, she wrote:

> The fruit of the peace testimony is love manifested in countless ways: refusal to take part in military endeavors, finding a manner of living that does not exploit the labor and resources of others, working for a more just and equitable social, political, and economic order, and sacrificial giving to those in need.[29]

She warned against separating political action from spiritual understanding:

> The root of this peace testimony is deep. It draws its nourishment from the power of God to bring transformation and healing into our inverted and wounded lives, from our deepening experience of Christ's love, and from our willingness to yield our lives to the guidance of the Holy Spirit. Only as this testimony remains rooted deep in its nourishing soil is it able to produce fruit.[30]

She also had words of warning for those who wanted to wait until their inner life was totally in order before venturing to tackle outer problems:

> Our peacemaking cannot wait until we feel completely loving. Feelings are notoriously unreliable guides. We are called to obedient love even though we may not be feeling very loving. Often it is through the performance of loving acts that loving feelings can be built up in us. We may start with small, perhaps very tiny, steps. It is only as we begin to allow Christ's love to act in and through us that it can become a part of us.[31]

She warned that ". . . Discipleship is informed obedience, not naive or ignorant action."[32]

For Friends, she noted, the sticking point is always that:

> Action requires discernment of God's will. Discernment requires that attention be focused on our Inward Guide who speaks to us through prayer, Scripture, the discipline of our Meeting, and the voices of our brothers and sisters in the church-community. From Christ we learn where our lives need healing and where they need re-ordering. We discover what we are called to lay down and what we must take up. We shall probably find that many of the accepted patterns of life in our society are inconsistent with those of God's kingdom.[33]

Her Father's Death

Sonnie's life was shaken to the core by the death of her father, Gary Arnold Cronk, MD, on September 28, 1983. The intensity of her suffering and pain was probably not recognized by her colleagues or friends. She felt that nobody listened to her, nobody walked with her through this deep darkness. It wasn't until two years later, while she was at Woodbrooke, that she was able to write about the devastation she experienced. Her account is very personal, illustrating an essential process of healing through telling the story of the events and their impact. A hospice nurse has described it as a marvelous essay on grief.[34] It is all there: the shock and initial numbness, the lack of energy and sense of purpose. It is not easy or comfortable to read such intense, private grief. At the same time we may find that doing so holds up a mirror to our own experience—and it may tell us things we've been unable to articulate for ourselves.

Readers may be shocked that Sonnie refers to her father's death as his "crucifixion." The initial context for this language seems to be early Friends' practice of "taking up the cross daily." They knew the inward, formational experience of having their self-will "crucified" and the Spirit of Christ resurrected within them. They also knew that this needed to happen every day in the myriad details of daily life. Sonnie saw the morning of her father's death as "his crucifixion—his ultimate giving up of all that he had and was."[35] Gradually the crucifixion as a symbol became increasingly meaningful far beyond the horror of death. Through it all she sensed God's loving presence, guiding and teaching her.

Sonnie's grief was compounded by her own worsening physical condition. The normal enervation of grief was added to her already high level of fatigue. The usual bewildering and debilitating stress of loss came on top of the stress of her own deteriorating health. Once more she had physicians who did not listen, were not helpful, and insisted on treating their small area of the human body (this time her thyroid) without regard to the whole person. She suffered tremendously, and possibly unnecessarily. Up until this point Sonnie had written very little about the details of her physical suffering. With the luxury of retrospection, she tended to emphasize what she had learned through illness. But now the pain and distress were fresh and ongoing, and what knowledge and wisdom might come was not yet apparent.

Sonnie seemed to handle her crises with apparent outward strength, resolutely fulfilling her responsibilities to Pendle Hill and her consultees or counselees.[36] Fellow teacher Sally Palmer later wrote of Sonnie's inspiring example, remembering "how many times I watched her teach classes even when she was terribly ill."[37]

Moving Forward

Healing began with a return to her grandmother's house in upstate New York in August, 1984. With the first anniversary of her father's death, she noted the gradual lessening of the physical debility, nightmares, and overwhelming waves of grief. But still she felt there was no one who was willing to listen *her* into a deeper healing, as she was listening to others.

The new academic year at Pendle Hill in the fall of 1984 did not bring a cessation of stress. There was the paper work of settling her father's affairs, and caring for her mother. Increasing amounts of spiritual direction were added to her work load. People sought her out, and she deeply, tenderly listened to each. She joined a little group organized by fellow Pendle Hill teacher Kathryn Damiano to discuss spiritual direction or guidance within the Religious Society of Friends. How could they explain what it was about, since there seemed a fair amount of ignorance and even resistance to the idea of "direction"? They finally settled on the term "spiritual nurture," which has caught on rather well.

In addition to the more overt sources of stress, Sonnie was beginning to feel some discontent at Pendle Hill. She always had to teach at what increasingly felt like an introductory level when she longed to do some solid scholarly research. She also recognized a budding leading to commit what she had to say to paper so that it would be part of a larger ongoing dialogue. The publication of her pamphlet, *Peace Be With You: Spiritual Basis of the Friends Peace Testimony* gave her new confidence.

Profound grief carries the burden of depression with its attendant characteristics, which Sonnie experienced to the full. Part of the suffering that she was experiencing also seems to have been the "dark night," the "*via negativa.*" This is a stage or pattern in the spiritual life perhaps better understood by earlier Catholic mystics (such as John of the Cross) than by modern Protestants. She came to learn experientially that this:

. . . is a time when we may experience the absence of God, the stripping of previous ways of making sense of our lives, and an emptiness that is often painful and confusing. Strangely, the dark night may come after a time of special closeness to God, when there has been vibrant meaning and a feeling of fullness of life. The dark night is a time when we are invited to let go of the gifts of God for the sake of a more intimate knowledge of the Giver. It is a time also when, in letting go of previous patterns of life, we can be repatterned by the One who works in secret and beyond our control.[38]

But these insights had not yet fully matured. In time they would result in her book on the *Dark Night Journey*.

Through the length and detail of Sonnie's catalogue of stress we get a sense of how overwhelmed she felt by her health issues, her workload, and the unexpected fragility of her heretofore sturdy and dependable family network. The need grew for her to get away, to take a sabbatical, to have time to reflect, do some scholarly research, and restore her soul. For reasons that are not clear, the Pendle Hill administration decided to send her to Woodbrooke, the British Quaker Study Center in Birmingham, England, as part of a "teacher exchange" rather than the true sabbatical that she longed for. Typical of her approach to life, Sonnie used the heavy-handed arrangements to explore how deeply she meant the internal pledge she had made when joining the Pendle Hill staff: to "treat the requirements of community life as my monastic superior." "The demands of my job would be my way of practicing obedience to God rather than my own will." It was not easy, adding another layer of stress. She realized that "much of the force of those negative feelings was coming from my woundedness, not health. And it was inappropriate to make decisions out of brokenness rather than God's desire for wholeness." She submitted with remarkably good grace, and in the end the year came together much better than she had dared dream.

A Glimpse of Ministry

Before she left for England, Sonnie took time in August 1985 once again to retreat to her grandmother's house near Syracuse. There she could escape the stresses of Pendle Hill and Princeton, and retire to the quiet of a room of her own not shared with her mother. She looked forward to the slower routine of her grandmother's house, enveloped in the "nice comfy, homey experiences of family love and caring." Her "time of deep rest, recuperation, and reflection" started with a mystical experience of her father's healing touch on her shoulder as she was walking one afternoon. It seemed so real she turned around to see who was there. From then on the frightening and debilitating physical symptoms began to subside.

As usual on her August visits to "Gram," Sonnie took along some reading that she wanted to do for herself. In a little booklet from Steve Mercer at the Bruderhof she found advice to go beneath the ego level of self-will to rest in that place of desiring to be in harmony with God's plan for our lives. The willpower of keeping a discipline was inadequate. Only by her aligning with God's will could God remove the "crippling thoughts" that imprisoned her. Eventually she came to understand, once again, the importance of letting go the need to control her spiritual path, because "we do not choose a path. We experience the path as given. Walking in trust, along the path that is given, is our way of saying yes to God."[39]

Another book, *Woman Wrapped in Silence* by John W. Lynch, led her to more fully imagine and live into Mary's experience at the foot of the cross, to "face more squarely what Mary had faced—the fact of death. She did not flinch and turn away—overwhelmed by horror. She stayed near the cross. And now rehearsing all the things I had felt regarding my father's death, I found I was able to stay at the foot of the cross for the first time myself."

Sonnie felt the parallels with her own grief, and was enabled to accept the pain. "Standing at the foot, Mary was given to John and John to her. Suddenly I realized this is what had happened to me." As Mary had been given as mother to John, so Sonnie was given to others as "mother, sister" and spiritual counselor. She realized her ministry of spiritual direction grew out of her experience of pain. She discovered her "rightful place was simply to be there in pain and trust that God would do what God would do." The crucifixion took on deeper meaning, resonating with and illuminating her own experience.

In the fourth week of her stay in upstate New York, Sonnie had a breakthrough experience of God's love. Walking along the towpath, with the sun piercing the clouds, she saw with new eyes the park that was partially built over an old dump. Seeing God there she knew her ministry was "there in the dump becoming park. . . . The power of the pain to cripple was taken away. A glimpse into my future ministry was given."

Woodbrooke

Shortly after her August in Syracuse, Sonnie and her mother, Margaret (Gartner) Cronk, went to Woodbrooke. During the fall term Sonnie taught a class on spirituality entitled the "Downside Up Kingdom." A Woodbrooke student explained the title: ". . . often misfortunes and tragedies in one's life may be providential—just when all is confused, upturned and overthrown and lost, then God is most at work. In the USA, packing crates are labelled 'This side up'; but for people being called by God, at times it is as if the directions on the outside should read, 'Downside up,' as the confusion and upendedness are just right."[40] Another student wrote that Sonnie:

> . . . has been a quiet member of the Woodbrooke community but her course has affected many of us deeply. She shared her insights in a way which showed a particular gift for words, words in which she helped us reach extraordinary depths in what would normally be regarded as a private area—the relationship of oneself with God. She seems not to have got tangled up in definitions, but in a remarkable way to have 'spoken to our condition,' despite our being a large and varied group.
>
> When I first went, I felt, How daring to try and talk about these things in a lecture setup! We were speaking of the *Dark Night of the Soul* in our most recent class, and Sandra herself said that it was audacious, and that it might be better to have an hour of silence together instead. In fact I found that, following her talk I had to go away and be silent on my own. . . . I certainly found her course a profound help—a sort of bridge between where one is and the direction in which one is yearning to go.[41]

Sonnie and her mother returned to Princeton in the winter to catch up on paperwork, then went back to Woodbrooke for a short series of lectures in the summer term. Although the resources for research Sonnie hoped to do were unavailable at Woodbrooke, she was able to use the time to write. The second segment of the journal stops here, while Sonnie was still at Woodbrooke.

Encouraging Others to a Deeper Life in God

Sonnie had long since moved out of the rational approach of her college years. Finally others began to move away, too. In the larger Christian world of North America a new interest in mysticism and spiritual life developed and spread. Friends were not immune. From the charismatic movement sweeping through Ohio Yearly Meeting (Conservative) to a fascination with Eastern, Native American, New Age, and other forms of spirituality in Friends General Conference circles, there was a heightened interest in deepening the spiritual life. Among unprogrammed Friends the renewal was strengthened through "new forms of teaching ministry, revitalisation of the work of vocal ministers and elders, and expanded uses of silence as a way of listening to God."[42]

Sonnie's own efforts through her example, quiet suggestions, committee work, and especially through her teaching in the Quaker Studies Program, joined with efforts of other Friends to encourage this renewal. Over the next few decades the movement would gain strength, nurtured by a wide variety of programs and initiatives. Sonnie's eventual participation in forming A Ministry of Prayer and Learning Devoted to the School of the Spirit became a major contributor to the renewal.

But Sonnie was not blind to the work remaining. She noted that the:

> . . . most difficult parts of renewal are still ahead of us. We have not yet recognized all the places where we cling to our own strength instead of to God. We have yet to face the challenge to our individualistic notions of religious life and have not accepted the centrality of mutual accountability in our meetings. We have not recognized fully the challenge to our comfortable ways of living demanded by our testimonies on peace and social justice.[43]

There was also resistance. Not all "liberal" Friends welcomed the new acknowledgment of Christian roots. Some resented a shift away from an emphasis on social action through political change. A number of Quakers clung to the idea that toleration for a wide variety of beliefs and even non-belief is the "core value" of Friends, and they dug in their heels against any threat to Quakerism defined as "whatever you want it to be." Perhaps most important, as Sonnie had noted, there was a deeply ingrained and stubborn strain of individualism that strongly resisted any move toward accountability to the community, or shift of power from individual to the body. In 1997 she wrote in a letter to a Friend, "Do you have a sense that there may be a backlash against a number of Quaker leaders just now? Quite a few people have mentioned deep difficulties. I wonder what is happening, perhaps something more than individual circumstances."[44]

Searching for a Quakerism more faithful to its original vision and the desire to define Quakerism as an umbrella under which very diverse beliefs and practices could find a tolerant home marked the fissures and struggles within the more liberal branches of the Religious Society of Friends for the next quarter century—and probably will continue to do so for far longer. Sonnie saw this, and made herself available as a tool for divine use in inviting Friends and others to go deeper into an obedient relationship with God through Christ.

In her hunger for a vibrant community of faith, Sonnie continued to reach out to groups of Plain People who still had strong communities. She wrote in her journal of her interactions with the few remaining Shakers and the Hutterian Society of Brothers. The Mennonite journal, *Festival Quarterly*, asked Sonnie to "reflect on issues in her church that are of particular concern to Mennonites— practicing spirituality in silence as a group, learning to forgive, cultivating leaders and looking to the past for guidance."[45] She wrote five articles that were published between 1987 and 1989. Although written for the Mennonite community, they contain observations and wisdom for Friends. They are reprinted in Part Two of this book.

In June, 1988, Sonnie participated in a colloquium on work at the Mennonite Brethren Bible College, Winnipeg, Manitoba. Her paper on "Work in Anabaptist/Mennonite Thought and Experience" was reprinted in *Old Order Notes*. She was asked to write an entry on "Ordnung" for volume V of the *Mennonite Encyclopedia*, published in 1990.[46] The following year she wrote a review, "The Mennonite Encyclopedia V: A Record of Paradigm Shifts" for the *Mennonite Historical Bulletin*.

Sonnie participated in an annual Quaker Theological Discussion Group [QTDG] gathering focused on atonement. Her comments were published along with the papers in *Quaker Religious Thought* in the spring of 1986.

Sonnie resigned from the Pendle Hill staff at the end of the spring term in 1989. She longed for an opportunity "to read, write a little, and just be."[47] She hungered for both more scholarly study and a chance to teach a deeper level of the issues dear to her heart: religious community, Quaker faith, the reflection or fruit of that faith in Friends' daily lives, and contemplative living. She felt that God was leading her towards new work, and wanted to be open to follow wherever God might lead her.

Prayer had always been an important part of Sonnie's life. Now she felt increasingly drawn to contemplation. She also continued to have health issues. She was "feeling terrible" with what her physician assumed was "a thyroid condition. But a new doctor diagnosed a severe case of anemia which, unbelievably, escaped detection earlier."[48]

In her journal Sonnie frequently alluded to people seeking out her listening presence. They were drawn to her wisdom and love. She was able to hear how God was at work in these lives, and draw the individual forward.[49] Much of the wisdom Sonnie gained in this work is summarized in her "Spiritual Nurture Ministry Among Friends," presented at the Quaker Pastoral Counselors & Chaplains Conference in 1993. As Sonnie observed to one person, with words that will echo for many, the greatest teacher will continue to be:

> . . . your own life with its ups and downs, its dry periods and oases. There is something very moving about that. It is so easy to talk of all the grand theories of spirituality. Yet our lives often take us to another reality. That other reality shatters the idol we constantly rebuild of a life full of great experiences of God. Those experiences are sometimes given.

But I sometimes think the opposite experiences are the most important because they bring us out of dependence on our mastery of the spiritual life and throw us in all our frailty toward growing dependence on God (not "growth" in the spiritual life).[50]

In the two years after Pendle Hill, Sonnie was able to write and publish two important pieces. She put in writing her growing understanding of the role community had played in the formation of Quaker spirituality in *Gospel Order: A Quaker Understanding of Faithful Church Community*, which was published as Pendle Hill Pamphlet #297. Her study of Christian contemplatives who travelled the classical *via negativa*, such as John of the Cross, combined with her own hard-won insights into the dark night of the soul, led to her publication of *Dark Night Journey: Inward Re-Patterning Toward a Life Centered in God*. One reviewer called it "a knowledgeable and sensitively drawn map for those who travel through the dark night and for those who seek to be their spiritual friends and nurturers."[51]

A Ministry of Prayer and Learning Devoted to the School of the Spirit

The contemplative-educational opportunity for which Sonnie yearned began to take shape. For several years she and Kathryn Damiano had been spending increasing time in prayer and contemplation. A vision began to emerge of creating an opportunity for Friends to gather for study, prayer, and transformation. Sonnie and Kathryn approached Middletown Monthly Meeting in Media, where they were both members, with the idea of offering programs in spiritual nurture and contemplation. Friends may not have fully understood, but they encouraged the women to proceed with what eventually became known as A Ministry of Prayer and Learning Devoted to the School of the Spirit. Kathryn drafted a description of their shared vision, from which the following paragraphs are taken:

> This ministry arises from two concerns. The first is a recognition that God is leading some Friends to a life centered in prayer as an active witness in the world. (This leading parallels the way in which God calls

certain Friends to work in such areas as peace and social justice.) This call to prayer is not a privatized or withdrawn life, but a life lived with God and shared with others. Prayer opens us to God's presence and draws us into Christ's work of healing the broken and wounded places in our lives and in our world.

The second consideration grows out of the awareness that many people, both inside and outside the Religious Society of Friends, have been yearning for avenues through which they might explore, more intentionally, the role of prayer and contemplation in a life of faith. Many Friends have also expressed a need for doing serious reflection and study on ministry and the call to live in faithful relationship with God. They would like to do this work within the context of a community of prayerful commitment.

Friends have always seen the connection among the inward life, religious community, and service in the world. Faithful living has entailed a balance of all three of these aspects of our faith. . . . Maintaining a true balance among these three aspects of our commitment is one of the most important and revolutionary witnesses Friends can make in our world today.[52]

The General Secretary of Philadelphia Yearly Meeting advised them to find a place in which to hold their school. But while still in the early months of feeling out the shape of this new ministry, they met Sr. Constance FitzGerald, O.C.D. (a member of the Baltimore Carmel), who advised them to pray rather than look for real estate. Pray for two years. This felt right to Sonnie and Kathryn, and as they settled into this discipline other teachers joined them, including Frances Taber and Virginia Schurman. The ministry came under the care of Philadelphia Yearly Meeting's Worship and Ministry Committee, and Kathryn received a grant from the Lyman Fund that enabled her to spend more time organizing the new endeavor.[53]

Programs began in late summer, 1991. "Contemplative Living and Prayer," taught by Sonnie and Kathryn was started with a long weekend at Pendle Hill, then the class met at Middletown Meeting one Saturday a month for an entire year. "On Being a Spiritual Nurturer" was an intensive, ten-month course that began and ended with a five-day retreat at Our Lady of the Angels convent, and met for a weekend each month in between. The core teachers were Sonnie, Kathryn, and

Fran Taber, enriched by a large roster of visiting teachers. After offering "Spiritual Nurturers" twice as a ten-month course, it was stretched out over two years. A short course on the prophetic tradition was taught by Patricia Loring, another Friend brought into the ministry.

The School of the Spirit (SOTS) answered a deep hunger among some Friends, and the "Caregivers," "Contemplative Living and Prayer," and "Spiritual Nurturer" classes, along with other offerings of the School, began to have a leavening effect on the meetings and yearly meetings from which the participants came. It provided a learning opportunity for students, teachers, and board members. Linda Chidsey served as clerk of the School of the Spirit board for eight years (from the late 1990s) during the tumult and struggle as it matured into a clear understanding of its role in support of the ministry.

The Shift into Being

Sonnie began to write in her journal again in November 1997. The third segment is very different from the first two. Now the careful construction of sentences took too much effort. Her entries are fragments of ideas, short-hand jottings of her internal experiences. Some are a bit cryptic. The intervening years are not described. We are moved from the beginnings of the School of the Spirit to a time when Sonnie felt confronted with three implacable "givens." One was the inward pull of the Divine; another was her mother's declining ability to care for herself. The third was Sonnie's own deteriorating physical condition. Fortunately, Sonnie was now receiving spiritual nurture/ direction, which was very helpful as she threaded her way among competing outward demands, decreasing energy and stamina, and the quiet incessant inward pull of God.

Returning to Princeton and living under her mother's roof perhaps reinforced the emotional habit of being the dutiful daughter. In whatever ways she experienced the change, Sonnie found herself at a crossroad, and struggled with what appeared to her to be the path laid out for her. Caring for her mother, who was gradually slipping into dementia, was both something she wanted to do and something that devoured her time and limited energy. Although years earlier she had deliberately chosen not to follow a domestic path, now she undertook caretaking and homey tasks as a kind of spiritual discipline, confident that she would find God within her shrinking horizons.

If it is true that each of us is given only a few spiritual lessons to be learned, Sonnie once again struggled with the notion that outward accomplishments are the measure of a person's worth. She noted that after a decade at Pendle Hill and the current course of SOTS she did not feel that she or her work were appreciated. Was this analogous to her disjunction about academic qualifications when she was a student? Was it a reflection of the reticence of Friends to speak words of praise and gratitude?

Taking care of her mother meant having to give up things she loved, including study and perhaps teaching. Sonnie grieved their loss, or potential loss, likening it to a kind of death. She wasn't ready to "retire" but it was physically impossible to continue full time with the School of the Spirit, work with a number of spiritual directees, and also give her mother the care and attention she needed.

Sonnie made a list in her journal to help sort out her priorities, possibly to discuss with her spiritual director. A life of prayer was central. Next came care of her mother. She felt released from participation in the major SOTS course on spiritual nurturers, along with the mentoring she had been doing. She also felt released from "accompanying" or spiritual companioning, even if those with whom she was working continued to want her. Increasingly she felt called to be with God and began to find fewer and fewer words to offer to others in this regard. She still loved to study as a spiritual discipline and as preparation for teaching, and she still loved to teach and write. But having written down all this in a list, she realized she could not do it all. If she cut her ties with SOTS to care for her mother as long as Margaret lived, she worried if she would ever be able to get back into teaching. How would she support herself? What would she identify as her career, her work, her purpose?

In early 1998 she wrote, "I can't believe nurture to institutions is vital," perhaps reflecting her frustration with both SOTS and the Religious Society of Friends. But a dozen days later, she wrote, "I still believe in ministry to institutions"—this time defining the institution she was ministering to and supporting as the critical one of family.

Even during this difficult period, there were times of great joy. Sometimes—in meeting for worship, in spiritual nurture conversations, or by herself—she was filled with gratitude and a sense of God's loving Presence. But there were also depressing times of tedium, self-doubt, and exhaustion.

In this time of "being," Sonnie discovered that intercessory prayer was changing so that she no longer felt moved to bring an individual or situation to God; God was already there. She was experiencing the inward movement from active doing to prayer, and then simply to being. This further step on the spiritual journey has been described in some of the classic spiritual literature. It culminates in an internal shift to the sure knowledge that simply being is all that is required or desired—being oneself in the presence of the unknowable, beloved, unfathomable, intimate, loving Presence. Sonnie responded to this new Life within her by cutting back on most of her teaching responsibilities.

As the months passed she continued to grieve her inability to study, and wondered if she was to give up teaching entirely. There was a sense of being relegated too early to aging and illness—and fear that without her ministry at this point, SOTS might disintegrate. In October 1998 she once again agreed to be a core teacher in the next spiritual nurturer course, delighting in teaching and being involved again. This would be the final two-year course with the original three core teachers.

Pulling Back

From their days at Pendle Hill through the establishment of the School of the Spirit, Sonnie and Kathryn had been yoke-fellows. They both felt drawn to a ministry of prayer and study, worship and teaching, in community with each other. As their paths began to diverge, tensions arose. There is pain in change, especially if one's close friend and companion is the one who is changing. Sonnie wrote to Kathryn:

> . . . your exciting, expansive journey reminds me of my time at Pendle
> Hill. That path is what I felt called to leave (despite its wonderful

qualities) when we started the School of the Spirit Ministry. So for each of us the journey of the other does not speak in a personally helpful way. We miss that mutuality of years gone by. We cannot be spiritual companions in the same way right now. It is genuinely not helpful for either of us. I think it would be good to recognize that and let it be.[54]

In February, 1999 Sonnie wrote an open letter to the board of the School of the Spirit trying to describe to Friends her situation. It included her resignation from future Spiritual Nurturer Programs, while intending to finish the second year of the present course, and hoping to continue with the Contemplative Living and Prayer offering. It summarized where God had led her, and the new life that she felt beckoning. Her own clear and careful words describe the experience that appears more inchoate in her journal. The latter no longer was being written in a clear narrative, and included her little missteps, misgivings, and grieving. The letter represents her mature reflection on where God had led her, and her response:

[Going back to 1997:] This was the first year that home required extensive attention. I tried to carry on both "jobs," home and School of the Spirit. It was an enormous undertaking. I don't think I've ever been in a situation that demanded so much from me. I wanted to do it. It felt like a sacrificial gift. It brought joy to me in the giving. The work done during that year gave us a foundation for our Spiritual Nurturer and Contemplative Living Programs now. . . . I did not want our work to suffer because of my new obligations. Looking back I suspect that some of the change in my path began then and I did not recognize what was happening. Unfortunately, as the months have gone by, I have been able to do even less than I did then. . . .

CALL TO PRAYER. Let me go over some of the changes in my path which I can better articulate now than I could then. It was in this "year from hell"[55] that the new, deeper prayer experience was coming into my life, an invitation from God to be in God's presence. It obviously was not the result of any special thing that I was doing. It was simply a call from God, in many ways an answer to the prayer we had prayed through all the history of the School of the Spirit to be able to enter more fully into a life of eremitical prayer. As I said in our board meeting, I feel the word "prayer" hardly gathers up the call. Prayer sounds like an undertaking we accomplish, whereas the call is simply to be with God. It is a way of being and living, not a special task. It is an on-going response to God's invitation. . . .

While one element of this new call is a deeper sense of relationship with Christ and with God, another dimension is the move away from "talking about" the spiritual life. This call does not look for new insights and understandings in books or even my own meditations. I seem to be moved away from study and reflection toward simply being with God. I am often stripped of words, concepts, images. By living into God's Naught (on one level), I turn more fully to God alone. I see that this stripping has been going on for some years. (For example, you will remember the times I have talked about satisfaction being stripped from the teaching experience.) But I still experience this change as new and sometimes confusing, even though the eremitical path has been a central call in our ministry. If people ask how to find God, I find Silence inside to offer them, for this is the place of God. I can no longer *automatically* be a person of spiritual nurture or companionship through words. The words simply are not there. Those who have known me primarily as spiritual nurturer continue to define me as they had known me in the past. Their expectations follow suit. They can be disappointed in the new me. To help myself understand, I think of the desert fathers' story of the visitor to the desert who goes to one hermit and finds no special welcome. The hermit continues to pray and the visitor joins in. The next day the visitor goes to another hermit who stops his prayer provides a warm welcome and a big feast. Later the visitor says each hermit's response was equally useful. I find myself as the first hermit, not out of any choice, but out of the reality of what I experience in my life. . . .

Generally when people want [the second hermit's] kind of response on the phone or in person, there is inside of me only Silence. I begin to experience these requests as grabbing the spiritual life, forcing it to come forth in words, a violation of my heart and God's work.

This is part of the reason I have decided not to go on with the Spiritual Nurturer Program after this offering concludes. . . . I do not know how long this leading will remain. [Kathryn and I] have both walked this pathway enough to know that sometimes one is called into a hidden place, rich in silence. Other times one is called out to share with the world. So I do not presume to know what God will call forth in the future. . . .

As I must deal with issues of aging, death is inevitably one of them. Close to the experience of death are the experiences of resurrection and ascension. But in a larger sense, it makes no difference where one begins the journey with God. One is taken to crucifixion, resurrection, ascension, creation, incarnation. Oneness with Christ brings us, through him, to each of these experiences. This has been powerful, freeing, and a pathway to God. My path does lead to a small outward circumference during this season of my life. Yet the whole world, the whole cosmos is in God. In that relationship one is related to all creatures and all of creation.

Interestingly, I discover that it is harder to find support in leadings that look small, than in grand things . . . we tend to ignore people who do what is small in our eyes. . . . My experience has brought me up sharply about some contemporary unanalyzed patterns in spiritual nurture work, including my own.

HEALTH. Another issue is my health. As you know, part of the change in my path comes because of decreasing energy and strength and because of a new attitude on my part toward my health. I've struggled with these issues all my life. In earlier years I've made the decision to grit my teeth, concentrate on work outside myself and try to do often more than was really comfortable. On one hand, this involved a kind of self-forgetfulness and involvement in the world which God often asks of young adults. On the other hand, it also probably represented a bit of overcompensation that many people with physical limitations make. I think God moved in my work and commitments. I draw much sustenance from what I learned during those years, now when I am not able to do as much. As part of my new maturing in the spiritual life I feel that this pattern of activity is no longer appropriate. I need to come to terms with who I am and accept God's love and acceptance of me. . . .

You often ask for some clear guide about how much I can do. My best estimate is that we have a window of opportunity to do these Contemplative Living and Prayer programs. These programs are closer to the work God is doing in my life these days. They are also less physically demanding than the Nurturer sessions. I think my health will make it this round. . . .

I continue to use, as much as I am able, the daily pattern I developed some years ago. That is, my active work takes place in the morning. The afternoon is for rest and quiet activities. . . .

HOME. Of course, a big change in my path arises out of my work at home with Mom. . . . As we know, life often is not fair. Life simply is. . . . I have had to make a choice, on the practical level, to look for God in this change, and much to my surprise (woman of little faith that I often am), I find God richly at work. The home has become like a monastic enclosure for me. The path centered in the home is what allows the prayer to flourish. I have had to learn how to love another in a way I have not before. I still have a long way to go in this work.

I find myself looking at other elements of fairness, too. I would not have been able to participate in the School of the Spirit ministry at all during these past years except for my mother's generosity, providing food and allowing me to live in the family home rent free. My sisters and my mother agreed to find a way for me to undertake the ministry work I felt led to do. I would not have been able to do that if I had to take a bread and butter job and do our work. For many years all my energy was directed outward. My mother helped me by doing all the home tasks and often spending hours collating, stapling, putting stamps on envelopes, etc. So I (and the School of the Spirit) owe her a great debt.

I know this change affects [Kathryn's and my] relationship very much. My new work is full-time. There are very few bits of time left open. . . . [Kathryn has] gotten short-changed. It is not my intention. This is the hand that life dealt. Unfortunately, not only do I have to deal with it. [She] do[es], too.

Out of this awareness has come a lack of faithfulness on my part. My unfaithfulness at home has been trying to do home tasks as quickly as possible so as to have more time for "my" work, "our" work. I have been slow to live into the new pattern and be more available to my mother. . . . I have only begun to know what self-giving means in caring for another. . . . I need to accept being here, knowing this is my current work. I do not feel God is telling me to leave the School of the Spirit work, just that its manifestation must be quite different now. . . .

I am no longer given to talking *about* God and *about* the spiritual life. But this is where I am now. God works in these daily events for me. . . . I have also come to recognize that I need to draw a line more stringently than in the past. . . . I understand the sense of "threat" that can occur when it looks as though there will be no one to do the work. . . . But I continue to follow our old adage, that ministry can come out of what we can do, not what we would like to do or dream of doing. We need to trust God to be in this process, even when we do not know what the outcome will be. . . .[56]

The Final Year

In April 1999 Sonnie was diagnosed with diabetes. It came as a shock to her, but she resolved to control it through diet. In May and June she jotted long journal entries in the form of questions and answers, themes, as she continued to wrestle with her path. Sonnie was having to set limits, and some responded with irritation and anger, which was hard for Sonnie to bear.

Her decision was not to stop everything. When Sister Kathleen Flood, O.P. (Dominican Sisters of the Immaculate Conception) of Stillpoint, a retreat center in Tennessee, called to invite Sonnie to be a presenter at Cullman (a monastery in Alabama), in October, 2000, Sonnie wrote that "the Inward Guide did not bring forth a 'no.'" Sonnie anticipated her series of lectures:

> Setting the stage would probably mean an understanding of cataphatic and apophatic paths and "emergence through creation". There would be a general talk on the dark night and learning to trust God in the darkness. Another subject is liminality and what it means to be a liminal person. Then maybe a closer look at some of the inward elements of transformation.[57]

These topics would form a recapitulation of some of Sonnie's most dearly loved and deeply studied topics. But Sonnie never had a chance to make her presentations at Cullman.

By the fall of 1999 Sonnie's physical condition was again deteriorating, resulting in diminishing energy and stamina. The physician brushed her off by informing her that these symptoms, plus the abdominal pain and excessive bleeding, were likely related to menopause. Simultaneously Sonnie was experiencing the inward shift into Silence, the nothingness of simply being in God's presence. She began to sense a new way of thinking about study, that one might reach a deeper understanding through an insight or an intuitive sense rather than only through the traditional method of study that had meant so much to her. It wasn't necessary, she again realized, to somehow prove her worth through study that was focused on an outward goal.

In the first months of 2000, as Sonnie became increasingly ill, her doctor insisted her situation was not serious. Diverticulitis was the diagnosis. By chance in early March her regular physician was unavailable and Sonnie met with another doctor. He immediately recognized that something was seriously wrong, and sent her to the hospital. Cancer was diagnosed in mid-March. Clerk of the School of the Spirit Board Linda Chidsey remembers:

> In March of 2000 Sonnie taught the second-to-last session of the Spiritual Nurture 4 program. Later in the month the SOTS Board held its meeting at Sonnie's home in Princeton, as she was not feeling well enough to travel. Although clearly in great pain, none of us knew just how ill Sonnie was.
>
> At this time the Board was fully under the weight of its role as stewards of the ministry. With each of the founding teachers stepping back from the ministry, the Board felt a strong sense of need to articulate the core characteristics of the ministry. With the guidance and support of Fran Taber who joined us by telephone, this task was accomplished. That day, in a very real way, the Board received Sonnie's blessing. Although in great discomfort, Sonnie's joy in knowing that the ministry would continue was apparent to us all.[58]

The Quaker grapevine came alive. Letters of love and support began to pour in. Fervent prayers were offered. Some of what Sonnie's ministry meant to folks whose lives she had touched is summed up in this letter from one of her students:

> . . . you have been a blessing in my life. Meeting you at the School of the Spirit, being taught by you, listening to you expound or explain with joy or enthusiasm on whatever was your subject of that session, seeing your infectious smile, were all *wonderful*. The depth and passion of your beliefs encouraged me to further depths and passions, and do still.
>
> I cannot help but do some railing against God ("but, God! We need MORE Sonnies, not FEWER!") and my heart grieves the loss of you already. But I rejoice and thank God that you were in this world, that you affected the lives of so many people, including me, and that I knew you even for a short time. Blessings and love, dear Sonnie, on your journey. I know God is right there with you and in you, and I trust and pray that you will constantly feel His presence and Christ's, too.[59]

Sonnie died in Princeton Hospital on April 4, 2000, with her sister Cindy at her side.

Post Script

The School of the Spirit went on, and completed the Spiritual Nurturer course. Linda remembers:

The final session of the Spiritual Nurturer program was held in late April. On the first evening of each weekend session of the Spiritual Nurturer program, teachers and participants gather to share how God has been at work in their lives since last they were together. All knew of Sonnie's illness and death, and the grief, confusion and disbelief felt by those present was palpable. It was decided that the following morning a meeting for worship in memory of Sonnie would be held. Friends gathered in silence out of which program participants spoke their questions, shared memories, and began to speak aloud their grief, their gratitude, their love. When the meeting for worship ended, teachers and participants felt released and at ease with moving into the schedule that had been planned for the final session. Over the course of the days together there arose a growing sense of deep joy, giftedness and celebration. Sonnie's spiritual presence became more and more real among us. At the open door to the room where Sonnie had slept we sang to her.

As I look back and reflect upon that final session I am convinced that we experienced a deeply personal object lesson that opened and revealed the reality of Christ's crucifixion, resurrection, and ascension. As I recall that first evening when participants gathered, I am reminded of the grief and confusion felt by Jesus' disciples following his death. When I think of the singing at the open door I remember Mary at the open tomb. Most difficult to put into words is that along with the growing sense of joy and celebration there was a deepening conviction that all was moving toward reconciliation, redemption, and resurrected life. I believe this was Sonnie's parting gift to the program.

A Lasting Gift

Sonnie had many gifts and touched hundreds of lives. Of course she was human, with a weakness for tuna fish, cheesecake, English muffins slathered with peanut butter, and marshmallow fluff on ice cream. She loved science fiction, and had an individual fashion sense that favored bold print shirtwaist dresses in greens, blues, and turquoise.

She struggled with times of depression and her share of private fears. But as she lived increasingly faithfully to the Inward Christ, she was drawn more deeply into the Wordless Presence. Those who have also been touched by that Silence were awed by her willing submission to Christ, and empowered by her example of faithfulness.

Sonnie's journal records her recurring struggles before she came to fully accept that she—and each of us—is loved by God, not because of anything we do, even to advance the Kingdom, but because it is God's nature to love. In the end she learned it was enough just to be, to rest wordlessly in God's love.

In the genre of Quaker journals to which Sonnie's belongs, the purpose was and is teaching. Without a written creed, Friends learn how to be a Friend by learning from others who are more consistent, more experienced, in listening to Christ Within and following divine guidance. Published journals are not intended to elevate their writers to the status of saint but to invite the reader to see the inward struggles and take heart: if *this* Friend, whom I admire so much, found it so difficult, perhaps there is hope for me.

Part One

The Journal
of Sandra L. Cronk

Sonnie with her father, Gary Arnold Cronk, and her grandmother, Dorothea Arnold Cronk.

June 1975 to August 1978

Sonnie began writing her journal in June 1975. She was living with her parents in Princeton, and was a member of Princeton Friends Meeting. The brief entry for June 22 interrupts the narrative flow of recollections about her childhood with an account of meeting for worship that day.

6/20/1975

The idea of keeping a journal of God's work in my life has come to me on several occasions. But each time I rejected the idea as of little worth and taking too much time. There was also a hesitation to write down very personal experiences and reactions which might sometime be read by other eyes than my own, a very disconcerting prospect. It also seemed that each stage in my pilgrimage was so clear and decisive that it would live in my memory without benefit of notes. But I now see that the months and years can blur the chronological sequence and other details of the most transforming experiences. Furthermore, I seem to need to learn many of the same lessons over and over again before they are really learned. Hence, I have decided that a brief record might be of great help in my journey. Keeping fresh in my mind where I have been and the openings that occurred along the way, will help me to know the next step along the path.

Before jumping to the present I need to review the path so far. My earliest experiences of God are lost with other early childhood memories. I have been told about some though. My mother says I always enjoyed Sunday School as a small child. I know I did as I got older. My grandmother says I used to talk about God and Jesus while we shopped in the grocery store so that she would feel embarrassed. My mother says I was very distressed at the crucifixion story. I remember none of these things.

I do remember when I became elementary school age that I was deeply interested in what the religious life was all about. The Dewitt

[Sonnie's spelling; also Dewitt] Community Church where we went to Sunday School had an excellent children's program. The Sunday morning program was divided into two parts. The first half-hour was a worship service for all age groups led by Mrs. Jordan. What a joy she was year after year! I can see her standing in the front of all of our folding chairs in the "gymnasium" wing of the old church now. She always wore a hat. She was not a young woman. But the gap of years made no problem in communication. Her joy in the Lord and her untiring efforts to bring this joy to the children were felt by all.

6/21/1975

How many times she wrote out the words and music to a new hymn on huge pieces of mural paper on big bulletin board room dividers. In this way the hymn could be seen from the back of the "gathered worship space." We learned the hymn to *Finlandia* this way. We also learned many Negro Spirituals. Another of Mrs. Jordan's favorites was "This is My Father's World." Those songs conveyed so much. Perhaps they were the reason I reacted so strongly against the purely formal "unfelt" singing that went on in the adult worship service when I got too old for the Sunday School program. Somehow that choir up in the front and the feeble singing of the unwilling congregation never expressed what Mrs. Jordan did with her mural paper.

After the first half-hour of worship we would break up into separate classes—each in an improvised place in the gym, set off by the same bulletin board dividers. The memory of most of the "classroom" teachers is largely gone. I do remember the texts we read and the workbooks we used. I saved as many as I could. I wonder what ever happened to them. I remember some of our special projects: the little booklet with the construction paper cover, with the cross on the front. We could choose any style of cross we wished. I was fascinated to know that so many styles existed. I can't remember what went into the booklet, prayers or poems I think. The cross was more important than the words. I remember vividly the little paper doll of King David we cut out of our workbook in some Old Testament history lesson. We had to dress him both as a shepherd and as a king. As a shepherd he had a tiny pouch of pebbles for his slingshot. As king he had a purple cape.

The classes were so arranged that in the course of several years one covered Old Testament history, New Testament history and church history. (We used Roland Bainton's *The Church of Our Fathers* for the latter. I still have it. Imagine my delight in later years to run into Roland Bainton again as an expert in the left-wing Reformation. I saw him interviewed on TV the other day. He is now an old, old man. He still has a sparkle about him and an amazing collection of stories to illustrate his points about church history.) The remarkable thing about this rather common Sunday School plan was that it worked. A faithful attender really did get a background in each of these areas.

One teacher stands out from the rest—Mrs. Lockwood. It was her whole bearing—such profound serenity and tranquility. This in spite of a busy life with a husband, five children, and a large home. I baby sat for her on one or two occasions when she had just had the last baby. Her quiet joy was Madonna-like. I certainly think of Mary with Jesus when I think back on her now nursing the baby, although I'm sure that image did not come to me then.

It was in Mrs. Lockwood's class that we used a lovely little booklet of children's stories published by a South African woman. Mrs. Lockwood had gotten her booklet years before. It was the only copy the class had. I wished I could have a copy to keep. So we arranged to write to the woman in South Africa. Mrs. Lockwood explained that the booklet was put out a long time before. She doubted any more could be obtained. Wonder of wonders I did receive a copy in the mail. I was so delighted. Mrs. Lockwood was happily surprised as well. It was wonderful to think of this lovely South African woman who had written of her deep love for boys and girls all over the world in her little book still living there and sending out her booklet to an unknown child in America.

In Junior High the Sunday School program began to prove inadequate. For one thing we no longer met in the gym with Mrs. Jordan. We met across the street in the Parish House. We had a similar arrangement of a half-hour of worship together and a half-hour class. The worship was good. The classes were not adequate. I think the teachers did not feel up to teaching the material. I remember a lesson on the trinity in seventh grade. The teacher said she did not understand it and it was not explainable. I did not understand her possible reference to a great mystery in the Godhead. I felt both bewildered at receiving no explanation and also that perhaps this was a silly doctrine, which should be purged from Christianity. The latter proved to be part of a most destructive pathway I was to follow for a long time.

One excellent spot in those years was the release time education program on Wednesday mornings when we had an hour off for church instruction. The Dewitt Community Church had a superb program run by their young minister of religious education, Robert Bolton. What marvelous classes. He lectured himself. He passed out mimeographed sheets of information on various aspects of church history—in preparation for confirmation, I think—which answered questions I didn't ask until Divinity School and which were also relevant to me then. I pasted those colored sheets in a notebook, which I think I still have in the attic. His enthusiasm was catching.

Somehow the confirmation was a disappointment though. I expected to experience something important. But nothing happened. I think I began to question sacraments and ordinances at that time. Of course, I now recognize the problem of trying to make yourself experience something and of too much stress on feeling in the first place. But the major problem here was not error on this side. It was mechanically confirming people because they were the right age with no regard to God's leading in their lives.

This was the same problem I experienced in the adult worship service when the Sunday School program petered out at the end of junior high or the beginning of high school. Somehow the reality of the world of the adult church membership had not hit me before this age. I cannot remember despair over church services before this time. On the contrary, I can remember crying one weekend when my cousin came to visit and I was asked to stay home from Sunday School to be with her. But suddenly as a high school student the Sunday School did not exist any longer, and I began to go to the regular Sunday morning worship service. I discovered immediately that there was no worship in this service, no communion with God, only talking about God. The whole structure of the service seemed designed to prevent any worship. It was full of different activities: hymn singing, choir singing, responsive readings, written prayer in the bulletin and, of course, the sermon. No one activity was really allowed to be an avenue for God to speak to you. Everyone rushed on to the next activity and the next, never taking time to listen to God. It was intolerable.

I also discovered, much to my surprise, that most church members did not take their faith seriously. It did not determine their actions in any area of life at all, especially not in social concerns. Suddenly it seemed that the rich heritage of faith and worship I had been given as a child disappeared. I knew I could not remain a member of this church. I began to seek out the alternatives.

There was no other Protestant church in Dewitt. There was a Catholic church but that seemed like a totally different world. The thought of going there never entered my head. This was true in spite of my love of certain Catholic forms picked up at my grandmother's house. The lovely blue and white statue of the virgin Gram gave me as a gift I just loved. (It never appeared again when we unpacked after our move to Princeton.) I also loved the "comic book" descriptions of the life of a nun, which my cousin Pat had. But the ritual of the mass was far too alien and only seemed a worse specimen of what I was trying to escape from for me to go there.

The only other avenue of exploring other churches open at that time was through books. I went to the tiny library in Fayetteville and read all the "Why I am a(n) Episcopalian, Methodist, Unitarian" series. I also followed the series of articles in the newspaper on the beliefs of each major religious group. No group looked particularly interesting until I stumbled across two or three ancient books on Quakers in the library. They were hopelessly out of date. I thought all Friends must still be wearing plain dress—a testimony I would not have felt comfortable with then. But there were several things which impressed me about this group. One was the strong sense of the experience of communion with God that pervaded all aspects of life and worship. The second was their relatively open position on what I came to think of as abstruse theological statements about the content of the Christian faith. I was growing toward a more liberal theological position. The

Unitarians were interesting from this point of view, too. But they lacked that concrete communion with God, which still remained important to me. I could do no more active exploring until we moved to Princeton, which had numerous different churches to explore.

6/22/1975

First Day—We had a beautiful outdoor meeting today (Princeton Meeting House). A glorious quiet presence was felt. I came to Meeting in my usual harried state wishing I could be more relaxed and quiet. I had listened to Ivan Rebroff sing German Christmas carols Saturday afternoon—an unusual record to play on a June day. It reminded me not only of Jesus' birth 2000 years ago but of Christ's presence with God before creation—and in creation—and also the presence of his spirit now transforming each of us individually and building a people and his kingdom through all of us together, with all our individual failings and strengths. Romans 8 was much on my mind ". . . the creation itself will be set free from its bondage to decay and obtain the glorious liberty of the children of God. We know that the whole creation has been groaning in travail together until now; and not only the creation, but we ourselves . . ." I kept wondering what this new creation would be like. Why can't I see it or feel it? Then in the meeting this morning I did feel it. I wanted to express it in words for all present. I could not articulate it. I decided it did not need to be said. All could experience it. It was the experience of that Being out of which our doing should come. It is that Being toward which so much of our doing strives frantically but never reaches because the Being is there already and we do not know it. The more we strive the less we find it. Striving is not wrong. It simply grows out of Being and hence toward it again. It is false and demonic when it strives out of its own nothingness. But I suppose even this is at least one step to God—maybe, through His grace.

After meeting, Tom and Heidi Abrams came home for lunch. We had a lovely conversation. Tom has gone through many of the religious pathways I have and has gained great insight along the way. It is very helpful to talk with them.

6/24/1975

Most of my high school years are a blank to me—all those years I was sick are wiped out of my memory. What horrible years! What horrible recriminations a person heaps on himself for being ill—all the guilt, all the feelings of worthlessness, being cut off from so many contacts. My life seemed to stop after a happy freshman year only to pick up again as a senior in Princeton High School. For a while I thought I would not finish high school. I can understand how easy it is for kids to drop out when they are faced with problems and have no help in overcoming them. Thank God for a supportive family.

The one ray of light in those years was the inspiration to major in religion in college. I remember the agony of trying to make that decision. Where was my life going? Where did I want it to go? When the answer came it seemed so obvious. As I looked back on my life it (religion) was obviously the constant major theme in my activities. A door had opened.

There have been periods of rapid growth or illumination in my life followed by long periods of quiet. (Quiet working out or dryness? It is not always clear.) The first time I can remember is at 12, 13, 14 years old. All of a sudden I seemed to see things from an entirely new perspective. Situations and problems were seen in a new light.

To a degree the introspection of the first illness was a second such period, although the harm done by the illness may have outweighed any good—at least at that time in history. Later reflection is a different story. God's hand is often hidden.

I was in Princeton long enough to make the rounds of the various churches before going off to college. I went to the meeting once. The benches were then arranged in the old style. I felt a very cold reception. I did not return. But I knew none of the other churches were possibilities.

That is not quite true. I wrote to Western Reserve [University] asking them if a Friends meeting and a Unitarian Church were close-by. They were my two requirements for any college. At that time I had not made a choice between them. I knew this would be my first task at school. And yet I think the choice really was made. When I first went to Cleveland I visited the Unitarian Church first because I knew I would end up going to the meeting and it would make no sense to go to the latter first only to later make a visit elsewhere.

The local Unitarian Church was impressive. But it lacked that stress on communion with God, which even at that time I recognized as necessary.

My first visit to the Cleveland Meeting was a joy. I had phoned previously to find out about the time of worship. I was told about the adult class before hand. I went early enough to take in both. I went with great timidity not knowing what I would find or what my reception would be. Vera Smisek greeted me at the door, took me by the hand and gave me a guided tour of the old home which served as a meeting house. She apologized a bit for the luxury of the furnishings, which had been donated with the house, as not quite in keeping with Quaker simplicity. Her warmth made me feel I had come home. I knew this is where I belonged.

Both Cleveland and 57th St. [Chicago] Meetings have done so much to help me grow through their love. I did not know the importance of the community as the body of Christ in the world before coming to Friends. I thought only of one's personal relation with God and social action. This third element in Christian love was revealed to me in action. I now see it as one of the great gifts of and to Quakerism. But in my early days I was attracted by only the first two elements and a fourth aspect: the non-creedal nature of Quakerism. I was growing away from orthodoxy at that point. I could not in good conscience join a group that asked acceptance of certain traditional doctrines. I remember running into Isabel Bliss in a department store one day. She invited me to lunch with her in the coffee shop. I had just about made up my mind to join the meeting but I was not clear if I could do this in good conscience if I could not accept the trinity. I got up my courage and asked her about it. She explained there were Trinitarians and Unitarians in the meeting and that no one standard was asked for. I felt such relief. It cleared the way for me to join.

I think back on this now that my own beliefs have changed so radically toward "orthodoxy" that I sometimes am impatient with the secular drift of the Religious Society of Friends. I look back and see what this openness meant for my life then. And I also recognize that the non-creedal position is not lack of standards but a different idea of where real commitment comes from. It is good to keep this fresh in one's mind to avoid the "formal professing" character of so much of Christianity which Quakerism originally rebelled against.

I also think back on the note Paul Miller, the clerk, wrote to me upon my acceptance into membership. He said he hoped I would not become disillusioned with the failings of the Society. It struck me as an odd thing to write to a new member, especially since I was uncritically proud of everything I felt the Society stood for. That note was prophetic. It still speaks to my condition today. I marvel at Paul Miller's insight.

6/25/1975

It seems to me now that my time in college was spent growing in the wrong direction religiously. At least on an intellectual level I could not understand the traditional beliefs of Christianity. I could see no sense to the idea of the divinity of Christ. God was no longer a personal being. I read Paul Tillich about God being the Ground of Being. This idea made sense to me. But it is virtually impossible to have any communion with the ground of being. Meetings for worship became dry and lifeless. How strange to go away to college, find the Friends and at the same time move farther from God.

The main joy in my studies at college was the religion department. It was wonderful to be able to study what I was interested in at long last and not what others thought I should study. (But I must admit I am glad I was made to take certain courses like art history and public speaking—both subjects I was ready to dislike, and both opened up new worlds for me.)

The religion department limped along with two men for my first three years at Reserve. This meant course offerings were inadequate. The Chairman, Dr. Wolfe was a dear man, raised in the church of the Brethren, I think, but by then a member of a Presbyterian, Methodist or Disciples of Christ Church—anyway a big mainline denomination.

Dr. Wolfe still retained that spirit of loving, gentleness, which characterized his original church home. I was fortunate to have him as an adviser from a psychological point of view. Dr. Wolfe's approach to religion was that of the 19th century religious liberal. As such my views were along the same lines. The ethical side of the religious life became of paramount importance. His teaching of the Bible was a generation or two out of date. While we learned about the historical and cultural background of the Bible, we did not learn any of the new critical techniques of Biblical analysis. All in all I was educated in the old liberal tradition, entirely ignorant of new scholarly or theological trends. And this situation only exacerbated my own religious lostness. I was given no help in understanding traditional Christian symbolism—or any other symbolism.

The other teacher was Ewart Bambury, a British Quaker, of orthodox views and a rather caustic personality. This combination was unfortunate. I felt his real concern through his brusque manner, but it made it difficult for me to relate to him. I am eternally grateful for his forthright presentation of the original principles of Quakerism and the introduction to Christian thought he gave in his courses. I rejected it all at the time, glad that Quakerism was no longer "that way." Since then I have realized the depth of that original Quakerism and have turned 180 degrees in my thinking. He was the first to present this view. I believe it was working below the surface ready to flower years later. Ewart Bambury had a heart attack and went back to England after I graduated. A few years ago I tracked down his address and wrote a letter just to let him know how much in his debt I am. I received a kind reply. His health is not good. He had been in bed for the past year, only able to work correcting papers for a free university. A second letter brought no response. I hope he is well.

My last year at Western Reserve saw the addition of two new staff members: a young Harvard student from the center for the Study of World Religions specializing in Hinduism and a Rabbi from Cleveland. Both offered an exciting array of new courses. I enjoyed the courses on Judaism. I wish I could have taken more. (The Rabbi came my last semester.) The "Harvard" instructor was an excellent teacher. In all my time in school I do not think I have ever encountered a better one. His lectures were beautifully organized and opened up the worlds of Hinduism and Buddhism. No course in the Divinity School came remotely close to his caliber in these two fields. It was from this man, David Miller I think his name was, that I conceived the idea of going into the history of religions.

Of course, the idea of graduate school at all came from Dr. Wolfe. This meant extra language study for three summers. (I hated each minute of it.) I needed one more language to graduate from the M.A. program at Western Reserve, and two more from the Divinity School. I took German first, and later French and Dutch. I never enjoyed any of them as much as the Spanish I took in high school and college. But no one seemed to think Spanish worthwhile for any purpose.

My first introduction to graduate study came in my last year at W[estern] R[eserve] U[niversity] with the experimental M.A. program. It allowed a student to graduate with a B.A. and an M.A. in four years. The fourth year was spent taking graduate courses. It was pure hell—too much work, not enough time to think. I was in torment the entire time and helpless to get out. My situation became clear when I had to take my final oral exam. I had told Dr. Wolfe my problem earlier, but there was no way out. Out of kindness they let me graduate. But the religion department did not participate in this experiment further. I did get a chance to take some courses I never could have otherwise. And I learned one unforgettable lesson about the need to keep one's priorities straight and academic work was not the first priority—God was—whoever God was.

Ewart Bambury was the one who suggested the Divinity School of the University of Chicago. His recommendation probably got me accepted. I chose the H[istory of] R[eligions] field in part because I felt any Christian study would be too narrow in my quest to find God and in part because I was afraid of any need for doctrinal commitments in the other more traditional fields of the Divinity School.

6/28/1975

The first year at the Divinity School was quite frightening because I felt I might not be able to do the quality of work required. As a result

I was afraid to take time away from studies for any extra-curricular activities. I did not even participate in any Meeting activities.

It was extremely hard to change meetings. I know other Friends who have felt the same way, especially about their first meeting. Cleveland Meeting had become like a family to me. I remember the little going-away celebration the Reading Group had for me. This group was made up largely of older women who were free to come together on a weekday for lunch and to read a work on Quakerism. Since they met in the meeting house right on campus, I was able to attend frequently. This group introduced me to the wide range of Quaker literature. On my last visit with the group they gave me a hankie, card, and two works about Thomas Kelly. One was the biography by his son. The second was his sequel to *Testament of Devotion* (which I think was out of print at that moment). I was totally surprised and very touched.

For a long time I did not feel I could transfer my membership to 57th Street Meeting in Chicago. It would have been like giving up one's family. But my first intensive year at the University (on top of that ghastly last year at Reserve) made me, forced me, to realize that I could not go on living this way. It was not spiritually or emotionally healthy to have academic studies become central in one's life and exclude all else. My second year (or end of the 1st year) in Chicago I had my membership transferred and joined the peace committee.

I did not know that my inner spiritual journey was just beginning at that little first step. It is hard to identify all the different ways in which God was reaching out to me. I saw them only as I looked back later from hindsight. One of the most important ways was in the loving care of the new meeting. As George Watson, leader of the adult First Day School class said once, "I have seen countless people come to the meeting afraid and closed in on themselves, and with the love they found there, they blossomed into new people." I think of Clarence Jordan's metamorphosis where the caterpillar becomes a butterfly. The meeting acts like a Cajon for so many people. It is indeed the body of Christ in the world today. He found me there when I did not really know Him.

The Divinity School was having its effect, too, both positive and negative. In most cases I am clear about what is positive and what is negative. But in one case the lines have blurred and shifted. This case is the requirement of passing a theology comprehensive (along with comprehensives in all fields of the Divinity School save one). I took historical theology all year of my first year in Chicago. The professor was Brian Gerrish, a gentle man and a very good teacher. His lectures were clear and well organized. I went through the whole first year virtually memorizing his words because I did not understand the inner meaning of theology as a discipline. In fact, I had decided to tackle the theological comprehensive my first year because I knew it would be the hardest for me. I wanted to get to work on it and get it over with.

My problem came essentially from my own rebellion against orthodoxy. Orthodox language created so many problems for me I could scarcely begin to perceive what difference it made if one said this or that slightly different statement about, say, the person or work of Christ.

At the end of the year I took the theology exam, was able to write about four pages in answer to the questions from my pages of memorized notes. I got a "C"; a "B" was necessary to pass.

6/29 to 30/1975

The next year I had to take it again. I could not afford the time or emotional pressure of taking more theology courses for credit, so I audited a couple of modern theology courses given by Langdon Gilkey. And something clicked. L. Gilkey made the theological problems more relevant. They concerned questions I pondered. Perhaps the language was easier for me to understand than the language and thought world of 2000 or 1500 years ago. Whatever the reason I could suddenly understand what theology was all about. What's more, I cared about the answers. The symbolism of orthodox Christianity lost its opaqueness. A new world opened up.

I remember going in to talk to L. Gilkey before taking the exam. I went with much fear, wondering if I would even be able to converse with him. We had a wonderful visit in his unbelievable office, books and journals covering every inch of floor and desk. The cobwebs betrayed the fact that a cleaning rag never entered the door. We did not talk much formal theology from his point of view. But we talked enough to give me much more confidence in this field.

I took the exam again at the end of the year. I understood the implications of all the questions, was able to write reams of relevant material, and got an A-. This is one field I'm glad I was forced to study. It helped to change the direction of my whole life.

I think I may have been open to Christian symbolism because my first year and a half had given me the chance to take some History of Religion courses. There I was introduced to the nature of religious language and symbolism. I learned to look for its many, often paradoxical, levels of meaning. I learned to look for the ultimate dimension to which the symbol pointed and which shines through this open window. This was made psychologically easier because we dealt with primitive symbolism of non-Western world religions. These posed no personal threat and I did not raise my barriers of defense against God working in my life, speaking to me. It was also a joy to be able to "catch" religious understanding from people like Marshall Hodgson and Charles Smith. The former was quiet and systematic. The latter was more active and, dare I say, disorganized. But if one listened between the lines or tried to catch the impression of the whole lecture one could grasp an element of religious understanding absent in the formal lecture. As a Friend, Marshall Hodgson became a model for integrating study of religion other than one's own and strong Quaker commitment. His death was a real shock. [Marshall G. S. Hodgson died in June 1968.]

All of these exciting openings did not take away my fear that I had somehow come to the Divinity School by mistake. In fact, they increased it. As my expanding horizons here became more important to me, the prospect of losing all by failing the M.A. exams became an agony. I felt all would be lost. What would I do with my life? What would friends and relatives think? I would periodically go into a panic state of fear.

At this time I had developed a new awareness of and interest in science fiction. I read all the things I could find in this field. One day I picked up a purportedly true book on strange lights and fires in

Woolworth's. It reported lots of strange incidents, including the phenomenon of human beings burning in a hot fire by an unknown form of spontaneous combustion. All my work with symbolism must have let this imagery speak to me. I felt this is just what would happen to me. One night I lay awake, petrified that I would burn up, that I would fail my M.A. exams, that all that was meaningful to me would be lost. Finally at about 5 a.m. I gave up trying to sleep and went to the laundry room to wash my hair in the big sink there. Suddenly as the cool water poured over my hair, I realized that no circumstance could separate me from God. Even if I failed my exams God would remain the center of my life. That could never be taken away. With God as center my life would have to be as worthwhile to God and as full as I could ever wish. There was nothing to fear. The fear of fire disappeared. But I saw them all in a new light. I could face them all calmly, and accept joyously what ever happened. (As it turned out I did pass my exams, and was not required to give up this particular avenue toward God. But by this time the avenue had become distinctly secondary to the goal itself.)

7/1/1975

Shortly after this time, I had a visit from a woman who worked for Intervarsity Christian Fellowship. I had been reintroduced to Intervarsity at Chicago through the many students from the "grass-roots" program, Chicago's attempt to attract students from rural areas out west as well as the big cities of the east. Most of the students were evangelical Protestants. I had had one very unhappy encounter with Intervarsity at [Western] Reserve [University]. Their whole meeting was devoted to a mission outreach to Jews with a "hit 'em over the head" approach—truly ethno-centric and narrow minded. It was a pleasant second meeting with Intervarsity in Chicago. The intervening years or the different location seems to have made all the difference. Here were strong, committed Christians without being obnoxious and without losing all sight of [the] social element of [the] gospel either. I attended their Bible study group with much pleasure. We worked on the book of John.

One week I was sick in bed with a cold. It was then that this Intervarsity worker called on me. I was particularly happy to get a visit while sick. Before she left she prayed that I might have a more personal relationship with Christ. This barrier against seeing Christ as God was the last and greatest barrier that needed to be broken down to overcome my years of "liberal" wandering and return to that close relationship with God I had had as a child—before I needed intellectual explanations for relationship with God. I felt her prayer and my accompanying/corresponding prayer were answered very soon because I did come to the realization that it was Christ—Christ, the Word; Christ, the Jesus of History; and Christ, the Risen Lord who was speaking to me now in my life. What a joy! I wanted to tell this woman about her answered prayer in months afterward, but she had married a pastor and moved to unknown parts.

The final element in what I can only describe as my conversion came when I realized that all the foregoing things were happening in my life, leading me toward a goal. This happened in a most prosaic way. One day, two girls in the school of social work came to me independently and asked if they could interview me for an assignment in school. They were studying growth in the adult and needed to interview someone over 25. Since most students on the floor were younger than that I guess I remained the logical candidate. They had specific questions they were to ask, but in preparation I was to think how I had grown in the last five years. In pondering this question all of the threads of the preceding pages fell into place. It was an exhilarating experience—not the deeply moving experience of baptism and peace which was so profound I could not speak of it for years afterward without weeping—but still the culmination of this long epoch in my life—perhaps the culmination of all my life until that point. It was certainly the turning point and base line for all that happened later. All else assumes this starting point.

With such grand experiences so recently in mind I had a naïve view of the ease of life continuing to be centered on God. The next stage of my life was to make me aware of my finitude and sins—perhaps a reversal of the usual order of spiritual growth. Through it all I was to come to know God transcending all the failures and sufferings of this world.

My immediate response to these openings from God was to dedicate my life anew to His service. For me this meant more active participation in the Meeting. After my first hectic year I had decided that even if it required more years [to] finish my program, I could not work exclusively at academic study as I had the first year. I resolved to take only two courses for credit a term instead of the usual three. Now this time away from studies became the primary interest in my life. I do not mean that studies ceased to be important, far from it. But more and more I felt how far they removed me from God—strange because they also were responsible for opening me more and more to God.

7/5/1975

I became active in the First Day School program in meeting, first as a teacher and later as a co-chairman for two years. It was an eye-opening venture. I learned a lot about committee meetings, the need for revisiting and not just attention to the problem at hand. I learned about the practical problems of child discipline, parental indifference, teacher "unpreparedness," etc. Most of all I came face to face with the astonishing departure from the traditional Quaker message by meeting members, many of whom rebelled against any orthodoxy. I also saw searching people who eventually grew to find. But I saw people who had already felt God touch their lives who went elsewhere because they wanted to be part of a committed church, not part of a congenial group of people. This sudden realization of the meeting's failing, after my earlier pride in Quakerism, brought an unbearable agony to my life—an agony which has never left. I recognize that it is my own spiritual journey, which has caused this change and not any change in the Society. Whereas I was once threatened by Christ-centeredness, I now felt betrayed to be denied it. For a long while I could not find the courage to speak out on these issues. Now I speak, but with great hesitation, hoping it is not my own agony, but God's love which is leading. But I speak into a void with either an indifferent or hostile response. A continuing problem.

A short while later I served on worship and ministry as clerk—a chance to serve, a chance to experience more pain. But I was able to continue in this position only a few months for I was becoming more ill from my allergy medicine. I was able to carry on less and less until it was all I could do to get through the basic activities of eating, shopping, etc. Ultimately, I was forced to leave school. I was in too much pain to get to the cafeteria and eat or to ride in a car without crying. Thank God for Ginny [Schurman]'s care in Chicago and my family's care in Princeton during the period. I learned what unselfish love is through them. What terrible agony to go to the doctor and be told that such symptoms as mine cannot exist. What a sense of worthlessness!! What fears of deadly disease! What discomfort. When I could not stand it any longer I would go into the bathroom and weep where no one could see me. All the things, which were important to me, were taken away: the meeting, school, friends, a sense of accomplishment. With all taken away there was nothing left to depend on but God. Finally, I slowly came to realize how many finite things I had put in God's place in the center of my life. In my desire to serve Him I really had made the meeting and our community faithfulness the most important thing in my life. The illness was an avenue toward God that I had closed off in my busy "healthy" life. I had to re-evaluate the meaning of human life. Did the person only have worth because of what he could do? That was how I had seen myself. What if a person could do no work in school, and worse yet could do nothing to advance God's kingdom, could not even take pride in being part of a faithful group? Even the grandest aims are finite. God is under, above, beside them all. God transcends this world of doing. God is present to/in our existing. How easy it is to judge others by their doing. How easy to withhold love. But Christ did not do that. My family had not done that. Yet, as much as I wanted, I did not love this perfectly. I had to learn to yield and give up all—again. I thought I had learned it in my baptism experience. Now I see I yielded only a small part. Now God was demanding the rest—or so it seemed. I suppose this is only a small part, too. To see a problem does not mean that we have the burden of solving it placed on us. We must be able to rest in nothingness and trust God's working.

One thing was left to me during my illness—a growing interest in religious community, especially the Pennsylvania German sectarian groups. I had decided to do my dissertation on the Old Order Mennonites and Old Order Amish. But I wished to know about all the other religious communities in this country, too. The illness gave me the time to read about them—a joyous experience. How much our fragmented individualistic world has to learn from them! I read about the Schwenkfelders, Brethren, Moravians, Shakers, Utopian groups (like Harmony, Amana, Oneida), Society of Brothers, Hutterites, Old Believers, etc., as well as the Amish, Mennonites and Friends. I read about their history, beliefs and practices. And better yet, as I was able I began to take trips to visit them. These trips will remain the high points of my life. What gentle, humble, warm and friendly people I met. I wish I had a record of the people I met.

7/6/1975
Schwenkfelder[60]

I made several trips into Schwenkfelder country. One was on a 4th of July Sunday when the rest of the family was away on a cruise. I attended Sunday School and worship at the huge Central Schwenkfelder church outside of Lansdale. When I came upon the church I was amazed by two things: its gigantic size, and its full parking lot on a holiday weekend in summer. The size still amazes me. The new church had only been built twenty years. Before that the congregation was worshipping in two smaller meeting houses, now razed. The old Salford Meeting house is still standing though; a quaint white structure is still used occasionally in summer. The people are very proud of their new institutional church. They take visitors through to see each room. But I wonder if their new direction is really for the best. Their minister wonders, too.

I was greeted with overwhelming warmth. One person invited me to Sunday School. Another showed me through the church. A third had relatives in Princeton, and was interested in the relationship between Friends and Schwenkfelders. He dug a book out of their library on an ancient joint venture of the two groups and let me take it home. (The return of the book became my excuse for a return visit.) He also told me about the meetings, which used to take place among the peace churches in that area. I had not heard of them before. They are long since defunct. Too bad.

After the service the minister's wife invited me home for lunch. They live in a lovely old colonial farmhouse near Valley Forge. We ate outside and talked about how far the Schwenkfelders had come from their traditions and how dead the local Friends meeting was. It was painful for all of us, I think.

On another occasion Mom and I went to Pennsburg to see the Schwenkfelder Library and museum and to find out the location of the various Schwenkfelder cemeteries. Claire Conway, librarian, gave us a lovely tour of both buildings, a nice painting of the St. Andrew landing in Philadelphia, a recipe for Saffron cake, an old Reformation era cartoon, and two Schwenkfelder Fraktur pieces. The library is excellent. I wish I could get back there to do some reading. The museum is fine, also. She was able to find us driving directions to all the cemeteries and a sexton from the Palm Church to take us to a family plot in Palm.

The sexton was a wonderful man. He had grown up in Palm and spoke with a slight German accent. He remembered the time when the town was all Schwenkfelder. Now the farms are owned by city farmers and housing developments are going up all over. He was glad to take the time to show us the cemetery because, he said, young people were not interested in such things now. He was happy to run across people who were. The cemetery sat on top of a high hill overlooking all the surrounding country side. A lone tree looked over it. It was in the middle of a farmer's field of corn. Luckily it was fall, the corn was cut and the ground was dry. Otherwise we could never have gotten in.

Shortly after this Mom, Dad and I took a tour of all the cemeteries, churches and meeting houses in Schwenkfelder country. Their living space is small enough to do that in one day. It is a rare opportunity to be able to encompass a cosmos in a one day trip—refreshing in a way. Mom took pictures of all the sites. I eventually made a little tour guide with driving instructions to all the places.

Only recently I discovered another Schwenkfelder burial ground in the graveyard of the Methacton Mennonite Church. We stopped on a

Pennsylvania German Society tour. A lot of plain groups had used this burial ground including Mennonites and Brethren. Christopher Sauer is buried there.

Amish[61]

My contacts with the Amish community are not as numerous as I would have liked. There was a brief visit to the annual Amish teachers' meeting in Zooks' barn, near Ronks. But I was too ill at that time to sit long on the backless benches. I had to leave. I continue to be sorry for that lost opportunity. I remember the line of little girls sitting on the benches in the front yard as I was waiting to be picked up. Such sweet children.

There was an interesting visit to an Amish 9th grade school in Saturday session during a Mennonite Historical associates tour in Lancaster.

Finally, there was the visit to Orus Bender's outside Goshen with the Clayton Sutters. The Benders had just had church in their "redone" basement. Most people had left, except relatives. The father fixed some popcorn on the basement bottled gas stove and the wife's oldest brother told us tales of life as a boy in an Amish community in Oklahoma (1903, I think). He still remembered contacts with the Indians. The Amish farmed Indian-owned land, the Indians not being much for farming, but being willing to rent the land for a share of the crop.

Old Order Mennonite

I have had some wonderful contacts with Old Order Mennonites. I made a special point to meet them because I felt I knew least about them. There was the visit to the Old Order service in Waterloo County, Ontario with the Archivist at Conrad Grebel College. At least five people must have extended dinner invitations to us. Unfortunately, I was scheduled to fly home that afternoon and could not stay. It was disturbing to see all the tourists who lined up across the street from the meeting house to see all the buggies come and go. The police had to come to keep the people from taking pictures through the meeting house windows and doors while the service was going. Interestingly, I met some people there I had seen a few nights earlier while interviewing some Mennonites in St. Jacobs. They had Old Order neighbors who happened to stop in for a visit.

7/8/1975

On that same visit to Ontario Wilfred Fretz took me to visit two Old Order Mennonite families: one buggy driving, the other automobile driving. We had a particularly lovely visit at the first family. We sat on the side porch where a cool wind helped relieve the high temperatures. They had just finished supper and the kitchen was stifling. The oldest girls picked some fresh strawberries from their garden for us to eat. J. W. Fretz steered the conversation around to Quaker customs as well as Mennonite ones. The husband was a song leader and gave me a copy of their hymnal, a completely unexpected gesture of kindness.

Two Old Order families in Lancaster shine brightly in my memory. The first is the Amos B. Hoover family near Ephrata (Weaverland Conference). They invited me to their home on two occasions and were very kind in giving information on Old Order music (he is a song leader) and other practices. On one occasion he invited the Daniel Martins to visit. He is a song leader from Groffdale Conference. We all had dinner one Sunday. D. Martin was kind enough to print a list of the most commonly sung songs from the *Unparteusche Gesangbush*, an invaluable aid, and an unexpected courtesy which involved a lot of analysis and work on his part.

The Hoovers came to visit us in Princeton in 6/1975 on their way home from seeing the animals at Great Adventure. We enjoyed the visit so much. We had a chance to see the interior of Princeton Meeting before they had to be on their way. He brought a copy of his newly reprinted Froschauer Bible, a beautiful edition which I bought. Later on he sent a map of the location of the plain churches of Lancaster County.

We have met two Old Order families in Dayton, Virginia, the bishops of the two districts there. The J. Showalter family seemed particularly willing to converse with me about their local history. Their warmth and friendliness drew in the rest of the family on the night

I first visited. Later they invited us to church, and home for Sunday dinner—a most enjoyable visit. I also visited Ruth Showalter's school to see her classroom and the class of the other teacher (Miss Betty) as well. Ruth and I have been corresponding since then. She writes full and interesting letters about their rich life at home. It is a joy to read them.

It is hard to express in a chronicle of visits what acquaintance with these people has meant to me. Such gentleness, humility, friendliness, warmth and hospitality. To be with any of these families is to feel oneself in the midst of deeply committed Christians who follow Christ with their whole lives and not just with words. It revolutionizes one's understanding of God's relationship with man to see this reality in person.

There have been so many visits with other Mennonites that it is hard to begin to list them all. The fine visit to the conservative Mennonite Church next to the Rockingham Motel [Harrisonburg, Virginia] where five of us were invited for dinner after church. The interesting visit Ed [Nowina] and I made to a similar church in Waterloo County [Ontario].

In Ontario the Fretzes went out of their way to be helpful in my dissertation work by driving me to visit Old Order song leaders with whom they had a close relationship. The archivist at Conrad Grebel [College] also went out of her way to talk about her family history, arrange people to visit and take me to an Old Order Church.

In Lancaster much help was received from Carolyn Charles and Ira Landis at the Mennonite Library and archives (Martin Ressler), also Eli Wenger and George Sauder, authors of the *Weaverland District History*. We have enjoyed many tours into the Lancaster area, as well.

In Virginia the people at Eastern Mennonite College were very helpful. There I also met William Rushby for the first time and had a long conversation about conservative Friends and *Gemeinschaft*. Anna Margie Lehman, with whom I roomed, has become a friend with whom I correspond.

In Goshen there were Nelson Springer and ____ Lehman from the library, Melvin Gingerich and Leonard Gross at the archives. G. C. Wenger and Paul Miller in interviews. H. Claire Amstutzs and Clayton (Elsie) Sutter as parents of Mabel and Sim[eon] Sutter from

U[niversity] of C[hicago] proved real friends. I also had a good conversation with John Ruth of Harleysville, [Pa.] while in Goshen.

7/9/1975
Brethren

Personal contacts with people from the German Baptist or Brethren tradition have not been as numerous as I would wish. But two trips to Goshen did produce two visits to Old German Baptist churches, first through arrangements by the Sutters and second through arrangement by William Rushby to Willard Wrightsman to Old Order German Baptist girls who were members of the congregation. We were received very warmly each time.

The church of the Brethren congregation in Sargeantsville, N.J. was the site for two visits at worship time. The minister there, ___ Landis, was extremely friendly and even offered to let me look over his book collection on Brethren history, a treat I have not had yet.

Finally Isaac Clarence Kulp of Harleysville, Pennsylvania, was the guide on my bus during the Goshenhopper tour (spring '75) conducted by the Penna. German Society. I.C. K[ulp] dresses in traditional plain style although he belongs to the more liberal church of the Brethren. He is an encyclopedia of knowledge about all the German churches in that part of Pennsylvania. His new museum is an excellent local collection of artifacts.

Moravians[62]

A couple visits to the Old Moravian buildings in Bethlehem had produced a deep interest in this church, but it was not until the German script course given by the Moravian archivists that I was able to meet and live in a Moravian setting. During the course in 6/1974 I lived in the Old Schnitz House next to the Sisters House. The house was occupied by Mrs. Walter H. Allen (Nancy), a most remarkable woman, originally from North Carolina, the widow of the former pastor of the huge Central Moravian Church in Bethlehem. Mrs. Allen was one of the warmest, most loving people I have ever met. In spite of physical problems and age she was active in many church affairs and was loved by all. She could always spare that extra energy to greet an old friend or a new acquaintance. What a joy to know her. I also enjoyed talking about Moravian history with her for she was well acquainted with the field. She was traditional in her approach to Christian life and hence we lamented together some of the far reaching changes secularism is bringing to Friends and Moravians alike.

My stay there also brought me into contact with some of the sisters in the Sisters' House, one of whom tended the traditional herb garden next to the church. I met a widow from the Widows House and several Moravian families.

The archivists who conducted the course were exceptional people, too. The Rev. Vernon H. Nelson, a young minister whose health forced him to give up pastoral work, was the head archivist. His health was not good during the course and sometimes he had to sit to deliver his lectures. Yet he never showed any irritation at this plight. Mr. Madiheim, assistant archivist, was a former Catholic monk, a brilliant older man, who married a widow with growing children. He was since widowed himself and had to raise the children alone. His manner was sometimes brusque and teasing/joking which made it hard for me to feel close to him.

The course was organized to allow time for lectures on history and for tours. We went through both the Bethlehem and Nazareth museums again. I was delighted with the director of the Nazareth Museum, a retired Moravian whose family was of French Huguenot ancestry. He conducts the most wonderful personal tours, telling anecdotes, playing some of the old instruments and taking a personal interest in each visitor. He is perfect for his new vocation.

My journeys have taken me to visit Ephrata, the Harmony Society in Pittsburgh, Snowhill in south-central Penna., the Dominican Convent in Michigan. But I have yet to visit such communities as the Society of Brothers, the Shakers, Koinonia, and the Hutterites. I hope these visits become possible sometime. Learning about each of these communities, either in person or by book has been a true inspiration. All have helped me to understand religious community and to contemplate what community means today for the Society of Friends and for all who wish to live as children of God. Some of the most worthwhile conversations on this subject have been with nuns while I was living in International House of the University of Chicago. Carol Wheeler RSM (Baltimore) and Sister Alma Marie Messing of the Adrian Dominicans have been particularly helpful in this regard.

7/10/1975

Yesterday evening we had a deeply "stilling" and "centering" mid-week meeting. Tom Abrams spoke out of the depth about the need to truly surrender to God. How often I have needed to learn it! How often I say it to myself! Yet that message made me realize anew how much my anguish over the faithless state of Quakerism is due to my clinging to an ideal and not to God. As once I realized life could be full without remaining in academic life, now I must trust that even the decayed state of our community cannot separate us from the love of God. Perhaps we need to recognize its death so that it can be reborn anew directly from God and not from our cajolings and preachings and teachings.

In the Divinity School I was interested in two major areas of study: mysticism, especially the mystical and spiritual traditions within Christianity, and religious community. (What a grand step that was from my arrival when I wanted to study non-Christian religions out of my feeling of rebellion against an opaque myth.) It was impossible to study both topics, so I chose the latter, which was probably most appropriate for the Divinity School and my barely emerging, primitive faith anyway. But more and more I have felt a personal gap in the other area which needs to be filled. I hope there is some opportunity to work in a systematic way on mysticism after finishing my dissertation, before I must go to work.

I have looked at several possible avenues in this regard. Ginny and I took a trip to Earlham School of Religion. Although we were met with great hospitality and personal kindness, we also felt hostility, anger, and ridicule at our quest. Our membership in the meetings we belonged to was seen as a sign of our lack of balance. Anyone who actively promoted silent meetings for worship was told, in effect, that they were disturbing the peace. Programmed or unprogrammed, it is all the same, officially, at E.S.R. We were put squarely in the "lesser" [Friends] General Conference camp. This is so strange, since we both are in physical and spiritual and emotional agony over our inability to accept the non-Christian orientation of so much of Friends General Conference. But the trip did reveal that E.S.R. was not a solution to our quest.

Since then we have talked with John Yungblut at Pendle Hill. He was the first person to give us encouragement and suggest what book to read. Unfortunately, his major project of "explaining" Christian mythology so that moderns can accept it was not helpful to us, since we had had our lives transformed with the old mythology and not the new explained-away version.

I have visited Douglas and Dorothy Steere at Haverford about this problem. They suggested using the Rufus Jones collection at Haverford Library. The Steeres are lovely people. I do wish I could work with them to learn more about their understanding of God's relationship to man. Perhaps it will be possible to go to Haverford, Pendle Hill, or even the Princeton Seminary Library for a while. It will depend how the dissertation comes along. I would hope to do more than read in this subject. I would like to meet people and experience the reality found in those communities which carry on this tradition in Christianity—and outside of it. Here I find my interest in community and mysticism (and even the ascetic tradition) blending in real life communities.

One area I have tried to explore a bit in the last year is retreats. In January '74 (I think) I went to my first retreat at Pendle Hill, a longed for treat—impossible while I was in Chicago. The retreat was led by Conrad Hoover, retreat director at Dayspring, the retreat center run by the Church of the Savior in Washington, D.C. He led a classic Catholic-style retreat. The retreatants were silent, while the retreat leader did quite a bit of talking. The weekend was very cold and I was constantly afraid I might be doing the wrong thing. All this did not help for a relaxed time. There was no grand opening during the weekend. But I was concerned to pursue my interest. Since I have written to C. Hoover to get more information on Dayspring. But I have never received a reply.

7/11/1975

My second retreat was at Quaker Hill Conference Center in Richmond, Ind. (4/1974), led by Francis and Pearl Hall, former directors of Powell House in New York. They were in Richmond investigating the possibility of expanding the program at Quaker Hill to allow non-degree students to study—a very worthwhile aim. We learned the Halls had once been members of the Society of Brethren. They had an obvious faith in God directing their lives, with many stories to illustrate his presence. But they did not live out of the traditional "silent meeting" understanding of Christianity, perhaps because they brought such riches from the Society of Brothers. Ginny Schurman and I, who attended together, would have deeply appreciated this richness in another setting. But it brought us the deepest agony at a Quaker retreat. There was so little silence, with what little there was, was programmed as to mental content beforehand. The discussions included socially forced participation—thus prohibiting someone from relying on God's leading about whether to speak and causing some great spiritual and emotional stress, and making others concoct a nice sounding speech. There was also an atmosphere which encouraged what I felt was inappropriate sharing of confidences without the consent of people intimately involved. The whole experience made me react strongly against the increasing threat to traditional Quakerism. Later discussion with the Halls brought no feeling of unity on these deepest issues. This was a serious obstacle to me because of my inability to accept people where they were, spiritually speaking, and not feel betrayal of my deepest principles—always "my" instead of "God's."

My next retreat opportunity came in 12/1974 at a gathering of retreat leaders at Kirkridge. The gathering, although called a retreat, was really a conference on how to lead retreats. Most attenders were Pennsylvania German pastors including Edward Ziegler, editor of *Brethren and Thought* who was starting a retreat center in his farmhouse in Maryland with his new wife, an ex-nun. Arnold Cressman, director of Laurel (Mennonite) Retreat Center was present. He was the only one who had the problem of arranging retreats for children, as 57th St. Meeting did. Also present was William Stilwell, (ex) Friend from Downingtown Meeting who was in charge of planning Caln Quarterly Meeting retreats each half year. We had some good discussion on their increasingly unprogrammed retreats, and this has led to further contacts later, first to talk about retreats at Doylestown Meeting in winter '75 and then to attending the June '75 Caln Quarterly Meeting retreat.

Of course, Jane and Jack Nelson were also present. They told us something of the history of their work at Kirkridge. Unfortunately, each interesting conversation at the retreat never was given time to be explored thoroughly. We all planned to meet the following December to share our growth. Jack Nelson recommended that all experience a Friends meeting and a contemplative Catholic retreat during the next year, if possible.

The discussion at Doylestown, mentioned above, was very worthwhile. Doylestown has one of the most active retreat programs in Philadelphia Yearly Meeting—going to Kirkridge and planning a Quiet Day each year. I met Helen Atkinson, a dear Friend who also went to the Steere retreat in April. I hear she is going to lead some Quiet Days at Pendle Hill this summer.

In March, I think, I went to a retreat in Mendham, N.J. at the Episcopal community of St. John Baptist where there is a girls' high school, convent, and retreat house. This arose after some excellent correspondence with several Episcopal sisters of St. Helena about going to one of their convents in N.Y. for a retreat. But distance finally made Mendham the logical choice.

7/12/1975

The retreat was led by an Episcopal bishop originally from India. His theme was the importance of transcendental meditation for Christians. (In this case he used transcendental meditation as a generic term and did not refer to T.M.) He gave a number of advices on meditation based on his boyhood in India—even demonstrating on the floor.

This was my first retreat with a private room—a great luxury for private prayer or just rest. Such rooms seem to be non-existent in Protestant circles.

After the retreat we were all given a tour of the convent by a very sweet nun. It was a highlight of the weekend, her sweet and yet alive personality, the lovely chapels with all their special objects and vestments. The retreat was a Lenten Quiet Day for Episcopal women (mainly). I would like to be able to go again sometime.

The next retreat (and I was trying to take advantage of my year back in Princeton to pursue this concern with a retreat each month) was the Dorothy and Douglas Steere retreat at Pendle Hill, in April, I think. Among other themes Douglas Steere spoke of Chas. Williams' novels *Descent into Hell* and *All Hallow's Eve*. Both stressed the theme of intercessory burden bearing—a concept which came alive for me as I read these novels for a second time. The Steere retreat follows the classical silent retreat model. But it did not seem as crowded and hectic to me as did my first Pendle Hill retreat. Even so I longed for more "open space." The Steeres always build in personal talks with a retreatant who wishes. I talked with Dorothy about the pressure I was feeling in fitting prayer time into a hectic schedule, thus making it one more activity. Through her talk and later reflection I came to see the problem was with my work schedule and not with the prayer time (not that prayer time was free of problems). This year I have really looked forward to the periodic retreats. I was in desperate need to get a better balance in life and feeling constant pressure. I was really surprised I should feel so pressured this year when at last I was away from school, classes and imposed time schedules. But the schedules I imposed on myself (mild though they were) apparently carried the weight of the whole academic program, symbolically. They felt crushing. I really worried about the effect on my health. Something had to be done. After the research was finished the pressure seemed somewhat relieved—in part because various extra activities like German transliteration and listening to tapes was also finished. I began to try to read a bit in my growing pile of religion books I wanted to read for myself. Sometimes this became just another item on the agenda, but often it was a real treat, so the situation is very good some days. Other days that overwhelmed feeling comes back. Can I possibly finish the writing, footnotes, typing, and rewriting in one more year? I thought I had been extravagant in my time allowance. But when I see how long it has taken me to get this far, I wonder. I should up my work schedule. But given the state of my health, it is out of the question. I pray to God for an answer.

In May [1975], or thereabouts, I went on a private, individual retreat, my first one, at the Cenacle Retreat House in Highland Park, a location I discovered through correspondence with Sister Rita Houlihan (whose name was suggested by Jack Nelson in December at Kirkridge) and Father Michael Sheeran. I had been looking for a contemplative retreat experience—á la Jack Nelson's suggestion. But neither Douglas Steere or anyone else could suggest a place close-by. This was second best. I was a little hesitant about the authoritarian nature of a spiritual director.

The retreat was by far the best I have ever had. Sister Anita Rourke was perfect in her attitude, "walking along beside the retreatant." Very understanding and insightful. Each day I talked with her an hour, usually recounting what had happened the previous twenty four hours as recorded in the diary she suggested I keep. After each session she would suggest appropriate passages to read before each prayer period (three or four each day). Isaiah 55—coming to the living waters as one who thirsts—was an opening door that let out a torrent in my first prayer period. Somehow in those few days so much came together for me. The culmination was Romans 8 and the glimpse of the new world that creation was groaning to bring forth. I had gone to the retreat assuming my dissertation and its scheduled work would provide my greatest problem. Instead, I barely thought about it. I thought about where God was trying to lead me in the future. In particular I thought of all the closed doors I had investigated during the past year as possible teaching locations.

7/13/1975

I had visited a number of Quaker schools and written to others to see about teaching positions. The recession meant that very few schools had openings. But this was not the discouraging thing. What was so disappointing was the lack of religious concern in most schools. Going to school at the U[niversity] of C[hicago] for so many years had convinced me that I did not want to teach in a secular school where academic excellence was the only goal. Learning is hollow if it is not done in the service of God, and a competitive, impersonal atmosphere is inconsistent with the Christian witness. Therefore I decided I wished to teach in a religious school.

From our visits to Richmond I knew that Earlham and the Earlham School of Religion were not the right locations. Even inquiring about which Quaker schools might have the kind of orientation I was looking for brought only a standard listing of all the schools and a threatened response, as though I were asking them for a job. A third trip back to Richmond for a conference of prospective teachers in Friends schools proved futile since practically no schools sent representatives. (They were not hiring.)

Still my desire to learn about the religious education at Friends schools was such that I wanted to visit a few boarding schools around Philadelphia, ones which Tom Brown had recommended at the above conference. With an occasional exception I found dedicated Quaker leadership in a secular setting teaching non-Quaker children in an atmosphere of caring concern. Many schools did not offer separate religion courses. They were excellent prep schools, but far from the guarded educational ideal of traditional Quakerism. The most notable exception was _____ where a guarded education was still sought.

A trip to Friends Boarding School in Barnesville made me realize I was concerned with academic integrity as well as religious content and growth, a worthwhile lesson to learn. Faced with the secular prep schools of the east, this balance had been neglected. I felt uncomfortable with the experiential approach used in the religion classes. There were other problems as well, including a negative feeling about the competence of the administration and a dislike of getting into the antagonisms between quietist and evangelical, new generation and older generation. Such factors would only create terrible burdens for an outside teacher. The trip did allow me to meet some wonderful older Friends in the area including the Doudnas (Kenneth, Lillian, and Chester), Elma Starr of Ontario, etc. They related details about Ohio Yearly Meeting retreats and also stories of Quakerism as it was in the past in Ohio Yearly Meeting (Conservative).

Also none of the letters sent to Catholic colleges produced any results. Thus, all avenues seemed to be closed. Yet I had a growing realization crystallizing at the retreat that perhaps ordinary academic teaching on high school or college level was not what I should be doing. I needed to be working in an area that dealt with the inner life, prayer, and so forth, although I still saw teaching as connected with that some way—possibly in an entirely new type of organization. (Pendle Hill was not hiring without experience and none of the retreat centers outside Quakerism seemed a possible location for me. Of course, Quaker Hill was ruled out by my experiences there.)

But at the retreat I had the feeling that God was guiding. All these avenues were closed because something new was coming into being. The prayer and educational community Ginny and I had talked about crossed my mind. Yet I did not feel a go ahead in working on it. (I also hadn't the slightest idea how.)

Soon after the retreat two unexpected areas of service dropped in my lap—a chance to be treasurer of the Princeton Interfaith Council and a call to be on Worship and Ministry Committee in meeting. I answered affirmatively to both—thinking this might be what God had in mind.

The retreat had also made me realize anew that I was called to be here and now with my family and myself and not just think about some future goal. This has made a difference in my working after dinner and my subjective attitude about the work which must be finished. I feel God's presence now without a call to be accomplishing something.

Yet Worship & Ministry has been a call to growth, for as soon as I got on it, I felt a deep need to express some of the concerns I had about our decayed state. I always discipline myself when these concerns come out of hostility to others or frustration. This has emotional consequences, although I think it is right spiritually. It means I bottle these feelings up, along with possible hostilities, and am not open to God speaking in the other people—probably the worst consequence. The first meeting of Worship & Ministry had mention of the summer meetings and what to do about them. I expressed my strong feeling that one community should have one meeting for worship. This concern became a long discussion, much to my horror. No other person felt the same way. I just hate to be in a position like that. I certainly did not want a long discussion. I did not even want a change to a single meeting so much as a realization of the implication of our decision to have two. Lots of subsidiary points were of agonizing import too: setting off a preparatory meeting to relieve too large numbers was pooh-poohed—the importance of corporate concerns was seen as a trampling of individual liberty. It was terrible. Yet I felt no other way was open to me than to express this opening from God.

Yet somehow after weeks of incorporating this terrible experience, I feel I have come to feel less called to take care of each misconception and ignorance and wrong notion. Not that things should be neglected as they come up. But at least a feeling that recognition of problems does not have to mean being faced with the burden of solving them. That may be given to others. I don't know as I have transgressed this in words because I have put on myself such a strong yoke. But the yoke was necessary because of the transgression in spirit. For a while I felt perhaps God was calling me to work in an area in which I had no interest, such as discipline and corporate concerns, because we failed so horribly there. I felt my own needs in the inner life were to be worked on privately. I now see the latter are being called forth publicly. And the former must be dealt with as they come up. But their massive failure does not signify inability to proceed on other concerns.

7/14/1975

Proceeding to work within the meeting also seemed like the best course because of the contact with the Northeast General Meeting of Friends. The October '74 gathering at Marlboro Meeting near Unionville, Penna. was one of the most powerful gatherings I have ever attended. The old meeting house was full of Friends from Ohio as well as from the east. As many as one quarter wore plain dress. We all felt we were participating in those powerful meetings of years gone by before secularism had taken its toll in unbelief. Local Friends provided hospitality in their homes.

The next gathering at Powell House in New York over Easter weekend '75 was a debacle. The setting was inappropriate. No facing benches for the ministry; no room to kneel in prayer. But what was worse was the spirit of self-righteous orthodoxy and evangelicalism which attenders brought along. The meetings for worship were non-stop talk marathons with everyone trying to outdo the next in scourges for not being faithful to Christ, and telling what Jesus had done in their lives. There was no waiting on the Lord, no silence, no experience of the Divine Presence. It made me realize how empty formal proclamation can be, how dangerous the evangelical spirit can be, and how important the traditional ways of doing things are because they grow out of dependence on the Spirit of Christ and lead to it. I wondered at the interest in hymn singing on the part of the new-Wilberite young people in plain dress. I wondered at the lack of reticence to speak, at the lack of humility. I was at fault, too—not saying anything through concern for adding another voice to the chattering and feeling a rising hostility and a real fright. I have never seen such a spectacle as that business meeting which went nowhere.

After this gathering I came back to Princeton and visited the Thursday evening discussion group in meeting for the first time. The sincere yielding to God's will, to be transformed from our selfish natures to God-centered creatures was so evident I rejoice in the Lord's work in Princeton Meeting. I realize that I was not being led to work with a "separated" group of Friends because this group had not really separated from evil at all.

These things all went into the Cenacle retreat, along with specific ideas about what areas of concern I could begin to take concrete steps on in meeting and how to be a more open and willing participant in the family at home.

The next retreat I attended was the Caln Quarterly Meeting retreat at Kirkridge with the Stilwells. It was organized much as the Marlboro gathering with only meetings for worship (this time no meeting for business). Silence prevailed the whole weekend. On Saturday I felt so dissatisfied I would have gone home had it not been for fear of hurting the Stilwells. I discovered at the sharing at the end of the retreat that they and others felt the same way. Only a few were content. By Sunday, I had become reconciled to the weekend, feeling that it is not always right to expect some extraordinary experience from God. Our faith does not depend on mystical "highs." It must develop an ongoing relationship of dependence and obedience.

The weekend almost made me aware that there were other formats for an unprogrammed silent retreat than this one. I also felt it was necessary to be extremely careful not to stress silence instead of dependence on God. On our introductory evening many words were said in the praise of silence. But I'm not sure God was ever mentioned. I also have qualms about the use of the open-ended meeting for worship traditional at Caln Quarterly Meeting retreats. The theory is that we are open to the Spirit all weekend. There is no end to the meeting. But in practice there is an end. One does not remain in worship constantly. With no ending there is self-consciousness about being the first to get up and leave and also about staying too long, perhaps keeping the Stilwells up.

A possible new format came into my mind incorporating elements of the Cenacle Retreat with the Quaker tradition along with a few criticisms I heard of the weekend. Some felt the real need to share problems verbally and were frustrated in this. I felt a reluctance to accept the communal worship/private relaxation dichotomy. That is, no time was allowed or expected for private prayer—a failing in all the Protestant retreats I have attended. Instead time away from meeting was to be used for rest or recreation or prayer if one wanted. Prayer was forced to compete with a nap.

7/15/1975

Possible schedule for weekend silent retreat:

Friday evenings: meal, getting acquainted, followed by short introduction to the weekend by a planner or past retreatant, setting up work details (may be done in advance), worship sharing: how God is working in my life now; what questions, concerns or problems I am wrestling with; meeting for worship (perhaps only a half or three quarters hour because people are tired).

Saturday morning: all meals silent unless a reading is desired, 1 hour of private prayer—journal keeping of thought, feelings, openings, etc., 1 hour of meeting for worship—perhaps an hour and a half.

Saturday afternoon: Free (sleep, walking, quiet activities, sitting), 1 hour of private prayer and journal keeping before supper, passage may serve as starting point of all prayer sessions.

Saturday evening: 1 hour or more (may be 2 hours or more for complete sharing) of sharing of journal and openings or problems in groups of two or three, meeting for worship—perhaps an hour and a half.

Sunday morning: 1 hour of private prayer and journal keeping, concluding meeting for worship and final sharing session for reactions and discussion about change in format for future.

The month after the retreat Mom and Dad were gone on vacation. I had a chance to plan a number of lunches for Friends in meeting. It was a chance to get to know people much more intimately and fully and has produced a much closer, warmer, more understanding and tolerant attitude toward meeting. In particular, Rose Scheider and I who have very different understandings of Quakerism, have developed a real appreciation and friendship. We discovered a mutual interest in Hasidism and are planning a trip to N.Y. to talk to a Jewish Rabbi who is interested in this movement. We hope to be able to visit in some of the communities themselves. Harriet Hitch and I, as well as having lunch (with her whole family, minus Ann) have gone to see Shenandoah in N.Y., a fun day. Lynn Sherwood and her family talked about arranging a trip to visit Quaker historic sites in England. They have made such a trip and are willing to share some names and addresses of British Friends. Tom and Heidi Abrams and I discovered much in common in our approach to Quakerism, a delightful surprise to be able to share some of our agonies. The meal with the Morgans was rather formal, but I learned more about Chapel House at Colgate and have since felt akin to them in a sense of impatience they expressed at business meeting, a feeling I have so often felt. Of course, the Davises are dear people whose friendship I value greatly. I feel I understand each of these Friends better and have a grasp of a bit of the suffering and yielding they have done to be obedient to God in their lives. What tremendous trials these Friends have gone through. I am in awe of them. It is helpful for me to know this for my own struggles against yielding. Suddenly many obstacles melt away because they were not real. I put them there in my imagined vision of what faithful Friends and a faithful meeting should be. The memorial meeting for Robert Macey, that dear Friend from New York who had to learn to yield his deepest life's goal to God was one of the most powerful meetings I have ever attended. John Howell's prayer was very beautiful. Thank God for His Spirit so vibrantly at work blending all of his children in the meeting (living and dead) into a faithful community obedient to Him, not just outwardly, but inwardly—not because of a desire to fulfill an external standard, but because we are inwardly led to the same. The visit of Amos Hoover this past month was also a real honor. It was a joy to see the family again. We went to look at the meeting house.

This summer I look forward to a lunch with Sister Anita Rourke of the Cenacle Retreat House to talk more about contemplative retreats and training in arranging the same. In August I hope we can take the trip to Syracuse, Toronto, Aylmer and Newmarket. All these prospective gifts grow out of past gifts of God—enriching my life to overflowing. His presence is so clearly present. I marvel that I ever despair or feel so much agony. It is really true that God is bringing forth his people. We are just blind to the action. We measure by strategies and results. God works inwardly.

11/25/1975

I have not written in this journal for six months or so. I guess I did not want any permanent record of such dark times. Inwardly these have been dark months. The oppressive burden of the dissertation has made a horror of many days. I try to accomplish at least a bit each day. I do not try much. I am ashamed of how little I do. But even this seemed to create a giant burden, pressuring me also, making me feel I could not accomplish even the most modest schedule each day.

In addition, the opening for further exploration of retreat work seemed to close again. This has been a time of negatives. I have recognized that I may never find that religious school or other educational position which I had hoped to have. Investigations of all school and retreat possibilities showed that. No way has opened to pursue any of the basic problems which afflict our meeting or the Society of Friends as a whole. My insights and evaluations are not widely held. Even those plans of mutual agreement reached by Worship and Ministry seem to fall through. The Interfaith Council is limping so badly I doubt its current worth. The fact of having no prospect at making any contribution on any of these problems was a hard pill to swallow.

Yet, I find of late, it has been swallowed. The burden of the dissertation is lessened, perhaps because I am making progress at it, perhaps because of Ginny's faithful prayers. Moreover, I realize my disappointment over lack of any way to make a contribution is the old problem of self worth. I thought I had learned. I see I did not. If this is the way life must be lived, then so be it. God must be trusted. How little I agonize over the true problems of the world and how much concern I have for my happiness. Such an attitude would not allow me to serve God or others in any situation. As always peace has come with the cessation of striving for self-fulfillment. I fear I will never come to leave God in the center. Always I must accomplish. Of course, it is hard to know when one should strive for God. Perhaps I should be trying to create a way to tackle some of the problems which He has given me to see. But the way is not apparent, so I will be content, not just to wait until a way does open, but simply to be, forever, if that is ordained. Perhaps this is God's greatest gift, the pathway to God, the pathway which will keep Him central. Any other path I fear would simply raise the head of pleasure in the recognition and approval of others or agony over lack of same. It is best to learn again, that perennial lesson, to be content with the human condition as it is, without the artificial supports given by social roles: wife, teacher, minister or whatever. How else can one really know others, if one is always evaluating by their spiritual role or religious worth? How else can one know oneself, if the true self is puffed up by some prestigious task? How else can one know God, if one of His tasks always stands in front of our eyes hiding Him? The nothingness and void which caused such agony has revealed God. How amazing is His guidance and His love!

1/13/1976

Helen Davis has been a real inspiration these past few days. She and Hal are about to leave on a long trip to Pennsylvania and Florida. The weather has been uncertain and the day of their intended departure turned out to be snowy. They both accepted the delay so gracefully. Helen, especially, was content to leave it in God's hands. She did not worry about staying or leaving. When their departure was delayed, she rejoiced at being of service to friends at home for one more day.

How I wish I had this trust in God and acceptance of all God brings into my life. I am so attached to possessions, achievements, and the love and recognition of others. I fear deprivation and I mourn it when it comes. But even the recognition of this mourning process is helpful to me. I can understand how I react to loss. I get angry and then I grieve. This is true whether it is an important loss or a minor one. I finally recognized the process in a trivial situation, the "graying" of a new, white article of long underwear in the wash. It was so nice to have something new, pretty, and white to wear even if it was only long underwear. I was so disappointed to see it looking like an old rag after its second wash and to think of having to wear it that way for another 15 years. I spoke of it with a hurt tone in my voice to Mom, which I should not have done. It just seemed like I was not to be permitted even the smallest pleasure. Of course, the "pain" (clearly too strong a word here) soon passed. And I accepted the situation. It made me realize that in my weakness I cannot hope to be totally non-detached to finite things. Instead I must ask God's help in working through this grief process quickly and to have the strength not to take it out on someone else in the meantime.

Again I see this year's main lesson in learning how to control self-will and suffer the pain of its infringement. I have learned that just by existing one imposes on others—even without any awareness of great or minor selfish acts. Living at home has been an imposition on Mom which she resents. I do not blame her in the least on an intellectual level. But, oh, the emotions. How hurt I was when through agonizing sacrifice I never once said where I would prefer to go on our Saturday evenings out for supper and then Mom told me that she felt I always was the one to make the decision. How hurt when she asked me to let her drive because she was afraid of my driving! Again, how can I object when I was in such an expensive accident last year! Although I try to be conscientious, I know on the level of pure skill, I am not an excellent driver. But it hurts because I do not believe I am worse at driving than she.

I realize that the problem of self-will is much broader than those acts we do toward others with the intent of getting our way over theirs. God, please give me the wisdom to see what I do to others and the strength to obey your will in all things. Let me see how others' fears distort my intentions and how delicate and fragile the personhood of others (and myself) is.

2/3/1976

The anger I felt about my situation has evaporated with the writing (facing) of it and with the answer to a prayer much grander than the one I prayed.

Mid-week meeting has been laid down because of lack of attendance. I started attending the Monday evening meditation group. What a wonderful opportunity to grow in God. I have learned much about my own impediments in relationship with Him, mainly fear of loss of self. But I also see how puny my definition of self is and how grand the vistas are beyond my narrow definition. I pray that I may go through the door to those vistas without fear (but go through the door, fear or not). The meditation has drawn the most diverse Friends in the meeting into a deep sense of love and caring for each other. Oh, the power of God.

Fear still licks around the edges of my being because of the dissertation. From the reaction of my advisors so far there is a real chance it will never be accepted. Yet I know the fear is a bit artificial—not rooted in truth. More and more I know my direction is not toward teaching in the traditional academic situation which stresses intellect over relationship—to God and fellow man. I'm not yet clear what the proper place for me is. But I now know I must take some steps, fumbling as they may be, for more light to be given. Until now I have felt I was called to wait and not strive, wait for an opening—or alternately look for a position already in existence. Now, I come to see that neither is quite the right road. But I must be looking for a way to do something new. A sense of wholeness grows.

2/16/1976

I went to 11 o'clock meeting yesterday to see how the children were managing now that they attend the first 15 minutes of worship each First Day. The furnace was off again, as it is about once each month. The meeting house was cold. At the beginning of the meeting, John Howell brought in two arm loads of kindling to build up the quiet fire. It was a loving act which drew a grateful response from all present. We began with a deepened sense of communion with each other. Our children were fairly quiet. Visiting Methodist Sunday School children were composed through the entire meeting. Several spoke while the children were present. Eleanor Werenfels spoke of how much we take for granted, just expecting we will be warm, fed, clothed, able to walk, talk and see. This message was very effective in our cold meetinghouse. John Howell then spoke of how glad he was that so many were not laid up with the flu and could be present. Later on Cynthia Fox added that many were not at all well, but we all came to be healed as sick people came to Jesus. Other messages followed including one about Plato's teaching that it is better to suffer than inflict suffering. No reference was made to the fact that this Truth is the heart of crucifixion. But, of course, truth is truth wherever it is found. After the meeting John Howell came up to Cynthia Fox and said how glad he was she had given her message, that his had only been partial and he was almost moved to add to it later on. It was a joy to see Friends so sensitive to the leadings of God. What a wonderful meeting! It brightened the whole day for me and will continue to illumine the week. What nothingness my own worries are in comparison with this great gift of love and communion and leading. Thank you, God.

7/14/1976

Can so many months have gone by since I last made any notation in this diary of spiritual pilgrimage? The most recent weeks have been a time of peace and greater interior restfulness. This new release has coincided with my beginning to read my books on mysticism, having finished all the others on religious community which I wished to read while writing my dissertation. Perhaps the two events are more than coincidence. I realized how labored my periods of prayer had become trying to conjure up some experience to no avail. Suddenly, I realized God's presence continuing to operate in my life in a way which did not demand more and more achievement. He was there. I could deepen my relationship with Him best at this time simply by being and not disciplining every hour toward some end. Indeed life is so much more pleasant this way.

This same opening has made me realize how closed in on myself such discipline made me. I would like to give myself more to those in closest community around me in a way that is still consistent with me—a way that preserves much of the silence given in this stage of my life—a way that allows *appropriate* concern for my studies, a way that does not create dependence in others, a way that is not "preachy."

So many times my expressions of God's will have contained more of "me" than of God. I have tried hard not to speak when this is the case. The result has been even more silence. But at July business meeting I felt freed to speak for the first time in a long while. The subject was a paid coordinator for Burlington Quarter. I voiced my reservations about the plan (although I have come to accept its "correctness" if done with proper understanding and care). The meeting clearly supported the plan. But I did not feel shattered. I felt only love for those in the meeting and a willingness to see the Quarter take this step which may be a betrayal of our message of Christ's relationship to men. The end is in God's hand. I was asked to speak. I did. I am content whatever the outcome. I am so grateful to God for this new love. I know it is His and not mine. I never had it before. He is working in me. These past difficult months in the desert bring this wonderful fruit. I would like to enter the promised land.

Weekly meditation was extraordinary yesterday also. The other two present had been supporters of the coordinator. I expected that fact to have no bearing on our prayer. It did not. I did expect another long monologue by one member, addressed to the other member and excluding me—a familiar pattern my old self has come to resent and anticipate before it even occurs. But this evening the conversation preceding the meditation was long and drew us all much closer together to each other and the meeting. I discovered one member felt hesitant about reading his letters to us because of my presence and my supposed academic background. Instead of arousing paralyzing fears of my own coldness, the remark made me happy that it could be expressed. We left the gathering feeling much more at one. And I resolve again to try as best I could not to let my personality, fears, or discipline of silence erect barriers where none existed. The meditation which followed was largely one of praise to God for these gifts. We all felt His presence. We all received His gifts. Praise God.

9/13/1976

I have just finished reading Rumer Godden's *In This House of Brede*. Sister Philippa enters the monastery, giving up her position of power in business. She hopes to spend the rest of her days there in the slowly changing cycles of the monastery. In the end, just as she finds peace by losing herself she must become Abbess of a new monastery in Japan, a job which will probably take the rest of her life—or close to it. In this sacrifice, seemingly returning to the world of responsibility she left, she learns to give up that last little bit of self. The book is an insightful look at the wondrous ways in which each woman works out the problems and unwholeness of her life. One nun who has mismanaged responsibility and hidden her despised low social background is given as penance the thing she does best—to write a book of poetry. The book becomes very successful, giving the nun not only confidence but conceit. When her subsequent ideas for a new book are turned down, she feels injustice. The subject for her next book finally comes from an old, dying nun. The first nun gradually learns to see who she is and can act accordingly. Each step is necessary for deeper maturity.

Now I know what Thomas Merton meant when he referred to a certain Buddhist monk as a completely formed monk. Carol Wheeler's talk about the formation period and procedure for new nuns takes on greater significance. However, true formation must take years.

9/15/1976

So often God is found in the hollow of the ritual. When we learn the importance of social action, we suddenly discover the need for waiting. Academic study may destroy the redemptive process for the Amish and be the stuff of the ritual among Hasidic Jews. To find God, to find redemption, to find ourselves we must go into that hollow, and through it to another level of awareness and being, a level which integrates both opposites and also retains something of the void. Each person has at least one hollow to find, perhaps more than one. But the number is probably not infinite because our human situation presents us with a finite social and psychological location for our lives, and more importantly because one hollow is related to the void. To experience it once is to know it always. The particular antithesis is only the path to the void. God is not the void, but comes through the void.

9/30/1977

Over a year since the last entry. I suspect the long period of dryness was the result of the grind to finish the dissertation. Now what I hope will be the final draft is in my advisors' hands. There were times when I did not know if I could continue. As the writing and revising drew to a close, a new awareness of God's work opened before me. I expect it was there all the time. My narrowed vision simply prevented me from seeing it.

Many new and exciting developments have occurred in meeting. For example, for the first time since I have been in Princeton there is strong support to return to a united meeting for worship. In fact, the idea is now suggested by a person who was a strong opponent. The single meeting allows for common worship among all members, extra Sunday time for breakfasts, discussions, worship-sharing, business meetings, and committee meetings.

This summer we also had our most successful adult program ever. Tom Abrams conducted a lecture-discussion group on Quaker journals over Sunday breakfast. He was excellent, both in presentation and content. This is the first time I remember Friends coming to any educational type of program in Princeton. The program has meant much to Tom, too. He has a vast, untapped gift for the educational ministry.

Harriet Hitch, Eleanor Howell and I went to Ken Morgan's Chapel House at Colgate University on an August weekend. The library was excellent. Coming fresh from my dissertation studies, I decided to by-pass the books and concentrate instead on the art work. Much to my amazement, I found it very moving: the painting of the head of Christ crowned with thorns—what agony; the life-size crucifix with the body which both grew out of the cross and yet seemed stiffly to resist the cross; the Jewish bas relief of Moses receiving the Tablets on Mt. Sinai—the crowded mass of humanity and tradition; the Zen mountain and sea landscape with only a hut and fisherman's boat with a line that reached to eternity; and the two calligraphers—the Muslim "There is no power and strength save that of the all-powerful and almighty God," in gold letters shaped like a mosque on a black background; and the Zen "Unattached, like a cloud" with huge curved black letters on a white expanse. The first so structured and social. The second so unpredictable and free. All the works revealed different aspects of the divine.

Harriet and Eleanor enjoyed the experience, too. I think it may mark a turning point in the meeting's attitude toward retreats.

Each of these marks of God's transforming power has come in areas I have been vitally concerned about. Yet each took place largely outside my initiative. I must admit it makes me question the skill with which I work. But I also recognize how joyful I am that they have occurred.

Indeed, I recognize more and more the profound gifts of meeting members: Esther's deep concern for others' personal difficulties; Tom's gift for education and teaching; Gale's gift for writing about the inward life; Rose's many diversified gifts.

In the Yearly Meeting the Worship and Ministry Committee work of the past year has brought welcome new contacts with committee members and very informative visits to surrounding meetings. I am particularly aware of the needs of so many small, dying meetings and the despair and courage of Friends who struggle to keep them going.

On this bleak situation a ray of hope has come from the Krisheim Retreat group which was sparked by a power to renew our Society—to let God once again direct our efforts for inreach and outreach. They plan a gathering in October of Friends from all local meetings to spread the Word.

Two more gifts in recent months were the retreats at Pendle Hill conducted by Mary Cosby and at the Visitation Monastery in July. What I took away from the first was a new concern about developing the gifts of all meeting members. The second helped me cope inwardly with my thyroid-testing which had given so much distress previously, but which has been put to rest in the larger network of God's loving care and community.

There are so many wonderful and miraculous events of late. I am almost afraid to enjoy them. After all the pain and purgation, I thought life held nothing else. I cannot believe the riches. So many openings here make me wish to stay within the Yearly Meeting, if possible. How this can be done professionally is not clear. The specific direction of any ministry here (or elsewhere) is also unclear. I think I just need to "be" awhile—free from the striving of the dissertation, free from any fear that God is not there if I do not "work" in the ministry. His hand is manifested wherever I look. Surely his direction for me in the future will also become clear.

9/1/1977[63]

After my brief account of all the activities and openings of the last few months, I felt the two retreats at Pendle Hill and the Visitation Monastery were neglected a bit.

Mary Cosby, wife of the minister at the Church of the Savior in Washington, D.C. led the April retreat at Pendle Hill. From an immediate perspective the retreat was not too successful. There was too little time for silence. Yet from a distance it is clear that God spoke through Mary's stories of her Church of the Savior experiences. That church has accomplished a great deal: welding disparate individuals together in community, talking about and solving huge social problems. Perhaps the most moving story was the account of the church's official recognition of gifts. They all were to meet one evening to publicly recognize one another's gifts. Mary was terribly afraid that not everyone would be recognized. She was especially concerned for a lovely rural woman in the group whom everyone loved. But this woman had no special education. Her gift was not an obvious skill. Mary's husband chided her for her lack of faith. But still Mary went to the "gifts meeting" afraid this woman would be hurt when her name was not mentioned or when the others had to "make up" a gift for her, out of kindness. Much to Mary's surprise, this woman's name was the first one mentioned out of the initial silence of that meeting. A man spoke about her phoning a New Testament passage to him that morning to help him with a problem. He said that this lovely woman had a gift for the pastoral ministry. The moment this man uttered these words, Mary said she recognized their truth. She remembered how many times she herself had gone to this woman for prayer or to share a very personal burden. The woman she had feared would be least among them, suddenly took first place.

I realized that Friends meetings were organized to function only through the gifts of its members. Yet we so often ignored them. We rotate people on committees—a fine practice in some ways. But it also ignores the life task and gifts which God gives to each of us. Our meeting has so many extraordinary people whom we do not use for the upbuilding of the body of Christ. What about the seemingly non-extraordinary people? How many riches do we lose because we do not recognize their gifts? I came away from the retreat aware that God had laid on me a burden of making us aware of this problem. Three small openings have occurred in this problem. The Tape Committee of the Yearly Meeting Worship and Ministry Committee asked Gale Smith to tape some of his letters on the inward life for the cassette library. Tom Abrams used his teaching gift for the Quaker journal discussion groups this summer. He now has invitations to speak at other meetings. And Princeton Friends would like to continue similar discussions in the future. Finally, three of us went to Chapel House, recognizing one of Ken Morgan's great contributions to contemporary religious life. I believe all three men were uplifted and encouraged in their ministry by even these small bits of recognition.

9/2/1977[64]

The week of quiet at the Visitation Monastery in July was a time of blessing. The visit was disturbed by some difficult hours resulting from the thyroid preparation. But these were overcome by the experience of the great love and warmth within the community. The sisters enjoyed life with one another. And they were so kind to Ginny and me—encouraging us to eat more at meals, explaining the Divine Office, and relating the stories of Our Lady of Guadalupe. (The community was founded by Mexican nuns who found in Our Lady of Guadalupe a symbol of God's transforming work among the Spanish conquerors who believed the Indians had no souls and the Aztec Indians who still made human sacrifices. Both races had their attitudes and cruel practices changed as a result of this appearance before a simple Indian.)

Ginny and I tried to attend as many Offices as we could. We found it difficult to follow until we got some special instructions twice each day to cover the next two or three Offices. We also found the biblical selections particularly warlike and oppressive. Even when understood metaphorically, they seemed inappropriate for a community so clearly living out of dependence on God. What room should have been left to fear God's enemies.

Still the communal Office was a great help in directing attention away from excessive introspection. I found myself able to come to terms with my worries about the thyroid condition in the atmosphere of participation in God's universal kingdom.

Ginny and I also listened to two sets of tapes from the Thomas More Association on meditation and prayer. The set by Dom Hubert van Zeller we found especially helpful.

We both came away from our week deeply impressed by the practical and spiritual lives lived by the nuns. We found life far removed from the rigid austere existence we had imagined. It was full of laughter and joy—along with silence. We could imagine ourselves living this life. The sisters were so "ordinary" on one level. This order does not demand rigorous fasts, sandals or straw beds and midnight prayers. The schedule had a good balance of activities. It was not a schedule of boredom—as I had also feared. The day was crammed full. For year-long living, I'm sure this is more healthy than extended hours of unprogrammed time when one could be bored or intro-spective (in an obsessive sense). It truly was a life in community, not solitary prayer. Indeed the one aspect of life which would have been difficult for me to bear was the exhaustion. Perhaps one's strength increases with practice. But I found the daily schedule more than I could comfortably handle. This problem abated a bit when Ginny and I overcame the culture shock of such new table manners and chapel behavior. We expended great energy the first few days deciding how we should act. This detracted from the retreat no doubt. If the Monastery would have us, we would like to return sometime to know that we have overcome these initial problems and I could more readily enter the life of the community schedule.

[undated]

Sonnie wrote the following on scraps of loose-leaf, lined paper, likely while pondering what to do following completion of her Ph.D. dissertation.

Things to do before I die:

1. Develop deeper prayer life and closer relationship to God
2. Be able to help others to deeper relationship with God
3. Be able to open up religion to secular people
4. Be able to bring Friends to deeper commitment and faithfulness
5. Know something about each branch of Quakerism and bring closer together
6. Learn about Catholic and other monastic orders—perhaps have some personal experiences with [them]

7. Promote discussion among community and contemplative religious groups
8. Learn more about above groups
9. Be part of committed community
10. Develop close personal ties with few individuals of like mind

How to do:

Teaching/personal study, talking to own and other religious groups, writing, reading and researching, knowing books in field, understanding and presenting different points of view, being part of Friends meeting, discussing travelling classroom, finding other Quaker academics, investigating religious orders, continuing personal development, retreats

Want to have or use:

Meeting people of different religious groups, prayer life, group worship, teaching, solitude-sharing, reading and study, writing, contributing to Society of Friends, understanding of religion, work with mature people interested in religion

Want to avoid:

Competitive pressure, too much togetherness, too little aloneness, no contact with Friends, having to attend Protestant worship as prime worship, constant busyness, researching alone, no religious community to be a part of, exclusively academic atmosphere, no chance for dialogue with other religious groups, travel, too much physical demand, internal Friends disputes

Skills:

Teaching, especially interested people, talking with people of other religious views, letter writing as a form of friendship/help/commitment, reading and researching, living fairly withdrawn prayerful life, knowing literature in my field of interest, suggesting books on areas of interest, fair presenter of views to someone of different views, better at understanding different religious views, advising in religious sphere, organization (e.g. projects) and determination

Job description (ideal):

Teaching committed adults who are seeking to grow religiously in context of and worshipping with community of Friends, frequent contact and dialogue with other peace churches and Catholic religious orders, chance to pursue interest in contemplative life and thought, chance to do religious research in general, chance to visit different religious communities

Achievements:

Developing a disciplined devotional life, conducting a First Day School, learning about each peace church group, learning that knowing people of different religious groups is important to me, contributing to [a friend's] religious development, joining Friends meeting

[The following list was not labelled, but appears to consist of significant experiences]:

- Deciding on religion as subject to follow in college—analyzing, beginning to know religious life, research, introspection
- Joining a Quaker meeting—making contact, radical break with tradition, first willing to go out on a limb
- Religious Education chairman—organizing, coordinating people, perseverance, calling on the talents of others, encourager, patience, applying ideas of others
- Ministry and Worship chairman—God centered, resolving and exploring divisions in ideas
- Speaking in meeting—recognizing what needs to be said, overcoming fear
- Passing exams for Ph.D.
- Coming to terms before Masters Exam
- Passing theological comprehensives
- Devotional discipline—knowing the goal, willingness to go through defeated times
- Convincement of a friend—talking ability, persuasion, acceptance of individual

- Reading German
- Illness experience
- Dissertation research
- Letter writing—understanding spiritual life
- Knowing other religious people—being able to talk with people about their concerns
- Life's work pursuit—acting on some goals, putting others aside, not being afraid to go look
- Getting "A"s in 9th grade
- Barb's college—knowing ideal, understanding religious values, research, analysis, persuasion

8/19/78

Almost a year has passed since my last entry. These months have seen the completion (at long last) of my dissertation. The burden of that task had become severe; it is good to have it behind me. I wondered whether I would ever be cured from the wound that dissertation gave: the sense of constant pressure, the continuous state of being on trial, the feeling of inadequacy. I needed a long rest before I would be in any condition to take on a job. Moreover, any job which brought that same external pressure would have been unbearable. I needed a job in which I could feel that I was obeying God's will not advancing my own or other people's projects.

Providentially, the task of job hunting did not oppress me. I felt God would lead me wherever I was to do. When the opening at Pendle Hill occurred, it appeared to be just what I needed personally and also just where God would have me serve Him and grow in Him. The small salary is a trial. But it may be a lesson in the obedient life which I need to learn. Indeed, the whole atmosphere may be a new school of service. I am happy about my imminent move there. I believe the next step in my religious life is in a form of positive service to supplement the "negations" of illness, study, and silence. Of course all those negations had positive effects spiritually. But I now am led to know what life in God means in health, teaching, and writing. These will provide an important balance. The key to both is centering in God.

The past few months have been both free and disciplined-free from external demands, but disciplined to the leadings of God (I hope). Serious attention to my reading, planning courses for P.H., visiting the Society of Brothers and the Shakers, undertaking the task of clerking the Worship and Ministry Committee all have been both cure for my hurts and opportunities to grow in love in the community and in God. Attendance at the Navesink Hill Public Meetings and the Conservative General Meeting in Middletown has deepened ties with conservative Friends. I pray these ties can help the Society of Friends at large regain their Christian basis and at the same time heal the frustration, anger and hurt felt by conservatives. The QRT gathering in Barnesville, although leaving something to be desired in the format, has opened the way for a regional gathering for serious study. I have prayed that God will make His people faithful to His Will. Sometimes, I wonder if our own narrow vision and lack of faith in His power is what keeps this prayer from being answered. For God is so clearly at work in many ways among Friends and other Christians.

My health is much better of late. Although, I still have periods of terribleness (tied, I think, to the hormonal cycle), they are not as constant and bad as they were. The daily thyroid tablets (the result of last summer's thyroid testing) have perhaps been partly responsible for the improvement. I am grateful to God for the increased health.

October 1985

Sandra wrote again in her journal in the fall of 1985 when she was at Woodbrooke, the Quaker Study Center in Birmingham, England.

10/2/1985

Pendle Hill is a remarkable community. The Spirit touches and transforms many lives there—mine included. From the cramped, stressful world of graduate school, I have entered a place of caring, giving, and nurturing. So many of my concerns are given outlet there that I feel a sense of direction, fulfillment, and self-worth. God is present and leading me. Among the "new" leadings has been both the teaching in spirituality and the spiritual direction. But all these areas of ministry and learning to be well were caught up in the unfoldings surrounding my father's death in 9-28-1983.

The unfoldings of this second crucifixion started long before the event. For my father they consisted of increasing pain and arrhythmia. The spiritual and emotional ordeal of his heart disease was not discussed out loud by him or the rest of the family. He was not one to share such burdens. And we did not know how to ask. But the disease was present for us all.

During these last years, I tried to get home frequently—at least one weekend a month. Especially during QSP [Quaker Studies Program] when I could combine my teaching at a far off meeting with a visit in Princeton, I would go each week. There was nothing that needed doing at home. I simply wanted to enjoy this precious time with family.

In the academic year of 1982–83, I found myself giving up most of my Philadelphia Yearly Meeting committee work for the sake of something new. I wasn't entirely sure what that new would be. (I did know I wanted a deeper involvement in my local meeting, rather than being on the "conference circuit.") My teaching did not have quite the same appeal. I longed to teach the same subjects, but more in-depth. Going over the same ground became a tiny bit boring. For the first time I wondered, but not too seriously, if I might be led to a different work other than that at Pendle Hill. Each consideration of the subject brought me to the decision to stay.

This year was also the time for confrontation with death. The death of our much loved "Pepper" (miniature poodle) had come earlier by a couple of years. In a real way, watching her through her aged years was a deep experience for each of us. She dealt first with the handicaps of deafness and blindness, then with problems we did not know when she withdrew from company to be by herself, and finally during her last few days she would have repeated and increasingly frequent attacks of unconsciousness. Each time she would come round, but a bit weaker and with breathing more labored. She stayed in my folks' bedroom, her usual night time home, going outside only to the bathroom. My last glance of her (I was returning to Pendle Hill) was as she lay on the bedroom floor, a short way from her water dish. Her head was up but her breathing was labored. Even rising to her feet brought unconsciousness now. I wanted to go in to pet her. But I forbore because I knew being petted was too hard for her. (It had been even before this latest attack.) She died that night. My father buried her in the back yard.

He had earlier thought we should (or thought we might have to) have her put to sleep lest she suffer through this last illness. (We did not take her to the vet for care. She was nineteen. We knew it was her last illness. The vet would only have been an unnecessarily terrifying experience.) But she did not appear to be in pain or fear. She managed to go outside regularly until her death. The rest of us resisted having her put to sleep and were glad it was not necessary. I hope my father learned something about the family's care—even when it did disrupt the routine a bit. We all had loved Pepper deeply. Her uncritical love of us, her willingness to surrender her life to our pattern of doing things, gave each of us a sense of what unconditional love is.

But the year 1982–83 brought other confrontations with death—involving people. None of the individuals was close to me. But I was close to their "grievers": Sallie Gordon grieving for Chuck Werts, and

Sarah Miller grieving for her mother. I knew at the time that these encounters were not accidental. I found myself weeping with Sallie one day over what I knew my own loss would be. I don't know how much "help" this preparation was. Even with its help, I later wondered if I would survive.

Both this not-necessarily-wanted preparation and the freedom from the many committees which usually occupied my time made me aware how much God was leading and supporting me for what was to come.

The last summer was a nice one. Dad, who was increasingly quiet in his physical activities at home, was able to make a trip with Mom to Iceland. They both loved their travelling and had decided to risk quite difficult and adventurous trips even if it meant that Dad suffered a heart attack far from home and far from medical care. In short, they wished to live during the time given and not just wait for death. In 1983 there was a real question about whether Dad would be up to the ordinary demands of the trip. (But this was also a concern for at least a couple years past—including the very demanding trip to China where he picked up such a dreadful chest cold that hung on for weeks, I wondered if he had the strength to fight it. But he did get to China and did recover from the cold—perhaps never quite as strong again.) So the trip to Iceland (July) went along alright, except for the usual bad nights—one especially bad, and another in which he slept so soundly, unnaturally? (and snored so loudly) that Mom could not wake him.

When they returned from Iceland, I spent a nice vacation month (August) with them. We planned what turned out to be a very symbolic trip at the end of that month to my grandmother's in Syracuse. We went up regularly (but not as regularly as my grandmother would have liked). Our last visit had been at Christmas time—the first Christmas we had been together for years and the best one my grandmother said she ever had. It was an odd occasion for a best Christmas. My Uncle John, Gram's youngest brother, then in his 70s, was ill with cancer. He was in the hospital. John liked being in the hospital, strange as that sounds. He appreciated the attention of the medical staff. Perhaps it made him feel secure. We at home truly had a wonderful time being together. We felt warm and comfortable with one another.

So this summer trip was the next one after that Christmas. Instead of going the usual direct route through Pennsylvania, we decided to drive up along the Hudson and across the Mohawk Valley. (That was the old route we used to follow before the new highways were finished through the Poconos and at Binghamton.) There was a reason for the trip. We did some sightseeing. But most of all we wanted to do a bit of genealogical research in Columbia County—the area from which the Cronks emigrated to Yates County—the Penn Yan area. We had fun poking around the small towns and church cemeteries of Columbia County. We stayed overnight in a motel—all squashed in one room— which turned out to be a cozy time. The next day we drove toward Syracuse, stopping to see an old college chum of Mom's. Our trip was beginning to take on the feeling of a pilgrimage back to my parents' roots.

That pilgrimage quality continued after we got to my grandmother's. All of us piled into the car one day, my grandmother included, to go to Penn Yan to do some more archaeological research in the county hall of records and visit some of the country Cronk relatives my father had known as a boy when he stayed in Penn Yan and helped work on the farms in the summer. (He still ploughed with horses!) Ida Cronk had just had her first bathroom installed in the house. The facilities were not completely functional yet.

It was at the County Historical Society, just as we were finding some interesting leads on Cronk family history that Dad came back upstairs to the record room on the second floor, sat down, and passed out. Mom went to him, holding him as he continued to sit in his chair while I flew downstairs, passed my grandmother who had waited on the first floor, rather than trying the long staircase, and out the front door. I stopped long enough to ask the office to phone for a rescue squad but the elderly ladies were in a dither to get the phone to work properly and could not get a call through. I raced across the street while they continued to try. The shops on the other side seemed the closest source of help in what looked like a residential neighborhood. But each shop door was locked tight. Was it Saturday afternoon?

Why was everything closed? I met a woman walking her baby. She promised to call from home when she got to her house down the side street. But that seemed time consuming. Returning to the first side of the street, now quite breathless and unable to run, I tried a couple of doors before I found a Red Cross office with a receptionist who knew the emergency number by heart. She phoned, and I chugged, now quite slowly from the effort, back to the Historical Society only next door. About the time I arrived the Rescue Squad did, too. They were superb. The leader seemed to be a competent and calm young woman who talked quietly to Dad, now conscious, and to the rest of us. She objected to my flying back down stairs for fear I would alarm Gram. But my purpose was just the opposite, to tell her promptly that all looked well. I sat quietly with her a few moments and then went back upstairs to see what was going on.

The rescue squad had put Dad in a chair (rather than a stretcher) to take him to the local hospital, only a few blocks away. We all agreed that would be best. Dad included. The initial examination revealed a heart arrhythmia. The doctors decided he should stay overnight while they brought his heart arrhythmia under control.

The three generations of women called up Donald and Janet Cronk, who live about a block from the hospital, to see if we could stay overnight. Donald and Janet were very welcoming and even managed to provide a separate bed for each of us. (We all made do by buying a few necessary overnight items at the drug store where Janet worked.)

The small town hospital was human-sized and friendly. The ICU had only four beds. Not all those were occupied. The doctors were trying various drugs to correct the arrhythmia. The hospital dinner was chicken and carrots, I think, all the things Dad did not eat. When we went to bed the arrhythmia had not been corrected.

It was a lonely, frightening night, each in our separate rooms, praying. This was one of the few occasions when I had come away with nothing to read. Back at Gram's I was reading Job Scott's Journal.[65] I had shared his touching description of his wife's "dissolution" with Dad who had an interest in the accounts of those who were dying. He was moved by it and shared it with Mom. Dad found, as did nineteenth-century culture, that there was special meaning given these times. Those who died well were a model for us all.

As a result of the lack of my own peculiarly appropriate reading material, I read widely in two nutrition textbooks apparently belonging to the daughter of the family who was not at home. The words were sufficiently removed from the situation to be distracting. After reading I lay awake praying for Dad. Finally about 1 a.m. a sense of peace descended and I knew all would be well. I learned the next day that this was the time that a new drug corrected the arrhythmia problem and Dad was able to rest peacefully.

The next day the doctor released him. He was weak. The whole episode had clearly taken a lot out of him. But the doctor gave him a prescription for the medication that corrected the arrhythmia and expected all to be well. Dad even got out of the car (albeit "wobbly") to say hello to Donald and Janet as we came back from the hospital and return to Fayetteville. He weathered the trip back. And we stopped at the drug store to pick up a big supply of this new wonder drug as we drove up Lyndon Road.

That night or the next I could tell something was wrong because my father was up so many times in the night. In the deep of the night my mother came in to say they were going to the hospital emergency room in Syracuse so my father could be catheterized. What we did not know then, but soon learned, was that prostate conditions are severely aggravated by the new miracle drug. And my father already had a prostate problem. The medication so increased the problem that evacuation was impossible. The doctor in the E.R. recommended that we go back to Princeton immediately, and check into a hospital, and see about prostate surgery—an undertaking the doctors had heretofore avoided because of the risk of the heart condition.

My father had a painful ride back home. We phoned the doctor along the way. He agreed that we should go directly to the hospital. He would meet us there. My father was admitted. The first order of the day was to do tests and to get the heart medication regulated. (The doctors had determined the cause of the first collapse was too much "beta blocker", which had depressed the heart rate to too low a rate.) And, of course, the new wonder drug was out. Making substantive changes in these medications required electronic monitoring of the effects. The danger of death was too great otherwise.

Both these hurdles were crossed successfully. The next problem was to decide what to do about the prostate condition. This difficulty was made worse by an erroneous diagnosis of cancer of the prostate. (A resident carried a test vial around in his coat pocket so long before giving it to the lab, that the results were skewed.) The treatment for this disease would have been (strangely) not the removal of the prostate gland (too serious) but instead a removal of the testicles to slow down the advance of the cancer. In my father's condition any operation would have been serious. This second one carried a terrible emotional burden as well. So for several days we faced a struggle with cancer.

My mother reacted immediately and wonderfully to the news, saying to my father that they had walked up a mountain in Iceland together and they would walk up this mountain together. It was the only time I saw his lip quaver on the edge of tears through the whole ordeal.

But my sisters, Cindy and Barb, came in to be with Dad. Cindy was able to be with him alone, and he was able to tell her about many unresolved issues in his early, growing up years. He never discussed these things when Mom and I (always together) were there. I think he was moved that Cindy flew in from Toronto to be with him.

Paradoxically, the dispelling of the cancer scare brought us to a decision about the ever more dangerous operation to remove the prostate gland to solve the chronic problem with elimination. Dad seemed to make the decision quickly. He did not want to spend his life in and out of hospitals, with catheters, etc. He wanted to chance the operation. Such courage was far beyond my grasp. The decision had to be his. The doctors would not recommend the surgery on their own. The risk was too great.

I could see the strain of these days on Dad's face whenever we visited him. And all waking hours revolved around our visits to the hospital, taking turns at different parts of the day and evening. His lips and jaw were set in a rigidly drawn line not characteristic of him.

I knew that Dad had all that he could handle and did not tell him about the thyroid surgery recommended for me when I went to see my own doctor during one of those hospital visits.

Dad came home once during that hospital stay in September '83 but returned again for surgery. The surgery was scheduled early one morning. We waited at home, Mom and I. It is the "newest" way. No more waiting at the hospital. There is nothing one can do there anyway. The doctor phones afterward with a report for the family. We went about a subdued morning routine that day. I spent most of the time in prayer. I expect we all did. All during my prayer I felt a sense of ease. The feeling that all would be well pervaded my being and my room as I sat on the end of my bed in prayer. I remember asking myself whether I wasn't being naïve. The operation was serious. But the sense of ease remained.

In due time the doctor phoned. The operation was finished. My father was alive and had come through well. The doctor recommended a round-the-clock special nurse during these first few days of recovery. It proved a good idea, I think, although they did not have to do anything heroic. Their reports were uniformly encouraging in the midst of the admitted gravity of the situation. They were almost hard for me to believe when my father's obvious physical situation was so poor.

But I had the assurance of my prayer. So after the first two or three critical days, I returned to Pendle Hill to participate in the fall staff retreat. I lived for Mom's daily phone calls, giving me a report. After the retreat I returned home. Soon Dad was to be discharged from the hospital. We could hardly believe our good fortune. He had come through all the dangers.

When he did return home Mom and I had fun trying to find good foods for him to eat. We went to Toto's to find an extra nice slice of liver which Mom breaded and fried for him. We tried V-8 juice, which was having a big TV campaign at the time. He hated it. (We all had a good laugh.) We scoured the supermarket shelves for tempting favorites. I remember thinking how much delight we took when I had always been led to believe that tending someone so ill was supposed to be a burden. Dad's recovery was slow. We changed bandages, kept written records of various medication doses, and marveled when he began to walk up and down the upstairs hall. He even caught up on his red ledger work for September and began to make a file of his medical expenses so we could go through the task of getting Medicare and Johnson & Johnson insurance reimbursement. One day we all went to the bank, Dad included, because he remembered an "interest coupon" from a debenture which was due to be deposited in an interest-bearing account. We joked about the long delay in depositing the rather rare coupon at our Savings and Loan. I said, "If I'd known how long it would take, I would have packed us lunch".

The end of September was near. Technically, staff reports back to Pendle Hill at the beginning of the month, although term does not begin until October in most cases. I had spent most of September in Princeton. With term so close to starting and Dad doing so well, I began thinking of returning to campus on 9/30/83, the start of our orientation weekend.

By Tuesday evening, the 27th, I had about decided to do that. We all sat in Mom and Dad's room for half an hour as he watched TV in bed. I could see it was a strain to have us in there—me on the floor, but it was such a pleasure that I stayed through one program in the early evening. About nine, I popped back in to see if he wanted the TV channel changed. He asked me to get him a glass of water. He seemed happy. He said he now guessed he had three or four more years to live.

That was a momentous statement. He had been feeling so badly earlier in the spring that he did not expect to live to see the season's opening episode of "Dallas"—the TV program that had ended its 1982–83 season with a big fire. We viewers all waited anxiously to see if our favorite characters would survive. Dad asked me to watch for him and tell him when we would meet again. Not knowing how else to reply, I said I would. Even on his 69th birthday in July, he said he never expected to reach that age.

Now "Dallas" was only three days away on Friday the 30th [September]. I thought he would surely see the program for himself. No one expected any special trouble on the morning of Wednesday, the 28th. Mom had gone downstairs to fix breakfast. Dad had been fine. "Fine" may be too strong a word. He was sitting in the bedroom easy chair trying to get up enough strength to take a shower. But all seemed well.

A few minutes later I took a breakfast tray up. It was clear immediately that he was having difficulty. He said in slow halting speech to call the doctor, and said he needed a pacemaker right away. That step was something the doctors had recommended in the hospital. But Dad had preferred to take one step at a time and postponed any decision about a pacemaker.

I did not even wait for him to stop speaking. I turned around with the tray and went downstairs. I told Mom Dad was having difficulty. She went right upstairs, saying he was fine five minutes ago. I started what was to be a long search for Dad's doctor. Only his answering service was available. (Wednesday was a day off.) It took them a very long time and repeated calls before he could be located. In the midst of my call Mom came downstairs and asked whether I had got the rescue squad yet. I had not, so I told the answering service I had to hang up to call the rescue squad. I remember telling the answering service my father was dying. Even then the fear had gripped me. Try as I might to enter that place of prayer, I could feel no assurance of wellness such as had come late at night at Penn Yan and again later during Dad's operation.

I phoned the rescue squad, giving the background about Dad's heart condition. I went back upstairs and looked into the bedroom from the hall. Mom had a basket or pail. Dad was sick to his stomach and throwing up a bit. I did not know whether to go in or stay away. Mom said later he was feeling a bit better then and thought the problem was subsiding. I decided to go out on the front porch to wait for the rescue squad. I think I tried again to reach Dad's doctor and found only the answering service.

The rescue squad arrived quickly, I thought. They thought they were a bit slow, they said later. It made no difference in this case. A policeman accompanied them. What a difference between this brusque, untactful group and the sensitive people in the Penn Yan rescue squad. These people set about their work, trying to get a blood pressure, etc.

By this time Dad was lying down on the floor. I'm not sure how he got there. Mom said later they asked him to sit up. But he could not. He said, "I'm sorry." The paramedics soon had contact with the hospital. The doctor was found. He thought the EKG was pretty good, I could hear him say. The paramedics said it was not—in Dad's hearing—a very poor practice, I thought. I also wondered about the ability of this doctor, whom Dad had never thought highly of. I was listening on the downstairs phone to the conversation. I could not bring myself to stay upstairs. I did go up once and saw Dad's feet raised on the little bedroom stool so they would be above his head. But I could bear to look no more. Even these few scenes so burned themselves into my memory that they replayed in horror for months and months afterward.

The paramedics with the doctor's advice or consent, decided to use a pressure suit to keep the blood in the vital parts of the body. Mom said later that Dad fought them. I wondered during my own many "laters" whether Dad realized that his problem might not be his heart at all. He was a superb diagnostician. He spoke on many occasions of the sometimes disastrous consequences that occurred when doctors assumed one problem—the long standing obvious one—only to discover later that there was another problem at work. Here we all (doctors, family and he himself, at least at first) assumed a heart problem. We were all wrong.

Mom who tends to be conservative about medical treatments questioned the pressure suit, especially when she saw Dad's resistance. The paramedics only felt she was interfering and asked her to wait downstairs. She came down where I was. I tried to reassure her that I had heard these pressure suits were wonderful tools. (We read only a few days later in an AMA Journal of a California woman who had an air embolus after giving birth to a baby. It was determined later that the use of a pressure suit probably killed her because it forced the air into her lung.) I do not know how much damage the pressure suit caused. I do know that my last memories of home that morning were of my father's loud groans as the paramedics tried to insert an IV in his collapsed veins—a very painful process. So his last memories were of that pain.

The doctors at the hospital finally decided to delay transport to the hospital no longer. They'd been hoping to get an IV started first. Mom went to the hospital with Dad in the ambulance. I was to follow behind in our car. I could not bear to be in the hall when they brought Dad downstairs. I am still glad that vision is not in my mind—those visions I did have were so terrifying. But, of course, I wish I had been emotionally able to confront the horror of that day more forthrightly. As it was I took the clothes we had earlier put into the washing machine out onto the line to dry as the cavalcade came downstairs and made its way to the hospital. There was something comforting about doing this homey task when the center threatened to fall out of our world. I do not remember driving to the hospital.

When I arrived I found Mom sitting in the waiting room for the ER. Dad was alive and being examined. All they could say was that [something] catastrophic had happened. They did not know what. A kind woman chaplain appeared and asked us if we needed to make any phone calls. We decided to call Cindy and Barb and reached them both miraculously. Both promised to set out for Princeton—Cindy by plane and Barb by car.

The next incident I remember was a rescue squad member or policeman saying they had left equipment at the home and would like to pick it up. I remember the bedroom was littered with medical bags and used equipment. So I rode back home with him so he could pick up his things. He inquired about Dad. I told him he was still alive. He drove me right back to the hospital.

Mom said they were going to try to implant a pacemaker to see if that would help—apparently his pulse was now steady, but he was not conscious. I am in awe of that poor sick heart to keep going in spite of all these odds. Mom had agreed.

The two of us went upstairs to wait in a new waiting room near the OR. I'm not sure how long we waited—not more than an hour. When the doctors came out, I could not tell anything from the expressions on their faces. But they said Dad was gone.

"He was a nice guy," they said. They were sorry. We found out later that Dr. Willard's office had a pall over it for the rest of the day. But Dr. Willard in his usual poor bedside manner said something about Dad being his own physician and wanting his things his own way (I think that meant refusing the pacemaker). At that time it was clear we were all thinking the problem was a heart attack. They asked to do an autopsy and we agreed.

The chaplain reappeared and said something soothing. There was nothing else to do but drive home.

Somewhere along the line we tried to phone back Cindy and Barb. We got the latter but not the former. Each said later they were glad it worked out that way. Barb cried all the way up in the car. And Cindy did not know. I alerted the hospital to have her phone home when she arrived, so she would not hear the word from a stranger behind the desk.

The only thing we could think to do was to go to the bank to draw out some money. We knew the joint accounts would be closed when word of Dad's death reached the bank. I was concerned that Mom have money to live on in the interim period. (It turned out I think that she did not draw on this money.)

Then we went back home. A strange world greeted us. It looked like the old familiar world on the outside. But it was not. We moved through this world like ghosts or beings from another dimension who could not fully materialize in this one. It was lunch time. But neither of us was hungry. Mom went up to lie down as she often does after lunch. I went into the family room and turned on the TV soap operas. What did one do after such a blow? What could be done? Mom, I'm sure did not sleep. I did not see what happened on TV.

Barb and Cindy arrived that afternoon—Cindy phoning from the hospital as instructed—to receive the dreadful news. I telephoned Pat and asked her to phone Gram. (It turned out later that the two of them later sat by the phone waiting to receive word on viewing and funeral arrangements. But we, assuming Gram would not travel, she hadn't traveled in years, did not consult her in making the plans. Hard feelings multiply at such times. I'm not sure Gram has come to terms with that perceived slight yet.)

The next twenty-four hours, when one can hardly function, one is asked to make dozens of arrangements. We worked with the young woman pastor at the Presbyterian church to plan the burial and the memorial service. We bought a casket. We contacted relatives and friends. The phone bills those days ran into the hundreds of dollars. Mom picked out two cemetery plots in the old and very interesting section of the church's cemetery on Witherspoon St. Dad, who enjoyed poking around old cemeteries, would have liked it better than the newer section. The cemetery has been the site of a historical ceremony—about a year ago. It seemed fitting that such an occasion should happen near Dad.

The burial happened on Friday. Could this be? The day I had planned to return to Pendle Hill? It was the last day before embalming would have been required. It seemed a shame to put Dad through that after all he had been through. And I, for one, would have found it emotionally impossible to go through the memorial service on Saturday knowing we had the burial immediately afterwards. The graveside ceremony was brief. Barb managed to stay by the casket after the service. But I could not. That didn't stop the tears but only made the eruption less violent. Cindy walked with me up and down the nearby cemetery paths while Mom stayed with Barb. Cindy said that Barb had had Dad for so much briefer time than we had, it must be harder for her.

At home, when I was alone, I would go to the pillow on Dad's side of the bed and to the easy chair and kiss them both as if he were lying or sitting there. Saying good-bye in that way was comforting over the weeks that followed.

The memorial service was lovely. The minister did a beautiful presentation. Wayne Geisert, President of Bridgewater College, spoke nicely of Dad's work there. And Bob Wilson of J. and J. [Johnson & Johnson, where her father had worked] spoke of Dad's contribution professionally and personally to that organization and its people. It was wonderful to hear about his reputation as the one who spoke for high ethics and responsibility to the consumer. The concern shaped Ortho into the fine company it is today. I had not heard Dad's work spoken about before. But it is entirely in keeping with what I knew of Dad personally: his great caring for persons, animals, and even so-called inanimate objects. He treated the latter very frequently as if they were alive and had feelings or at least an identity and being of their own which needed to be respected. He was an honest and just and generous man. His dealings with other persons or organizations were always carried out with honesty and responsibility. (The memorial messages did not speak about characteristics such as Dad's love of trains and horses—perhaps inherited from his father, an engineer with the N.Y. Central, and from his farming summers in Penn Yan.)

The messages did speak of his sense of humor which was unique, sometimes teasing and even off-putting to people who did not know him—strange for such a gentle soul.

We picked out the music and hymns for the service. I was pleased with them. Bridgewater College had sent a large floral arrangement which we put at the front of the church. We did not encourage flowers. (Many came to the house anyway.) But Mom was glad there was at least one in the church. I could not keep from weeping in the middle of the service. Cindy's children did the same. [Uncle] Bob tried to be comforting.

Many people attended the service. There was a touching sign of honor and respect. After the service, the family departed through the front of the sanctuary. It was good not to have to greet everyone. A few came back to the sitting room behind the sanctuary to give their respects and condolences. That was enough, and comforting.

Relatives and close friends (Ginny Schurman was there) came back to the house. Many people brought food. And we had ordered a big platter of cold cuts from the Acme. We did not need to cook for days. But of course, we were not eating either. But the "company" ate. Ann Whitney and Gigi did all the dishes. It was quite nice to have everyone there, if we didn't think about why they were there.

When they left we went back into our numbed shock. The numbing sensation is a protection, I think. It wasn't a very successful protection. Anything could break through it. I opened the cupboard door and saw the special cans we had gotten because Dad would like them. And here I was eating them. (It took me a while to be able to open one.) Television shows about hospitals, doctors, police, etc. were too painful to watch—not that we could concentrate on a plot anyway. I watched the premiere episode of "Dallas" on that Friday of the burial. But I couldn't keep track of what was happening. I'll have to watch again in the repeats so as to give Dad an accurate report when I see him.

Day and night, no matter what else was happening, my mind replayed the events of that August–September—especially the day of the 28th. It was like a film projector that turned itself on even if I didn't want it on. It is only now, at the end of the second year of grieving that I realize that the projector does not turn on by itself any more.

The tears, mostly in private, and the utter desolation then would sweep over me. The acute sense of loss, the wish to be caring for Dad as we had been. It was hard to be in the house because it reminded me that Dad was not. On the first day my wish was to be with him rather than here separated from him. I have never felt such all encompassing loss of a loved one. From being a constant feeling it became an intermittent upsurge that could overtake me anywhere. It was only months later that I could separate out feelings of my own aloneness and loss. In the beginning my thoughts were only on Dad.

Why? I had always felt emotionally close—as though we reacted alike in many situations (not all); not that we shared a great deal by phone or letter or did a lot together. We were close because we were alike, strings tuned to vibrate at the same tone. When I went off to college, I remember feeling as though Dad were present with me or that what I did I did with him in mind. He never judged what I did. I never felt I hadn't live up to his expectations in an oppressive way. It was just a tie that was. That's all. I never knew how he felt. I have no indication he felt the same bond. It had nothing to do with his depth of love for Cindy and Barb. He had a special relationship with each. He talked about different things with each. This was just how the bond felt on my side. Very early on after his death, I vowed to live my life as fully as God led and by doing so I would be embodying and continuing his life. I didn't have to do his activities, read his books or watch his TV programs. By being the best "me" I would be continuing his presence in the world.

In the pain and loss, which were acute, I had a curious experience of God's presence. That was true at the beginning and it has remained true these two years. It was curious because I had heretofore assumed that such pain and emptiness were incompatible with a strong sense of God's presence. But that is untrue. Those people who recommend a stronger prayer life as though grief is synonymous with loss of faith in God are quite mistaken. I could and did have experiences of joy and loss at the same time.

I found as Mom did that many ordinary activities lost their sense of meaning and purpose. They did not carry enough depth of meaning to speak to me. Perhaps this world had receded in significance.

Yet out of that receding came new involvement—the ministry of spiritual direction. When some ground was left empty, a new plant could grow. The pattern of my life reshuffled a bit. The implications of that new pattern and the new involvement are part of my contemporary questioning. But that is to jump ahead of the story. The one element that might be mentioned here is that the ability to listen to pain may have come out of my pain. No one listened to me. After a few short sentences, conversation would turn in another direction. I felt no one could listen deeply enough to be with me in the pain. And I was somehow now given to be that listener for others. I was released to be mother, sister, friend of others.

An element, perhaps even a block, in the grieving process for me was my unwillingness to acquiesce to my father's death. I did not want to say good-bye. I did not want him gone. I was not ready to give up the grieving.

At the same time I recognized a strange kind of "rightness" in the time of my father's death; all the while recognizing alternate scenarios that would have allowed him longer life. I recognized even God's kind providence while at the same time I could not understand a God who allowed such a horror as death. Death contravened all that I knew of love and caring between people. There is still nothing but mystery for me there. But given the fact of death, the ordering of Dad's was very special. He had had ten years since his heart attack—a wonderful gift which we always accepted as a gift. These last couple years he was getting much weaker. The autopsy showed that an incipient colon cancer would have appeared in six months. He would have then had to undergo a surgery he probably could not have born or a radical treatment that would have made his last time a hell. How much "better" to go like this. Moreover we had had such a wonderful final summer: Mom and Dad's trip to Iceland, the retrospective trip to New York. The visits of Barb and Kim and Cindy. It was as though God delayed the end of that summer as long as possible—almost to "Dallas." On top of that, we knew from Dad's choices of the past month, his wish not to be so disabled as to be greatly impaired in his living. (At the same time his courage to live with whatever pain came to him was extraordinary in this age of "rational suicides" and easy ways out.)

I saw his death morning as his crucifixion—his ultimate giving up of all that he had and was—in such a gentle way—his final words of "I'm sorry" to the rescue people. Out of that surrender of all, I can only trust in God's care of him, to bring him to a new home in peace, untempered by the pain and ills of this world. In those early days my prayer was that God would take care of him as we had. Our whole lives are pointed toward this surrender. Each of our smaller crucifixions brings a resurrection to deeper life unknown before. I believe this happens at death. But the pain of separation was so great for us. I could only imagine what it must be like for him. There must be learning how to live this new resurrected life there as there is here. I hoped there might be a small silver gray poodle waiting to help and perhaps some friends and dear ones already there.

We called on Dad many times those first days as the business/arrangements end of our new life began to descend on us. We needed papers and more papers, forms filled out in proper order—an avalanche, a tidal wave of such work that kept up for close to two years. This inundation was the hardest to handle of all both practically and emotionally. For each time we faced it, we were confronted with the loss and our own insecurity at handling this mountain of financial paper work.

Sometimes there were pleasant times of talking to Dad explaining what was happening, pointing out a view, an occurrence, an interesting TV show—all done inwardly, of course. It was hard not to share a bit with him after all the years of sharing.

Right after Dad died Mom put her arms around us all on her bed and asked us never to forget Dad. It was very touching. But forgetting would be impossible. He is part of us and will be as long as we live.

Mom stayed home the first couple of weeks to tend to all that needed tending. I drove down to Pendle Hill for my classes and to see my consultees. Then I would come back to Princeton. After about two weeks, Mom began to follow the same pattern. She would come to Pendle Hill with me for half a week and then we would both go back to Princeton to take care of the load of business. I blessedly cannot even remember now what all that business was: will probate, contacting insurance companies, medical and funeral bills, initial meetings with Bill Porter at Horizon Trust. He was most helpful and under-standing in taking us through all the steps we needed to take.

We marveled at the time that we were both well enough to do this travelling back and forth and to carry on the responsibilities at both ends of the road. But we managed with no ill effects.

Mom was very shaken during these weeks. She said later it was like a physical blow. I knew what she meant. She looked physically shaken and unsure of herself and her world. I worried about her health. She was also shaken emotionally—to state the obvious. I was unfamiliar with the disorientation such an emotional upheaval could cause: the memory loss, the inattentiveness, the confusion, the lack of any energy to be concerned with those closest (i.e. on an emotional level. She was very helpful in an everyday sense.)

On top of all these difficulties she had to face the problems con-nected with learning to do so many of the things alone which she and Dad did together or which Dad had done for them both: looking after the car, yard, house repairs, and most of all the bookkeeping (check book balancing, bill paying, C.D. recording, tax filing). These new jobs she slowly began to undertake with increasing confidence over these two years. But the pain of this new life was intense at times. I think we both wondered if we could do it.

I am convinced we would have been able to manage all these changes quite well if it were not for the intervention of my thyroid surgery at the end of that fall term. The prospects for the surgery were in themselves more than I could handle on top of the stress already in my life. But matters were made worse by the vastly increased synthetic thyroid hormone I was being given in preparation for the surgery. In the early weeks, while the dosage was being slowly increased, my body tolerated it well.

In later weeks the amount of medication was having serious effects on my ability to function. The first "attack" occurred on the way home from a trip to Friends University in Wichita, Kansas, to prepare for a Friends Association of Higher Education (FAHE) meeting. I found myself sick to my stomach, with a queer shaking, and pounding heart. When the plane landed I could not walk to the car. A friend secured a little electric car driven by a porter. When I reached home, I had to lie down for two hours while the symptoms subsided. I remember being very cold. Mom piled blankets on me. I was not upset by the symptoms, imagining I was airsick or had picked up a bug.

The next full blown attack did not come for another month. But in the meantime I was getting more and more tense and nervous. By the end of November I was having increasing problems with physical symptoms. I feared taking so much hormone, really wondering if my body could take the strain of such severe reactions. But the doctor kept insisting. Who was I to believe, him or my body? He kept telling me to disregard the symptoms and even gave me a beta blocker to block the symptoms. It worked after a fashion, so I tried to follow his advice, until I was at the point that I felt I might be killing myself with reactions I was having. And the few days before surgery I stopped taking so much hormone.

Unfortunately, the symptoms did not let up. My doctor called it thyroid storm and said 90% of thyroid patients had that reaction before surgery. The fear associated with the intensity of the reactions increased. The doctor replied that the fear itself was one of the symptoms of this increased thyroid hormone. The remark had only limited comfort value.

I left Pendle Hill at the beginning of Festival Week in order to enter the hospital and have the most recovery before winter term. The weekend before surgery I had a sermon to deliver at a Mennonite church in Franconea Conference. It was a progressive congregation. I was glad to be with them—especially so at this time because it gave me something else to focus my mind on than the surgery. But the logistics of the day were a horror and probably a good picture of the distressed state of Mom and myself.

I had asked her about three times the day before to plan to get up early so we could get going in plenty of time. But when the day dawned, she was up later than usual. (Later she said she hadn't heard my earlier requests. I think instead they had not registered.) The day was miserable—a horrible rainy snow. We set out with Mom driving and me already upset about the late start. Things got worse because of our slow progress in the storm. If it hadn't been important, we probably would have turned back. As it was, we lost time as we drove. What's worse, we lost our way. I was nearly frantic inside. Finally, I felt we must stop and ask someone for directions but Mom felt it was too early on Sunday morning to disturb anyone (8:50 a.m.). So we drove a bit further with no success in finding our way across country. Finally I burst out with a dramatic plea to stop so I could ask directions. She was astonished at the uncharacteristic outburst. Uncharacteristic it was. But it showed my general condition, my frustration with Mom about our slow start and the prohibition at asking directions at an hour which, while early, was not too early from my point of view. She stopped at a house. I asked directions and we were on our way and eventually reached the church at just the right time. My fears of being late were groundless. My body was in such a jumbled state that I had to request permission to deliver my sermon seated. I did not think I was able to stand for that length of time. For all the problems of the day, I was glad to have done it.

The hospitalization was short and basically a good experience. There were only minor exceptions: a nurse in the middle of the night telling me (quite rightfully) that she could not offer any advice on my not taking medication I thought I did not need. But her curt reply that I must ask the doctor was no help to a frightened patient who obviously could not phone the doctor in the middle of the night to see if harm would come by omitting a medication. The kitchen was also unhelpful by sending a regular lunch—sandwich and all, the day after the operation when my throat was so sore I could barely swallow. But I was hungry. Over the course of an hour, with plenty of chewing of small bites, I ate the lunch. But otherwise the regular checks were comforting, the grogginess after the surgery was a relief to a body which had been racing for a month. The doctors released me after three days, two days after surgery.

Then came the wait for the pathologist's report on the two nodules removed. The report was delayed because one nodule was unclassifiable at first. So I got conflicting reports from doctors—one saying all was fine, the next that things were suspicious. Call-backs did not come promptly. All the waiting and conflicting information over the course of a week succeeded in frightening me all over again. The all clear came over a week later with one nodule being clearly benign and the other at least not cancerous. That was a relief. But it still left the question of whether to take the thyroid hormone to inhibit growth of future nodules. The doctors would have liked the continuation. But my attitude was so negative that it was decided to go ahead without the use of external hormone.

Post surgical recovery was strangely far worse than the hospital stay and even worse than the pre-surgical time. The periods of body racing continued coming on me quite unexpectedly. By this time they produced not only the physical symptoms themselves but great fear as well. My heart would pound arrhythmically for hours, I would wonder what damage had been done or would be done by this battering. The doctors seemed unconcerned. Take more beta blocker was all they would say.

But this symptom was accompanied by another that appeared on the Thursday after surgery. I remember its sudden appearance. My left side arm, under my arm, shoulder all began to shake internally at the slightest movement. It felt as though something were dreadfully wrong. I suspect, and my doctor felt too, that something may have happened to a nerve in surgery. But he was not concerned. Many people had it, he said—no problem.

I was incapacitated by it. At night I would sleep with the left arm away from my body so that the shaking would not affect the rest of me. The racing syndrome, set off by too much activity at any time or getting too tired meant that several hours were necessary to settle down at night for sleep. Moreover, all these effects so shattered my already strained life that I began to have nightmares—along with the already recurrent showings in my brain of the events surrounding my father's illness and death. I who always slept through anything and everything could not get a good night's sleep—shaking, nightmares, racing or memories were always there to wake me up or prevent sleep in the first place. Even ordinary amounts of physical or emotional stimulation were more than I could handle. It was as though the bodily mechanisms for handling overload were out of kilter. They would shift into high gear inappropriately and I had to go with them even if I was not feeling that way in my mind or even emotions. There was a discontinuity between my emotional state and my body. I say this in spite of the obvious upset on the emotional level. It seemed as if the body's manifestations went further than the upset of the emotions.

This physical upset only increased the emotional burden. Fear remained the dominant feeling—fear of my body not working, fear in this new world with its many demands.

Returning to Pendle Hill Mom and I continued to live in my apartment. Our disagreement at the end of the fall term was reassuring to me in a way. I felt we no longer felt so emotionally insecure as to avoid arguing. She was a great help in my recovery. For there were times I was literally afraid to move—even to get a sandwich, e.g. my internal body workings would be shaking on the left side or the problems of "racing" would be so severe that I did not want to aggravate them by moving. For even relatively brief movements, would make both problems worse. But I longed for solitude. I have always needed much aloneness. Now, especially, even the physical presence of someone else was so burdensome on my nervous system that I wanted to scream. I think I might have recovered more quickly if I had been given that quiet time sooner. But on the other hand, I could not have managed alone.

As it was I was awakened nightly when Mom would go to the bathroom. This was devastating because my nightly routine was so upset already. It was not just being awakened. It was that her presence at that odd hour was a reminder of the extremity of our recent situation. Instead of normalcy there were signs of abnormality at every turn.

(Right before and after surgery I had told Mom and Cindy that I needed lots of time alone and even asked them to leave when I felt their presence too much. But one cannot continue in that discourteous way for week upon week. I tried to be quiet and scream only inwardly when the presence of another became too great. I was acutely aware it was not really Mom, but the whole tense situation which was too much.)

How I managed classes and consultees I will never know. I literally got up for class—took lots of beta blockers and then went back to bed again. Dyck [Vermilye],[66] Pendle Hill's dean, kindly assigned only two or three consultees to me. (I suspect I was not much help to them.) As it happened my Quaker Studies Program (QSP) was scheduled that first term after surgery. It was at Willistown, the closest location I'd ever had. It was in the afternoon. (Evenings were bad times. It seemed my body was too tired to react properly.) And Pendle Hill and local Swarthmore people were attending, so I could get a ride easily with them. I remember I had to sit through the classes at first because of these scary bodily symptoms if I did not. In spite of everything, I did get through term.

The following term was better during the days. I even managed to go on class field trips (although I had to stay in the car during some stops.) Mom had a room of her own on campus (Dyck's suggestion). But nights were still bad. It was about this time that I began to be able to grieve for myself and not just for Dad. In fact, it seemed as though there were two grievings to do. The first one, which remained after the other one was gone—"Dad dead." But there was also the second one. My own loss. One nightmare was of two bulldogs wearing shoes. Each had one shoe of ox-blood red and one of very light tan (or perhaps two of each as befits a dog). In a completely surprise move the older (father?) dog kicked the younger. And the younger dog in astonishment and horror went down a huge pipe or tube into the ground. Here the younger dog was lost, not the older. The image was terrifying and woke me up in a fear that took a long time to settle again.

Indeed, the one task which obviously had an emotional impact was any of the Princeton financial book work. A visit to Horizon Trust, trips to the bank or a couple of hours work on the red ledger were enough to bring on an episode of racing. Mom felt the same way, I think. She often went to bed with a headache when we had to do such work, which we had to do constantly. The stream of financial and paper work seemed never ending. Each time we thought we were getting close to having all matters under control, new demands would arise to demand attention. For both of us this work was not just stressful, it was so full of emotion that it was physically damaging.

Fortunately, this was about the only specific task which had this effect. Otherwise, the physical symptoms mentioned above came with physical exertion—especially at night (I had to be very careful what time of day I walked) or with tiredness in general or for no reason discernable to me (and hence even more frightening).

During this time I ate ravenously. It seemed I was always hungry. Whether this was an effect of the upset hormonal system or whether it was a way of searching for some security in a world of chaos, I do not know. Perhaps it was both. Only now am I able to think about eating normally again—although dieting still seems too much of an effort. So one legacy of this period is a large unwanted weight gain.

By the end of the school year I was managing pretty well without extra help. I was not taking beta blockers regularly. Racing symptoms generally calmed down by themselves. I even went to Wichita, Kansas for the FAHE meeting I had planned in the fall—although I did not get to any evening gatherings. We had made a big push to have Pendle Hill people present at this largely evangelical gathering. It was a great success.

My single biggest gain was made in August when I spent the month with Gram. I had been deeply aware that we had neglected her terribly from Dad's illness and death. We had not been able to visit later. It was the first time I was brought face to face with the fact that I could not act on a need I so badly wanted to meet or fulfill a priority which was so high in my list. It was a physical and emotional impossibility. So I promised her and myself that I would spend the month of August with her. I knew even before I went that it was as much for me as for her. To be back in her house and with her would give me the security I so deeply needed. And the quiet of her routine and the long walks on the towpath of the [Erie] canal would be restorative and strengthening. This proved to be the case. By the end of the month I had made great strides.

Of course, the month was not easy. I would come from walks with my body shaking and having to sit in the living room chair a while before I could talk to anyone or eat supper. The nightmares continued! Ghosts and other scary things to disturb my sleep.

But gradually I was able to walk longer and longer. And if I didn't go too late in the day, the shaking might not come or if it did it might not last all night. It was lovely to be with Gram. I have such warm memories of growing up in her house—her cooking in the kitchen, walking into the woods together, playing on the canal ice in winter, Thanksgiving, clam bakes (annual family reunions, etc.). I had that continuity again. I was not constantly reminded of our loss. For all that I got out of it, I think she felt better too. She ate more regularly and sensibly. Her hours were given a bit of structure. There was someone else in the house. She physically felt better when I was there—even if I did make us eat up leftovers instead of letting them grow stale in the fridge.

At the one year anniversary of Dad's death, the loss was new and still acute. Yet we had survived and traveled some way out of a pit toward new life. The tears which would utterly overwhelm me no longer came daily but every several days. They were still as intense—entirely encompassing. But the storm would last less long. It was as though the release brought a more immediate relief rather than a plunging into a deeper sadness or an expression of a constantly renewing spring which never lessened regardless of how much it overflowed.

After a year I was beginning to do some external and interior learning. In an external way I was beginning to learn how to do the financial affairs and be more comfortable with them. And Mom was taking over more and more of the day to day work. That was a great help—not just that she did the work but that I did not have the worry of her confusion about daily affairs which was an emotional strain of its own.

Internally, I had learned that I now had three households for which I had a key responsibility: my own at Pendle Hill, Princeton and Gram's. But responsibility did not mean that I must shoulder the burden of making sure that all came out all right at each location. There was a delicate balance. At Gram's there was little I needed to do—or at least little I was able to do. The most I could bring was myself. That was what was needed most. That was lovely. In Princeton I was needed for some skills or at least attempted skills with the books. That was not nice because "I" felt missing in the equation. I did not have a chance to be me, express how I felt, etc. But I also felt the work was appropriately mine to do. And a part of me was even pleased to be able to pick up new skills in an area so totally removed from my usual activities. I gained more confidence. But the work remained the most distasteful and emotion laden of all. So the biggest learning was to do the work and yet not get too tightly bound to the problems, results, etc.

At Pendle Hill things moved along more or less normally at the beginning of 1984–85. As the year progressed I recognized I was moving into a new area of ministry not previously so pronounced or recognized in my life: spiritual direction.

Over the years at Pendle Hill I had grown in my place as a consultant. From the early years when there was little I could do in those consulting hours, I found myself paying attention to what God was doing. More and more I began to see how God worked and how people experienced that transformation and God's work. Suddenly patterns and pathways became clear. Not that everything was reduced to a neat formula. Mystery remains. But chaos does not. I haltingly learned to listen to people's stories and to see God. Even more haltingly I groped for ways to help persons see the same thing in their lives. Sometimes the Spirit would blow powerfully for us both.

In the last few years I was drawn to people whom I felt would appreciate a listener and an encouraging hand. People were drawn to me. I became part of the little Quaker spiritual nurture group organized by Kathryn Damiano. I began to read more literature in the area of spiritual nurture. My understandings of familiar literature deepened.

This past year an explosion of spiritual nurture opportunities poured out at my doorstep. Beyond the usual consultees I had taken a few off-campus nurture conversations as a regular part of my life. These were not burdensome. However, the unplanned and hence uncontrolled encounters were a torrent. They were rewarding for me because they helped me see God at work in so many ways. They also highlighted for me this work I was doing and made me own it in a way I had never done before. But they also made me question my ability to enter this work. It was so uncontrollable as to be physically overwhelming. Of course, my physical state was not good any way. So what might have been all right under ordinary circumstances was very draining at this time.

I looked at questions of whether I encouraged people's dependence on me. Just the opposite seemed true. Too much looking toward me has always brought a distinct negative emotion in me. I have had several often difficult encounters initiated by me with consultees over the years when I refused to go along with their wishes for increased consultation or even continued consultation. So this did not seem to be the problem.

I was not over scheduling myself. So this was not the problem. Rather people just appeared in the Pendle Hill dining room or they called on the phone or they came to the door. Their problems and concerns were always so serious or pressing that it just did not feel inwardly right in each instance to say "No, I can't talk." So I did talk. But the result was that by the end of the academic year '84/'85 I was left with literally no strength to put out anything at all. I have never been in such a low state on that level. Contributing to the extreme situation were all of the events and physical symptoms already described.

Some dramatic step was necessary to further the healing of the wounds of my father's death, my surgery, the demands in Princeton and this year of heavy outflow in spiritual nurture. The first step was just to stop. The stop came in August when I again went to Syracuse to be with my grandmother. It was a time of deep rest, recuperation, and reflection. Many strands came together in a way which seems to issue forth in a new period of my life.

To see all that came together there, it is necessary to have a few other strands of the immediate past.

First, it is important to name for myself some of the other stresses of this year. They range all the way from small matters such as sleeping on my back to major events such as Pat, Cindy and Mom's physical situation. The sleeping was the result of the thyroid surgery. It had not occurred to me after the surgery that I would not be able to sleep on my stomach—my favorite sleeping position since I was a child. I had never slept well on my back. It took quite a while before I could master the art of this "strange" sleeping position. It may be that the sleep disruptions were and are due in part to this change. As my neck began to heal, I would try sleeping again on my stomach—only to wake up with severe neck pains and a sense that something was pushed out of line in my neck. Next best normally was sleeping on my side. Sleeping on the left side was out of the question. Whatever had happened to that side since surgery made that impossible. If that side were not shaking already, sleeping on it would get it started or would cut off circulation to the arm after a very brief time in that position. Sleeping on the right side became possible after some healing months has elapsed. When the left side shaking was so bad, it could not bear to have my left arm on my side—a requirement of right side sleeping. So I would try to sleep with my lower body in the side-sleeping position, but the upper body with my left arm extended on a second pillow. It was a relief to be able to move into a slightly different body position. But all of these restraints only reminded me of the whole cluster of horrors of the past year or two. In fact, the nightmares and disturbed sleep seemed to be directly related to how poorly my body was doing. If it were shaking or racing at bedtime, the night would be poor. I never knew whether this was simply a reflection of stress or whether the bodily distress triggered the dreaming and fitfulness more directly. As time went on, the nightmares would have less power to terrify. I would be awakened. But my reaction would be "Oh, another one of those. Bad night" and go back to sleep—as though the dreaming were no longer deeply related to the working out of grieving or fear or stress.

(One unfortunate consequence of sleeping on my back is snoring, which I'd never done in such a disruptive way before. This snoring wakes me up, disrupts others who might be sleeping near me, and even continues if I turn my side. I am self-conscious to go to Sadsbury Retreats or even to go to Quaker summer gatherings where one must share a room with others.)

This year also saw a series of serious physical problems among family members. Mom broke her hand which mended well. More seriously Cindy ripped apart two fingers, wrist and forearm on a glass canister in the trash. Barb and Kim were present and so was Ed. That probably saved her life since one phoned for an ambulance and the other bound her hand and wrist to stem the bleeding. It turned out that the major artery to her hand was cut beyond repair. After a harrowing night at the hospital when it was not clear whether the bleeding could be stopped, micro surgery was performed on her hand restoring her thumb and little finger as well as medical science could. The event took us all too easily back to those emotions of 9/83 which were never far below the surface. Barb was in tears over the incident and spent a long time on the phone with me late on the night the accident had occurred. None of us had any reserve for coping with such threats to us as a family. (Here was an example of a spiritual nurture call which came unexpectedly.) I wondered if Mom would have the strength to cope. As a matter of fact, she did quite well. Perhaps better than I.

At the same point in time Pat Thompson [a first cousin] was afflicted with a serious case of rheumatoid arthritis which runs in her family. The bout left her joints red and swollen. She could not turn over in bed, rise to her feet, or walk without help. Medical science has developed no cures, although a few drugs are available to alleviate the symptoms of this painful disease. None was immediately effective for Pat. The best hope the doctors could give was that initial bouts usually subsided—only to come back later, sometimes never to go away again.

All of this was terrible for Pat and her family, but even more so for Gram who depended on Pat to do the wash, grocery shopping, banking, bill paying, etc. Suddenly we were confronted with the problem of what alternative living arrangements Gram might make. Ever since John's death, a few months after Dad's, Gram was alone. (Her own year must have been hell, losing her last son and having to nurse her youngest brother through the last stages of a terrible disease—nursing she was not up to performing.) This was a problem which had come up before as Gram advanced in years. Gram considered various alternatives: an apartment, a nursing home (the most hated alternative), living with Pat, living with Cindy. Each time the decision was harder. This time most of all. She was alone now. She disliked being alone in the house. She thought about and even made some attempts to find a roomer. No success. But even this prospect was not a happy one. It meant taking in a stranger whose honesty and living habits might provide as many problems as answers. Having someone else in the house had a lot to recommend it though, especially when she was having fainting spells which would leave her on the floor unable to rise by herself, waiting sometimes for hours until someone visited the house and found [her]. (Putting portable phones in each room lessened the fear a bit on all sides. Gram could phone out—if she were able.)

Of course, these decisions are really Gram's not ours. But the whole family took them on—getting in each other's way in the process. This was particularly so with Cindy and Pat, both of whom offered their houses. Cindy perhaps not realizing Pat's role as the central care taker, offered out of love recognizing Pat's illness and Gram's need. Pat felt as though the offer was taking her mother away from her, since Gram was more like a mother than a grandmother. There the matter rests: Gram not accepting either offer, perhaps to avoid hurting either one, perhaps because neither felt just right (fears of intruding, having too many demands placed on her, longing for home, etc.). So again she has decided to remain home. This may indeed, be best all around as long as conditions remain the same.

But all of these events caused an increasing sense of chaos and the dissolving of traditional networks for security and real risk of losing those we loved. Mom and I went to Syracuse to see Pat and Gram in the midst of the crisis. It was just spring break time. Barb stayed on with Cindy to help her and the family when she got out of the hospital.

Yet another element proved both disruptive (and ultimately a path of healing). This was the invitation to come to Woodbrooke. There had been a brief discussion of it in earlier years: sabbaticals and exchange teaching. I always said exchange teaching was not my idea of a sabbatical. Woodbrooke was also not my idea of a place for a sabbatical. I did not want to do anything Quaker—at least unpro-grammed Quaker. I would have preferred a time among Evangelical Quakers. I would have liked even more a time in a contemplative monastery. Alternatively, I was itching to do some good scholarly work again. The level of Pendle Hill was not satisfying that element in my heart and mind. So I wished either to study or to write. The writing wish came as a bit of a surprise to me. I had never had much desire to write before and still don't on a basic level. That is, I do not particularly enjoy the craft of writing. It is not satisfying on any deep level. I have no flair for style. But I do now have some things I would like to say, to be part of a wider discussion of issues of the religious life. The way to do that seems to be by writing. Even to think about taking that on represents a break through—a giving up of concern about a "good" "finished product." It is a move away from concern about how such writing would reflect on me and toward a focus on the community of dialogue—trusting in a larger process. The writing of the peacemaking pamphlet for the Tract Association [*Peace Be With You: Spiritual Basis of the Friends Peace Testimony*] gave me some hints at least, that I could put down my thoughts in a way that others could understand. This was the most central need for the kind of writing I envisioned. But in the press of other demands, writing always was put at the end of the list of priorities. But I had no writing at any advanced stage which made a sabbatical make sense. Woodbrooke did not appear to be the place to undertake research either. The Princeton library system would be better than that.

When the invitation came from Woodbrooke via Dyck [Vermilye, Dean at Pendle Hill] in the fall of '84, it felt like everything about it was wrong. All the above issues were still true. Moreover, the timing was now terrible. The family was in such a state of disruption, and my own inward state was in such disharmony that the thought of a move was horrendous. Just leaving the apartment was worst of all. I needed some stability badly. Of course, I would have to vacate the apartment for Pendle Hill's use while I was gone. The idea of giving up home, when so much else was threatened was awful. It made matters worse when I realized that no one took me seriously when I tried to raise these personal questions or apparently had even heard me when I raised the larger questions about a sabbatical. In fact, no one asked in all the planning whether I wished to go.

That was the rub and the leading. For when I first came to Pendle Hill I had said to myself that I would treat the requirements of community life as my monastic superior, so to speak. The demands of my job would be my way of practicing obedience to God rather than my own will. I had been confronted by a number of such situations. I had followed this "rule." But none of the previous situations had been as extreme. I wondered whether I was being naïve to expect a decision arrived at in some administrative process to carry the weight of obedience. No one who conceived of the scheme had that in mind, I thought. And I was angry at not being consulted. This was the last straw in a life over stressed already. Yet I had made that promise about obedience. How could I disobey now just because the going got rough!

I talked to my spiritual nurture group about it (a bit after the fact). Their rather psychological advice all seemed to say that I should press my negative feelings more strongly and not keep quiet and agree. Yet my own clear feeling that this advice was wrong was a sign to me that I must keep quiet (if I could) about the depth of my negative feelings. I recognized that much of the force of those negative feelings was coming from my woundedness, not health. And it was inappropriate to make decisions out of brokenness rather than God's desire for wholeness. Moreover, while Woodbrooke would not have been my choice of places for a sabbatical, I had nothing else in its place and would be unlikely to have anything else in the near future (given my state). Only later did I discover the Woodbrooke year was not to be considered a sabbatical but a teacher exchange. Yet when it came down to practical experience, Peter Bien was the actual exchange for David Gray who came to Pendle Hill. So I was never disconcertingly clear what I was—except freer to do what I wanted than I thought—if my teacher exchange were my only definition. Early on in the process before many of these later clarities, an inward awareness came to me that I could best deal with the problems of this invitation by owning my own needs in relationship to it and seeing how I might meet them there.

What were my needs? To have a time away to recuperate and reflect where I go from here; to have time for silence, solitude, prayer, and reflection—lost in the busyness of the last year; to do research or write; to decide how best to live the call to spiritual guidance; to find a way to help Mom into a new life; to be as available to Gram as possible; not to burden myself with the demands of running two households (Mom's and mine) from across the ocean for a whole year—remember the horror of the bookkeeping already facing us in Princeton; to honor the final year of QSP and a commitment to Laurelville Retreat Center in winter.

Not all these needs seemed immediately satisfyable in Woodbrooke. Yet a number did—a surprising number. With only a little prodding the 1-1-1 plan appeared to me. Fall and summer at Woodbrooke; winter and spring at home. The pattern seemed to answer almost all concerns. By going home in winter, I could look after the financial affairs that would just be out of hand if left a whole year. We could look in on Gram. (We probably wouldn't have gone up sooner if we had been home. Cindy had also modified her invitation to include an extended visit if Gram wished in the fall of '85. That was nice. Also Pat began to feel better. But these things happened only later, confirming my decision.) It is hard to write this account in chronological fashion since decisions were made only to be confirmed by facts later instead of the other way around.

The same is true of Quaker Studies Program [QSP]. I envisioned I could do it in winter. (Laurelville was already set.) It turned out I could and in Princeton, no less. That seemed too convenient to be coincidental.

I realized I could not do any of the research I longed to get into while at Woodbrooke. The resources were not available. But it occurred to me that I could write about some of the areas I had already researched—a way to nudge myself into writing.

Wanting also to protect just space and time to heal and reflect on issues of ministry, I wrote to ask Woodbrooke if I might do a class the first term (Spirituality), be in Princeton the second term and do a short series of lectures the third—giving myself some weeks when I would have no classes. A bit to my surprise Woodbrooke agreed easily. Well, there seemed no hesitation in the letter. Otherwise the correspondence was so sparse as to make planning an ordeal all during that preparation year. I was ready to throw up my hands on that score alone.

I felt good about the arrangement. It fit all needs so perfectly. The shorter stays seemed to appeal to Mom, too. So she agreed to come along (and is enjoying the experience very much).

But the abstract beauty of the plan did not take away the pain of not being consulted in the midst of that difficult era of my life and not being listened to when I did try to speak of my deep personal needs. It did not help the stress of having to pack up the apartment—a job that was made more difficult by Mom's cataract surgery. Yet another strain. But on a practical level it meant I was back and forth to Princeton frequently and could bring a load from the apartment whenever I came. (Of course, my schedule was so tight it meant exercising great discipline to do my summer conferences and gatherings, pack a load for the car, go to Princeton, see Mom, unpack things at that end, and go back to Pendle Hill for the next round: Lacey conference of teachers in Quaker schools, FAHE in Oskaloosa, Iowa; Quaker Theological Discussion Group [QTDG] in Barnesville; Quaker Spiritual Nurture Group Retreat, and those constant phone calls, knocks at the door, interruptions at meals, all the conversations. I could barely maneuver by the end of the final activity in July.

So all these strands are part of what I brought to Syracuse. Mom felt already quite alone during the period of recovery from eye surgery, although she had done little to try to clear a more convenient date with us. She also felt abandoned, I think, when I went to Syracuse. The surgical after effects were disturbing and frightening. We had tried to postpone the surgery as long as possible, knowing that she was not ready for much more strain than she had had in the last two years, if my own situation was any guide. This summer of '85 was about the final time of delay. Her eyes were getting worse and she needed to be recovered by the time we went to England.

I felt caught, unable to be in two places at once. But I knew I needed some space away from Princeton stress. There were no "if's and's or but's." And I felt Gram had my allegiance for this one month a year. I wanted to spend time with her. I did not know how much we might have left. It was about the one gift I could bring to her—myself—for long enough time that it could influence her eating, sense of being alone in the house, sense of purposelessness, etc. Mom did not protest too much. Her trip to the Canadian Rockies overlapped my stay a bit. And Barb brought Kim up for a visit while I was away. I was grateful to her, as to Cindy who came to be with Mom during the surgery. It gave me more peace of mind to be away during both times. Doing my things I felt were an important part of my getting well and of Mom being independent.

The second trip to Gram's was as healing as the first. On the first trip was general strengthening and a renewed sense of security in the world. There was also a definite improvement in the left side shaking.

It happened suddenly one day while walking on the canal. The shaking of the left shoulder to side was often a problem in walking. On this occasion as I walked along I had the distinct impression of someone coming up behind me and a hand laid on that left shoulder. Inwardly, I felt it to be my father's healing touch. I was so sure someone was present that I turned around to see who was there. No one was in sight. I was very surprised. From that moment on I felt the shaking to be improved although not completely healed. A few weeks later I learned that at about the same period (none of us knew the days involved) Mom and Cindy had had the distinct impression of Dad's presence as they were coming up the front walk of a house in Newfoundland. It took them both by surprise because they never dreamt of such an occurrence. There was no visual, auditory, or tactile sensation in their case. I was moved later on hearing of it because it was so close in time to my own experience along the canal in New York State.

The second trip in the summer of '85 proved just as healing in a spiritual level. I could never remember being at such a "strung out" place—an expression which is appropriate for the way I felt. All had gone out of me. I was stretched way out of shape so that I could barely operate as a human being. Now I had a month in which to begin to resume my shape.

The best advice I received for this month came from a little booklet from Steve Mercer at the Bruderhof. It spoke of how to free ourselves from sinful thought. And indeed, I did need to be free of all the thoughts that were crippling my life: thoughts of Dad's death, Gram's death (sometime), Mom's illness, Cindy's accident, Pat's illness, the financial paperwork, the sense of being lost in the flood of being and wanting a spiritual friend, anger over the way the Woodbrooke invitation had been handled—NIGHTMARES most of all and all the fears connected with my own illness. The list was endless. This little book recommended going below the level of our own ego and will—well below our will and there seeing our wish to be in harmony with God's plan for our lives. This spoke to my condition. I was good at exercising discipline. I had been making myself do all the right things. But that discipline alone had not reached deep enough inside me. I could not free myself from these crippling thoughts. But God could. I only needed to get below the "me" of the discipline and feel that oneness of will with God's will.

This advice came at just the right time and spoke to my condition. The other advice coming my way was to take up a much more active prayer life in my month retreat. But that would simply have repeated the pattern of ego-based discipline which was not reaching deep enough. What I needed to do was just the opposite—stop trying to make myself follow a pattern and see what God was doing. That is what I did. I let myself be—at most levels. The only discipline I continued was to read the annual collection of books I put together for every summer. I knew that would be my only opportunity, going to England in the fall. Besides reading books I wanted to read (rather than those I had to read) was a symbol to me of reversing the outflowing stream, allowing something to enter and nourish. This discipline also helped keep the part of me that found it hard to unwind continuing with a helpful work. With that lifeline to the world of activity, the rest of me started to relax.

"Relax" should be put in italics because no sooner did I arrive than Gram's house was full of activity. The Thompson children, getting ready to [go] off to college, were over frequently to do shopping. Every friend Gram had seemed to drop in for a visit. The toilet seat broke and we had to get a new one. Susan stayed overnight for a few days. We celebrated her birthday by going out to dinner and another night, having ice cream sundaes. Gram went along to both events. Margo stopped over for supper while at her new job at G.E. Pat stayed all day while the children shopped. The kids broke down in their car at the Lyndon Road corner and on and on.

At first I was resentful of the lack of rest. But I realized that I was so much better physically than last year, I could manage these things and still manage to have the quiet time I needed personally.

For about three weeks, nothing happened spiritually—or so it seemed—no great experiences of God as such but lots of nice comfy, homey experiences of family love and caring. But by the fourth week much was coming to the surface.

I had outlined the quandaries as I saw them on paper at the beginning of the month for V. Schurman whom I had asked to be my spiritual director earlier in the summer. I was pleased that she agreed. She is a deeply committed Christian with deep spiritual insight. She listens well. I badly needed a spiritual friend to listen to me. All the usual avenues seemed closed. I realized how much listening Dad had done for me and how little Mom either had done or was now able to do. (Cindy commented on the same thing.) With so much built up inside and so much going out, it was necessary to have someone to turn to. The writing down of my problems and questions was a helpful sorting out procedure for me—although I did nothing to try to answer the questions I posed.

In the fourth week of my Syracuse stay, I was reading John W. Lynch's *Woman Wrapped in Silence* about the life of Mary. I had been to meeting for worship at Syracuse Meeting on a day when there were many prayers for those in the meeting who needed healing. There was also some helpful sharing on the source (Christ) of this healing.

In reading Lynch's long poem I felt each feeling that Mary felt in connection with Jesus' crucifixion. The book seemed to help me face more squarely what Mary had faced—the fact of death. She did not flinch and turn away—overwhelmed by horror. She stayed near the cross. And now rehearsing all the things I had felt regarding my father's death, I found I was able to stay at the foot of the cross for the first time myself. Standing at the foot, Mary was given to John and John to her. Suddenly I realized this is what had happened to me. But I was too far away from the cross to hear distinctly. Somehow out of my father's death I was now given to be mother, sister, and friend to the people who looked for spiritual guidance. I was given away from my old life and being to others. I realized that throughout the last couple years I never felt far from God in spite of the pain. And I was more deeply involved with people than ever before.

Mary had faced the chaos splitting a world that was long ago cracked with pain. She accepted her emptiness and pain. She saw the abandonment of God in death. I could never face Dad's death, its horror and pain made me shield my eyes. But now I could look at the crucifixion he had undergone. Jesus' hands and feet were nailed to the cross, never to be free for his use again. Dad also had been called on to surrender all. He had even apologized to the "rescuers" for not being able to sit up. The freedom to function was not his and would never be again. The would-be rescuers might even have brought about his death. Those who loved him most were implicated as well. There is nothing that takes away the horror of death. There is only the terrible emptiness and pain.

Yet precisely in this emptiness and pain Mary found her ministry. By not fleeing from it, she could be given as mother to another. She could now be with those in the greatest extremity of human life.

Now I could begin to see why all the spiritual nurture work had come in the midst of my pain and even why the family spiritual nurture work appeared. The pain and emptiness made it possible—a pain and emptiness coupled with an owning of who I was in health and fullness of human life (i.e. what I had learned in the earlier years at Pendle Hill.)

My problem had been in not recognizing that something below the ego, place of discipline would minister out of its relationship with Christ. My problem was in not accepting my own pain in a more straight forward way—not the pain of grieving. I had always accepted that. But I had not accepted the pain of being stretched out on a cross to a point where I could no longer function. My rightful place was simply to be there in pain and trust that God would do what God would do. In this case, God gave rest in August and rest for a year. My squirming about being stretched only showed my lack of trust. More and more I see my ministry with others and myself being given from the cross—mine and Christ's—to be able to see the pain and wait for God's new life.

After reading the *Woman Wrapped in Silence*, I walked along the canal, needing to let all of this soak in before going on to make dinner for Gram and me. The late afternoon sun was sparkling on the water (the second wide water near the fruit stand—not the one by Burdick Rd.) in an arrow pointing to me from heaven. The wind was blowing and the leaves were showing their white underneath sides. The walk reminded me of the occasion as a child when I looked out Pat's window at Gram's on the first wide water to see the canal and the whole world dazzling in brilliance. At that time I felt privileged to see a special divine world that had somehow burst through to this one. I felt again that at this location of healing, the divine world was breaking through, showing it was just on the other side of this world if we only looked.

As I walked back home I came to the park bridge, rays from suddenly heavy clouds filtered sunlight down in visible strands so they spread out on the still fenced dump right next to the park. I remembered that the whole park is built on a dump. I had been walking close to the area where we dumped our trash when I was a child. Now I saw God there. I knew my ministry was there in the dump becoming park. The sun came out again as I crossed the bridge. It shone down on me fully.

The power of the pain to cripple was taken away. A glimpse into my future ministry was given. I had a nightmare again that night and still do from time to time. The dump is still there. But so is God there in the pain, bringing new life. I can be in the pain with myself and with others without dying in it. More importantly, I can see new life coming forth—not life that I create. But life given by God.

I have not solved the questions about the demands of spiritual nurture work. I don't know what the demands of Princeton family life will be or Gram's needs. Right now I am grateful to God for the rest given in August and for the deep healing and restoration which this year at Woodbrooke promises. I am learning to accept both the stretching out on the cross and the restoration. Both are given by God. Each condition makes faithful living and ministry possible. WE can bring or relieve neither one. We only love and trust.

10/14/85

In the rush of recounting the experiences of the last couple of years several important developments in the Society of Friends and in my own life were not mentioned. They are especially important as carriers of continuity from the journal records of ten years ago.

At that time a great inward agony was the lack of Christian content and experience in the faith of Friends. In a way that I would have thought impossible at that time God has brought the winds of renewal among us. It is evident in many ways. When I first came to Pendle Hill

I could not speak about God or Christ in classes without much explanation and overcoming of many emotional barriers in students. Each session was a struggle in that regard. Now there is much more openness—even yearning for the heart of the Christian gospel.

A major contributor to this change, as well as an expression of it, has been the Quaker Studies Program [QSP] of Philadelphia Yearly Meeting [PYM]. A brain-child of Samuel Caldwell, now Yearly Meeting secretary (with input from many others) the program included three terms (one term each of Bible study, Christian thought, and Quakerism) along with retreats, a spiritual friendship and the opportunity to learn about and practice many spiritual disciplines (journaling, devotional reading, etc.)

The program is now in its fifth and final year, having covered almost all geographical areas of P.Y.M. The idea is being transported to other yearly meetings in various adaptations to meet the needs of geography, interests of participants and availability of teachers. The effect of the program in opening up participants to a new depth and understanding in Quaker faith has been enormous. The attendees of this program now constitute a sizable pool to draw on for further religious education, ministry, service work, etc. Those yearly meetings which have not yet been touched by the renewal have a distinctly different flavor from those which have. To visit those meetings is like going back in time a decade or so. All that I wrote then about Friends is true there today. I believe that the renewal is spreading. It may take a generation, but I hope it permeates the whole Society.

Unfortunately, there are forces at work in the opposite direction, e.g. attempts to change the discipline so dramatically that it may never be possible to return to a Christian understanding. Already one sees clashes in these two movements. We can only trust the movement of the Spirit to lead us through these shoals.

There is also a concern, presently slight, but still there, that the renewal may bring us to a kind of Protestantized Quakerism which will have lost many testimonies as quaint and irrelevant. Of course, clinging to past forms is not admirable in itself. Not all forms are to be clung to. But when forms of worship, as example, give way to patterns accepted by the larger society they usually are manifestations of more basic changes in understanding which are part of the critical core of the Quaker message.

The renewal is evident at Pendle Hill not just in the changed atmosphere in classes but in the general seeking for silent retreats (as groups, e.g. Sadsbury and solitary opportunities in our spring house hermitage).

The Sadsbury experiences have been very popular over my years there. (Parenthetically my own attempts to be the "leader" of a retreat in a more programmed fashion have always ended badly. This has encouraged me to continue with the more radical and Quaker silent structure which the Stilwells pioneered. Bill Stilwell's death this summer is a shock to us all. I think that his work will be recognized in its fullness only after his death.)

The hermitage movement is growing rapidly. We have found that the eremetical [reclusive] tradition is usually closer to Friends experience than the cenobitic [communal]. Fran Taber is currently studying retreat ministry to work more effectively with this concern at Pendle Hill and to help enhance our offerings in this area.

Bill Taber has brought many gifts to the Pendle Hill expression of renewal. Among others his revival of the "opportunity" and his apprenticeship of younger ministers in his classes and in his own travels have been very important. His whole intuitive approach to discerning God's will regularly open people to deeper levels of the work of the Spirit and is a challenge to the rationalism of most of contemporary Quakerism.

So many of my interests in the contemplative side of religious life are being nurtured by those around me and my own movements toward a growing discipline of prayer and a growing ministry in spiritual direction.

My second major religious concern: religious community has also had an opportunity to broaden and mature. In the first part of this journal, I see that I had not yet visited the Shakers or the Hutterian Society of Brothers. Warm contacts have now been made in both communities.

My first visit with the Shakers was at the invitation of Virginia Schurman. We went to a "Friends of the Shakers" weekend commemorating the arrival of the Mother Ann Lee to North America. It was a lovely weekend in August some years ago. There were interesting talks. I can remember one given by William Patterson on early Shaker Spirituals. There was a delightful barbecue on the lakefront. But best of all there was an opportunity to speak to the Sabbathday Lake Shakers themselves. We were both struck by the love given by the "family" to all who visited. Non-Christians who would ordinarily have been disturbed at the use of Christian language accepted it here (and even sang it themselves) because of the love expressed behind the words by the community.

Some while later three Shakers (Br. Ted Johnson, Br. Arnold Hadd and Sr. Francis Carr) came to Pendle Hill as part of a Spring term Monday evening lecture series planned by Jackie Coren on different traditions of religious music and the Quaker tradition of no music. The visit of the Shakers was a wonderful highlight in a program with many highlights (including Martin Ressler, Zalmon Schachter, the Goschenhoppen Sing Gemeinde and Don Yoder). The Shakers stayed the weekend, gave a public lecture, spoke in my class on Plain People (really just answered questions, a bit of a disappointment) and had a wonderful Saturday of teaching the community songs and dances. Many people from Lancaster County came—some in spite of strong hesitations about the rightness of it. Nora Hoover was gently brought into the dancing upon her arrival. She did not seem to mind. Lancaster bishop Noah Hershey looked on with no spoken word of disapproval. In the evening we had a dinner at Brinton House for all those from the plain traditions—a special treat for us all.

Last year Brother Ted asked me to help chair a discussion period at another summer conference at Sabbathday Lake, this time commemorating the deaths of Mother Ann and Father William. The papers were generally good, especially that by Sister [____] on the feminine images used by Mother Ann in her understanding of her faith. But over all the conference was so full that the wonderful atmosphere of the community could not come through. Mom and Ginny were there too. It was Mom's first visit. She was disappointed. I felt so badly about the experience I wrote the community a long letter saying I thought they missed their calling in that worldly style conference. No reply ever came. I don't know how my letter was received. I hope it did not damage relationships. The community is so special. I would hope for more and deepening relationships in the future.

My contacts with the Mennonite and Brethren communities have continued and have enriched my life and that of Pendle Hill students. The spring class on the Plain People has always included field trips: 1) with Martin Ressler to Amish and Mennonite sites in Lancaster County; 2) with the Central Schewenkfelder church (and Salford Meeting house) on their tradition and with Isaac Clarence Kulp on the Dunkard heritage; and 3) the Moravian heritage either in Bethlehem or at Old Man's Creek. Those trips have been very important to many students. In later years we have included a visit with the Old Order River Brethren, especially Myron and Lois Dietz, David and Naomi Fidler, Stephen and Harriet Scath, and David and Emma Sauder. They have sometimes come to dinner at Pendle Hill. Sometimes we have gone there. They always issue an invitation to go to worship with them.

My own experience has been deepened by attendance at the EMALA [Eastern Mennonite Association of Librarians and Archivists] meetings—although my non-productivity regarding papers or books has been weighing more and more on my mind. Perhaps this Woodbrooke year will allow some work in this area to come forth.

Before leaving Pendle Hill I felt strongly a leading to try to arrange some avenue for Friends to come more deeply into contact with their own witness on faithful community. I wonder if a joint endeavor with I. C. K[ulp] and others in that tradition might be an avenue. Ruth Pitman, who has grown to appreciate the Anabaptist tradition, has strong parallel interests (often independent of mine, not always overlapping mine). This year again may bring forth a new birth.

An exciting new friendship has opened with the Hutterian Society of Brothers at Rifton, New York through the invitation of former Pendle Hill student Steve Mercer. Two visits have unfolded for me with that community—one last summer when I was still recovering from surgery. Mom came too. We were hosted by Carmen Stanaway and her daughters Ruthie and Edna. They made us feel at home right away. The community was so thoughtful of my limited energy, providing a little electric car every time I needed to change buildings. A good visit with Hardy Arnold, in spite of his own illness, was much appreciated. The challenging, provocative and caring support of this community as Friends struggle toward faithfulness is a blessing. In the spring of this year a number from Pendle Hill made their way to Rifton. Many had very positive visits. Contact does not produce instant friends. Even when people think they have much in common, much can be perceived to divide them. Many issues of cross cultural contact were raised by these visits and remain for me as I think about the future—not only future Pendle Hill-Bruderhof relations but future avenues for helping Friends confront our own unfaithfulness where such unfaithfulness is now seen as a normative part of American culture or even Quaker culture.

November 1997 through January 2000

The following was transcribed from a final journal Sonnie kept while at home caring for her mother in Princeton, New Jersey. It covers three years before her death and addresses major transitions in her life during that period. It is significantly different in style than the earlier journals, e.g. sometimes written in pencil, sketchier, fewer complete sentences over time, some notations and sections indecipherable. Her earlier journals, while also handwritten, were remarkable in that they were done entirely in pen with no cross offs, or corrections. There is significant editing of many of the original entries in this third journal out of respect for the privacy of other individuals whose own spiritual paths were intersecting with Sonnie's. Words within brackets have been added for clarity. CN

11/5/97 (Journal during Spiritual Guidance time with Carolyn Jacobs)

Noticing points where God is at work, present. First meeting with Carolyn Jacobs—real joy, comfort, way to proceed. Real pleasure with home tasks: store, check book. This is a change from an earlier attitude. Pleasure in living through the day. Health is improved—more energy. Trip to Lancaster in one day for EMALA [Eastern Mennonite Association of Librarians and Archivists] meeting which was also a pleasure. Still pressure of much to do: home, callers, SOTS [School of the Spirit], computer courses—can't do it all well. About visitors/callers—feeling "on call" all the time. Enjoyment and hair tearing at computers. Enjoy something completely different from religion; "sweetie pie" [dog] walks.

SOTS—many questions about core group, survivability of program. I would love to do new teaching if that materialized in area of CLP [Contemplative Living Program], i.e. if possible within SOTS group and possible in my life. Unease at doing nothing in area of study/ teaching. Prayer on bed after suppertime to be with God.

11/21/97

Fun, enthusiastic, satisfying happenings. Doing reimbursement sheet with new Excel program. Writing letter to [a Friend] after her turmoil in solitude. Speaking with Virginia like old times. Problems, interruptions, phone calls, letters, long essays, poems. How [to] distinguish [whether should] phone, write to, visit. Critique if I narrow phone hours; critique if I separate from friendship; don't want [it to be for too] long. Spiritual direction, nurture, formation, [I] want to talk about other things. No space for own study. I put [study] on back burner because there is no immediate time pressure. Study is a way to God.

12/3/97

Very fruitful meeting with CJ [Carolyn Jacobs] today regarding more levels of discernment about correspondence and visitor overload. She suggested God is a jealous God. God wants all of me first, not my doing, even where He is present in doing. It is unfaithful if work blocks deeper springs of life, relationship with God, call to prayer, gifts of healing God wishes to bring. God has more to bring than we know. Put this way, I knew all these things, but heard them in a deeper way from her—with promise, not judgment. She felt it was OK to accept calls only during certain hours. She says these calls/ letters may be temptations—discern on each one. Regarding different advice from others, CJ suggests they may be in a different place. What is right/works with them may not be for me and so they can't know my situation (also their journey may not be in this place). This helps to know what to do with very different advice. The whole session brought a joyous expectancy about what God may have in store— rather than a fear of more demands. CJ also recommended all the naps necessary so as to come back refreshed. All this suggests another image than death in retirement. But rather the image of deeper life. Without knowing it, I was feeling this call to prayer, but [also] an undertow of retirement and death departure, not newness. That has changed!!

12/15/97

Lovely gift of prayer with Leanna [Goerlich] before and after her session. Rich Presence in our midst. Meeting for worship is also lovely these days. But I am much overwhelmed with activities—Christmas preparations, present shopping, cards, food shopping, dog is sick. No time for my reading. Episode with Mom looking for lost address book and I went off to meeting telling her I'd search when I got home. We did that and found it quickly but in the meantime Mom called Barb to cry and complain. Barb told me to be more patient. Much losing (keys, scissors—still gone, papers). I often do the same, so we barely manage. This is full-time for me. Probably little time left for study, teaching. I am sad at that prospect.

12/23/97

Vocations Book seems to talk about doing work, ministry, leaving home. All that resonates with earlier steps in my life, but not this one. [The] book is helpful in back door way, book moves me to say how I do feel. I would still like to do teaching. Feels like I am retiring and preparing for death. But prayer now has a drawing forth to new, full, whole. This is experience of new life—promise of it. [Still a] fear of being cut off from Friends and activities. [SOTS] Program is short-handed and may not survive. God will provide. If I leave now, I may not be welcomed back. My colleague feels it as abandonment. I often feel that I have failed each "image" and maybe actual reality before me. Not [to take up a career as a] full academic in college, although that was never quite right. Never a full pray[er] or spiritual nurturer. Now I am led to model [that] which is least in my eyes and eyes of others—care for mother, no career or self-support. Letting down people involved in ministry. Even mother and sisters let down. But God more present in "non work" for me. Lack of competence, lack of respect never a problem. Well, yes it was and is. How much is in me and how much out there.

12/30/97

Troublesome passage [reference to p. 39, Vocations Book?[67]]. The amount of harvest we reap will depend on the amount we sow. The more we allow ourselves to be used as divine instruments, the more God will fill us with the capacity to give of ourselves more adequately and generously. God is the one who loves, cares, gives and serves others through us. Helpful [reference to p. 27] God has chosen us and not the other way around. God calls us through the Gospel for the following purposes: to save us through true faith, to make us whole and holy by the Spirit and to share the glory of Christ Jesus, our Lord.

12/31/97

Another day of frustration—not being able to do the few things on my agenda because of time-consuming bank stuff. I recognize in prayer that I need to be with God in the midst of this stuff.

1/2/98

Move not only away from apostolic ministry, also away from insights. Tired of being insightful. Solution is not just telling people I'd call back. But a whole other emphasis.

Moses not accompanying—like dying. What if I live and not choose to give up teaching—accept another place? Dialogue with Kathryn and Board members. Some accept where I am. Ended up with dialogue with self and God about my ambiguities.

January meditations:

Month busy with attempts to learn the computer, e.g. Excel program. Gladness at learning something new. Feeling alive if frustrated. Thinking of uses for School of the Spirit.

Mom's situation—Visit with Barb who said Mom ate a lot. I realized she had to have the food put out before her to eat properly. New realization on depth of care of Mom—more full-time.

Meditations on Moses not entering Promised Land but dying ahead of time (not helpful). Not accompanying (helpful). If this is a time in preparation for dying, then it is lovely. Great gift of God to slow down and be with God. Why don't people talk more of this gift? If human life is arranged this way, it is beautiful. I had wondered about this as preparation for death/or as retirement. But what if this is not preparation for dying, but living. Then what? The image made me sad to tears. Taken away from much that I love. Ten years to regular retirement. Prayer started to change, dry up. Very much into computer learning to show myself/God I wasn't ready to leave work. Found I was trading off prayer to get back to work. If gift of prayer was what came when work was gone, then no thank you. I knew that wasn't true from last year's experience of prayer as I worked. But on some immature, infantile level that is what I felt. I took hold of [my] self and said I do not believe this. Richness of prayer and experience of God returned and love of work and deepened understanding of caregiver at home.

Not sure how to discern about giving up work. Seems given, but I cannot conclude it is what God wants. If home situation was different, I would continue ministry.

1) Life of prayer is center.
2) Call to care at home. This is a spiritual path as rich as any. Learning how to love more deeply.
3) Called to lay down our major spiritual nurture program and a lot of mentoring with SOTS group.
4) Not called to accompany even if it feels to them and me like a bad thing [to stop]. Maybe need to see more dimensions of this. How it is morally good? Call to be with God.
5) Still love study as spiritual discipline as well as teaching.
6) Still love to teach/write—maybe more in the area of contemplative life not spiritual nurture per se.

Issues

There is not space to do it all. But I am not ready to say some of it is not important. Some may need to be put down now but not by preference but yes by choice. But I must live one life, not parts of several. How to pick up again if circumstances change. Burn bridges? No career? For SOTS, it may not survive if I stop altogether. It's not that

I am so important, but we are a small group. For me to live at home as long as [my] mother is alive. If not at home, [I] have to work elsewhere to earn enough to live.

Usefulness—being used by God—favourite expression. I do not feel used, except for this month . . . don't want to go back to being used by God in old way. How to perceive uselessness? Solidarity and oneness with many who are not perceived as useful. Study and teaching [may] take other forms in the future. Do I trust God to provide? Half-hearted attention is not what is called for. Pray for clarity for sifting out. Don't close the door or you will stop praying about issue. Wait for movement of spirit. Greater trust, dependency on God, living in God.

2/4/98

What was not helpful today. My best analysis should be set aside as lack of faith that God will give all back in a new form. Half-hearted attention is not called for. This feels like a call but not one I wish for. Give up silence at mealtime and during the day. Take on another calling which is almost more than I can do. But each previous activity has become filled with God. Why not these too? Also means any outside work is out. I feel call is mourning current loss. It may be given back. I have no assurance that God wishes it back. Maybe not. Loss of all that has meant so much brings sadness. Doesn't mean I won't give it up—just hard. Little status or recognition involved. I have done no public speaking, have had no sense of appreciation after a decade from Pendle Hill or classes in SOTS this time around. My unfaithfulness was in Mom's care, not in School of the Spirit [SOTS] requirements. Prayer of not knowing—yes—but can't live in both expectations easily. I make myself and others unhappy. I can't believe nurture of institutions is vital!

2/16/98

Prayer gifts this period rich in midst of painful dilemmas.
1) Recognition of how much this new life will entail and how I
   have resisted—coming slowly, feeling I could do old life and

this. After Dad's death, I wanted to help Mom but not take over Dad's role, feeling she needed to build a new pattern for herself if possible and I needed to live my life. If it is no longer possible for her to build that life on her own, my old decision no longer applies. I saw a world of homemaker stuff, e.g. freezer to be reordered, cupboards a mess. I have never enjoyed homemaker things. Hated [the] idea. But I was given a great sense of gratitude to be able to help my mother. Great gift of privilege to me. I can certainly do those small things I don't enjoy with enjoyment. We have different likes and interests. Many of her things I could not do. But some I could. Pennsylvania flower show, little birthday lunch trips.

2) Recognize that old life is the old life. I must lay it down in my head, mindful of what you said about opting out of tension & Prayer—But I am in mental tears if not physical tears trying to do both. I must mourn loss because it is a loss to me. Was thrust of all my working life till now. Can't jump to ["]this is just fine["].

3) Coming to terms with implications of this. Possible demise of work and K's extreme hurt. Cannot move, as you suggested, directly to ["]if God wishes to keep it going it will keep going["]. Maybe should—please say what you think—of course God could keep it going or close it [regardless of my actions]. Story of high schools in 1880s[68]—Dad's death—not God's will, apparently, but still it happened. I need to see and live into this possibility [that SOTS might die]. Society of Friends on cusp of significant change. Much that was treasured about the past will be gone in order to go into future—understanding of institutionalization, possible it [SOTS] will die because of where we are now and my choice. God may wish it [but] doesn't want it. Someone will die in traffic accident or [get] hurt in [the SOTS] program But I doubt it. But may happen. Our actions have consequences. Must live with that. Problem was sense that I was not faithful and therefore [causing the] demise [of SOTS]. That I could be faithful & [still have the] demise [of the program] for my action is poss[ible] to live with—No way to go back.

4) I still believe in ministry to institutions. My life with Mom now is nurturing the institution of family.

5) Board meeting—wonderful—decided life of prayer was what all wanted to affirm. All Board/teachers felt led there as primary call. Possible wonderful new teacher volunteered. *[There was a difference between Sonnie and Kathryn over the choice and the process of identifying a potential new teacher.]* Kathryn is very angry still. I felt terrible when I left. Terrible for days. Why so angry? How can every step of mine be so bad? How can I help? Where am I so unfaithful? I felt finally a letting go of "me" and therefore both letting go and deeper caring for Kathryn. Stopping putting my discernment of right thing and where I was wrong in center. Maybe [I] am wrong. Here [I] will have to trust in God to let me see that. Maybe I must trust God to let me see that Kathryn is hurt more than I. Maybe [we] will not be able to be colleagues again. Mourn loss of this informal covenant relationship. [It] is gone now. But I should try to both initiate some more things [and] Wait. Trust God for our healing.

3/22/98

Last session with Carolyn Jacobs on prayer. Her recommendation—pray that no images, expectations, pre-set ideas limit my reception of God in prayer. First Meeting for Worship—my love for God—great outpouring. Second Meeting—joy overflowing—delight with the world—abundance, opportunities. Loss, pain still there, yet this great gift.

3/23/98

Prayer after dinner. I was cranky, out of sorts, tired. Light bulb out, new pan scrubbed to death, timer not working. I told God I wasn't fit to come into his house. I should stay in mudroom or corner of kitchen. Door was opened and all the out of sorts feelings disappeared.

[At the] Board meeting, I found myself resisting. This isn't me. I'm the cranky person there. This is someone else. God said I could go back to cold, damp mudroom if I wanted. I felt this was an invitation to go deeper with God, yet it felt who I was, was gone and I didn't like it. But a moment in the mudroom and I could see myself as a petulant child. Why wait out here when I could be in the warm cozy kitchen. I went inside. This is the gift—not a radical disconnect from my life and feeling, but a gift that how I feel is not dependent on the light bulb or the frying pan. I really can accept the gift of life with God even when the stuff of life seems ordinary and wearing.

3/28/98

Awareness of prejudice and hostility, difficulties faced by older people.

3/29/98

Meeting for Worship—feeling sad and depressed. This time God didn't just invite me in. God came outside to where I was to let me see the joy, glory, delight of yard, porch, outside things, family reunions, walks along the canal—as much at home with God inside and outside house.

4/4/98

Prayer image of loved old dog next to stove. Gram's house. I am the dog. Brought tears in face of death maybe but has more to do with loved dog not required to do anything, loved and treasured by owner. Is this what God gives me? It is both a gift and a sadness not to run, play, etc. But I think now all that activity was important and necessary on one level, yet irrelevant on another except insofar as it brings me/ one to God.

5/5/98

First meeting with [new spiritual director] Sister Barbara Wittemore. Told [her] my spiritual journey. She suggested looking at roots to see how God has worked in [the] past and paved [the] way for this move. Sr. Barbara said to be ready to be in transition even if it is not comfortable. Be faithful. Much joy during rest of the day. Delight at finishing [SOTS] brochure and getting it to Old Hights Print Shop. Fun to do that, again.

5/27/98

Reflection on last several weeks. Looking at roots. Experience as young child with Jesus connects now. I as "Innkeeper"—God in Gram's kitchen inviting me in from cold pantry. Being with me on porch and lawn. Pain of loss of money, work, ministry, relationships. Possible future dissolves again in prayer. Not clear if this is grief that dissolves or the path itself. Felt called to give up path for first time. Many visitors this month after [a] time of few. They like quiet, prayer. Fragile, beautiful time.

6/1/98

Remembering Gram's house as place of God's presence. Kitchen: welcome/love, play as a child; dining room (back yard): big family gatherings, matriarchy tie; living room: small family conversations, forgiveness; porch: listening to concerts and fireworks; bedroom: prayer time. Reading—found treasures on bookshelves. Typing—as an adult—in sacred space. Canal and woods walks. Experience of family at Gram's helps to know trinity of family now. Continue to see how roots have expanded, grown, been transformed. God waits for us in the not knowing place.

6/16/98

Joy in preparation for program. [Ministry] Work feels like it is being done for another. Work at home feels like it is being done for me. Getting through the day is all that I can do. This feels same way. Just manage the basics. Try to do more. Which may be more doing or less doing: quiet, prayer—not life of demand for her [Mom] or me.

7/1/98

Anguish over non-teaching. Mrs. Willis [neighbor] asking Mom what I do with my time. Not so much concern with Mrs. Willis as my own. Entering into prayer, God is there. There is nothing to say or do. Nothing to teach. No insight to share. Looks "non-productive." Used to come to prayer as intercession, to bring in world to find Christ. No great teaching, only God.

7/11/98

Prayer has new feel in solitude. Used to be that I brought intercessory prayer into my time with God. [God would initiate it.] But part of this made prayer seem useful. I didn't think of it this way consciously. But now I do not bring others/the world into presence of God. I find God already has them. I am brought more deeply into God's love for them and all the world. All already exists in prayer. Reality of God's love, healing presence is already there. Not insight but reality. Learning to live that here and now.

More on Study and "no's." In change of living pattern, I love much though [what] I regret most is lack of study. This is [a] longer time change than just now with my mother—has to do with demands of ministry. In fact, I wondered if it could be in the same situation as prayer—crowded out by people demands, [i.e.] study crowded out by doing demands. Carolyn [Jacobs] used to say that was the way I used to find God. Now it will be another way. True, but I miss it. Sister Barbara said maybe a taste was possible. That was like a cool drink of water for one parched. I couldn't fathom why study should be gone. People at [SOTS] ministry said I was unfaithful not to do it vigorously. Didn't ring true. But I also felt guilty for not being able to give up the desire for it as though I was clinging to something less than God. Maybe I am. But recent experience shows how much fuller life is for me with study. Helps me to articulate, see afresh. My study is important for Mom ... not just to focus on her. So I think just for now I am not ready to give up this desire. Maybe I should, maybe not. But I am feeling I need to acknowledge it and act on it when possible.

God's "no" will take care of itself. I will go only as way opens. The call to prayer is paramount. Call to my mother. But this is third and this Third feels like it needs to be there. If God doesn't want it, it will not happen. I can live with the no of God. I trust it is what is best. I cannot live with a no of mine to what still seems very deep. I must acknowledge and trust God to lead me further if this is not to be. You [Sr. Barbara] said life of prayer is never what you imagine. Maybe life of study isn't either.

8/3/98

Just read above. It has [a] hopeful feel when I wrote it and now. Why such sadness in my life? Sense of being relegated to aging and illness, too early. I do only survival things with a bit of reading. Impoverished, narrow feel. Sense of no purpose outside myself. Sense of loss of SOTS. Best discernment of "me" and leading that I know has changed. My sense is that I belong even with changes, but not wanted. May be not able to earn a living, able to live in retirement.

8/early/98

Prayer gave memories of playful/joyful things. Walk in woods at Gram's. SOTS conversations and planning were fun for me. Vegetarian food. Strawberries and cream. Meeting visiting teachers.

10/18/98

Opening session of Spiritual Nurturer. Wonderful to be involved again, teaching, meeting [the] part[icipants]. Enjoyed it even though I had felt Spiritual Nurturer was not cutting edge. But new requirement of staff meeting each evening [while a] good idea [was] too much physically. Just demands of day and demands afterward.

EMALA meeting next weekend. Wonderful at Messiah College. But exhausted at end—with much to do for Oversight Comm[ittee]. Too busy to be present.

My frustration, my anger over supermarket—keeping cash register receipt at home after I put it in her [Mom's] purse three times. My sorrow and realization this schedule was wrong. Mom great. My creator made me this way. Her [Mom's] availability in street—neighbors.

I said no to new person wanting Spiritual Nurture. Did say yes to [a SOTS] participant. Stuffing [a mailing at the SOTS] board meeting—noisy, [I'm] tired—can't keep up banter.

12/7/98

I was unfaithful at the Board Stuffing Day by saying yes to [a] request [of me] to do more letters, when I needed to say no for the sake of my health [and] being at ease with Mom. I was persuaded by argument that I agreed to teaching therefore I need to do promotion work.

Lots of house jobs this month: new fence, outside repairs, end of year finances, new wills and powers of attorney.

A terrible day at the supermarket when Mom told me I was using a bad tone of voice to her and when I apologized she said it was still a bad tone of voice. It was a very busy day before a storm. My cart and I were hemmed in by people and fallen canned goods from shelves. I had asked Mom about five times to help and she hadn't done it. So I was frustrated and tried not to be angry, but she read my frustration anyway. This is not the only such incident. I weep and ask God for forgiveness and pray that it does not happen again. Yet it does. I feel awful about it. I ask God why I cannot change and be more generous in spirit. Do I really want to go back to old life or want to hold on to former pattern? I see conversion will take much more time and is beyond my "best" efforts or so it seems.

One thing I did learn was that this is connected to the former incident above. I was tired, at the end of what I could do. I needed rest and no hassles or demands. I took that for a few days and felt better. I need to take care on this point and to recognize [my mother's and my] diminishments more quickly. My only other leading was to make hard jobs actual prayer time so God can do it when I cannot.

I feel as though I must still squeeze to get everything in despite massive cutbacks. I resent things that feel like they make the squeeze, e.g. store, mail. I need to give up yet other things to be able to live into these needs, both the ones I dislike and the ones I like.

Which brings up silence and solitude again. Have always felt a drawing yet life needs another way—at Pendle Hill, SOTS, Mom. Carolyn [Jacobs] said other things were temptation (not Mom, but phone calls which I do not initiate but which come from others). When I have expended myself with needful things I dislike new demands. It is too much. Trying to see interruption and [the] unexpected as of God just isn't so. Sister Barbara [says] do not cut off anything nourishing. I will need them.

3/1/99

Good weekend of Spiritual Nurturer [program]. Free to be available for participants. No presentations. Still exhausted at the end. Resistance in prayer ... why? Path of service to make enclosure and not prison. Embrace life to find joy. See places of need when you can help beyond immediate situation. Brings satisfaction.

4/3/99

Hard trip to see Barb [sister in Virginia]. May not be able to do again. Mom mistakes dog's brush for hers. Couldn't keep pills straight even though I put dailies together, follow up on bills, etc. Discipline to paying attention to my body, to do nothing if it feels [necessary not to]. Recognize paths of desert hermits—solitude, illness, service.

4/6/99

Sister Barbara said my intellect was well developed. Never saw it this way. Never excelled. Never validated. Also chose specific life element of study and teaching. Explicit therefore seen as soft intellectually. Always felt maybe I did not do it well enough, although I knew university role was not mine so this change does bring this regret on intellectual front. Also no movement toward working with aging, writing about aging. People changing identities. Maybe because it moves toward project, working toward change in the world. That is lovely but is not mine. Subject not quite right. Have to do something but all this feels backward. My life as it was. Maybe this will never be. Not move to another topic but another way of being. Talked some time ago to Kathryn about need for work and said anything would be fine. Didn't need to be a "religious" thing.

4/24/99

I learned I have diabetes and probably high blood pressure. Quite a shock. Hope to treat through diet. Scary. But through the month a deep sense of being held—all rightness of beauty of prayer—joy of being with Mom. Mom is mixed up more often. Mom had opposite idea of medicine for asthma and was sure it was right. I talked to nurse and doctor. Dates and obligations hard [for Mom] to keep straight. My father's last pension stops soon. Must adjust use of savings. We do more together. Hair cut and perm. Stop for sandwich after for fun. Birthday party across the street. Thought of street dinner. Probably not possible. I asked her about visiting a garden or going out to lunch with a friend. Maybe [I'm] not up to it. May try EMALA meeting. May session coming up. I have lots of work. Awkward timing. Too much.

5/23/99

Oversight[69] of me as an eremitical prayer. Strange for Friends but this is [at the] heart of what this ministry is about.

Formation pieces:

Solitude. Not to be a role. Be with God. Filled with God—taken to any role.

Health/Illness. Long term path—dynamic formation. Find life in God's love, not necessarily in doing. See that at new depth now. Prayer possible because of bed rest.

Service. Once a month conversation with Sue Krass. No time of one's own. No building of [my] own, separate work.

Study. Strange partners—cataphatic—via positiva. Place of spiritual nurture always grab at as [I] can. Not much place these days. Need to have others encourage that. Maybe one day write about Christian prayer in Trinity. God, Christ, Holy Spirit. But that's not now. Value now simply for living it.

My Spiritual Nurturer, a Catholic Sister, says eremetical prayer is never as we imagine—hermit, e.g. unless one is ill or caring for one ill. That is me. So maybe my life will look like this image after all.

Three models of Desert Tradition. Apophatic via negativa. Always beyond words, images, empty places. God in darkness. Recessive gene of spiritual journey. But needed as prophetic witness in Nurture. Hard to find folks who know this path.

Fruit. Prayer. Being with God—plain, ordinary witness to God and life in God in world that doesn't speak about such things.

Outward Work. Care of mother and myself, Spiritual Nurture work, letters especially for apophatic led folks, study, teaching classes somewhere/sometime, writing about prayer or pathway questions for Spiritual Formation Oversight.

Solitude. What is happening in reflection—what integration? What is happening in new repatterning? How to move to deeper relationship with God and foundation for self and community? How do you respond to call to be with God as most important call? Do you let it be? How are you addressing [the] need not to be available as well as available, especially handling phone calls? What insights/understandings of Spiritual Nurture grow out of [this] path? Do you continue to be led to do some Spiritual Nurture work? How to decide what is at question? You travel an apophatic path. What is that like? How experience [its] underside?

What are [my] demon battles? Accept my physical situation. Accept anger of ones close, one's companions. Deepest surrender of meaning and purpose. How to deal with tiredness?

Health. Are you letting tiredness take you to Quiet? Do you truly believe you are of worth and are loved because God created you, not for what you do? How do you deal with anger, frustration of co-workers when it confirms your worst fears? Do you take care of your health? Do you know God sustains you even when you cannot pray? How does care for yourself keep you grounded in real world? How to plan for long-term complications? How to plan for your mother's situation in own life? See God at work even in diminishment? Preparing to meet God after death. God in diminishment. God in whole person, not mind, not body, deeper than that.

Service. Do you grow in patience, compassion, love? Where you are impatient and irritable—why? How to [help] make Mom's life have times of delight? Do not own times. Sue Krass says embrace the path that calls you to be for another. How does that embrace happen? Where is it difficult to let go being the owner of your time and effort? How to meet each new demand, e.g. bookkeeping, reading aloud, pill count/ordering. How [to handle] grieving over the loss of teaching? Is there a call for [providing] additional help in any way? How does care for your Mom keep you grounded in prayer? Your path is largely apophatic/cataphatic. Why is it important? 1. Apophatic/cataphatic 2. Nurturer 3. Spiritual discernment not head knowledge. Part of teacher. Helpful on apophatic path.

Study. This is a via positive spiritual discernment for you. It nurtures you. On this demanding path of service it is necessary to recognize and make use of nurture and nourishment. Do you allow or are there bits of time for study? What are your current topics and why? Medieval mystics, Trinity, Eastern Orthodoxy, language of prayer. What do you learn/see about [your] spiritual path, walk with God, life as a result?

Ministry. Being an ordinary person. Frailty. Foibles. Find God in daily life these days. Is it conceivable you want to be led to teach or write about any of the above at some point? Not wanting to negate the being piece. Care of mother. Life of being with God. You still do some spiritual nurture work even though that is not major call. How much spiritual nurture work are you doing? Are you careful to discern acceptance of each conversation? Apophatic style → contemplative—feel call.

Conflicts. Are there places where these threads seem to conflict?

6/23/99

Themes during summer

A) Talking to the board about my commitments now has helped me take an important inner and outer step to be faithful: quiet prayer, health and illness, care for mother, study, i.e. if no space for quiet morning that comes before many requests, if no space for study, then it must have a place—not just no place. Claimed silence and solitude in work part of day. Allowed more leisurely space for Mom's errands and I could hear her needs. Yummy hamburger and ice cream cones. Write in journal in the morning. Wonderful—open to God. Other way is unfaithful.

B) [A needy person who wanted to be a consultee] had a real need, so saying no to her may not have been right. We did talk on phone. I do need to see her over the summer.

C) Kathryn is leaving the ministry. The [SOTS] Board will need to scramble to allow next year to go. We would like to complete program if possible, e.g. CLP [Contemplative Living Program]. Maybe with clerk as new teacher.

D) I accept non-continuation of SOTS at least in any way related to old form. Seems OK, obvious, even necessary. Unthinkable only a short time ago.

E) My life is filled with aspects of human experience I would have spent little time on previously: exercise, homemaking, cooking, bill paying, finances, rearranging income with stop of my father's last pension.

F) Call to prayer, being with God, in not easy places: waiting for doctors, waiting for my mother in visits, etc.

G) Mom not able to go to church one day. I found her back in bed fifteen minutes before we were meant to leave, too late to go to meeting. I was upset she hadn't told me, so I could go. Then realized this was her morning, whatever she did with it. And I was given the gift of a quiet morning. Something I had longed for. It was lovely. Had my own meeting for worship, meditation, reading, just being—a real treat. How often do I not see God's gifts because they do not conform to my preset ideas?

Ending Times

A) Kathryn's lovely news about [joining the Friends of] Jesus community [in Wichita] and possible marriage. May she find love, appreciation and joy.

B) SOTS ending, I imagine. Feels [like] it. Hard to imagine saying that, but it does.

C) I feel like [I did at the] end of [my] dissertation. Big void. Although even [the] few things to do from last session took me a month or longer. I have so little time. So it is clear that I could not go on.

D) I feel no call to other ministry, no sense of being called. Maybe meaning, purpose and direction are not the only ways God works with us—we can clutch at meaning and purpose and lose God. It is a good year to be a creature of God, child of God, a woman of God. I recognize God in parts of life I didn't tend to. These parts aren't so much gifts, but possibilities. Open, empty now has a sense of empowerment. Purpose is just being me.

E) Feel life as full of points of human existence. I never paid much attention to body needs, exercise, homemaking, cooking [chose against suburban life]. [I feel like] Almost a different person or in a different country. I have been a walker, but not [spending] this much time. Recognize God in parts of life I didn't tend to. These parts aren't so much gifts but possibilities, almost alien possibilities like a science fiction adventure/planet where people do not see and hear as we do but have mobility [by] using sonar locators and "talk" using rhythmic taps on skin. And much to my surprise I have some dormant sonar ability and can painfully learn rhythmic taps language. It's interesting, even exciting, but still not me. I want to see and hear. Now as a matter of fact, a quieter schedule does mean a possibility of reading again = seeing. [Has] Not [been] possible for a long time.

F) Rose Garden day [with Mom]—tired and not able to walk around historic Rocky Hill—fascinating. Mom urged me to walk slowly admiring each flower. I had walked through fairly quickly and had to sit in the shade. Couldn't be her partner in enjoying the garden, although we talked about it some after-wards. We noticed the same things. Mom said OK when I told her I had to sit down. So different from [a colleague's] anger over my limitations. Made life so pleasant. Allowed me to take care of myself and not feel awful about it or only slightly awful. Healing for me.

6/29/99

G) Healing of [a] relationship [with a Friend]. I feel no call to active work there. Was a question with new way of life. So much is over my head there. I don't think I would be better now than then. I tried to fill a need—be available. She would be pleased. I couldn't keep up pace—fell in hole; when I needed to regroup she would be upset; can't call regularly—[a phone call] would be my main task [for the whole day]. This is not [my] call now. Maybe there is more I need to learn later. But for now the recent phone call shows me this is not good.

[A colleague's] questions about me have not gone away. But I feel I am not called to try to answer her accusations once more. To try to explain that Mom is not keeping me prisoner feels like answering the question of whether I stopped beating my wife. Can't share about health. She is too fearful. I told her about [my] diabetes. Linda Chidsey, clerk, had to deal with fall out. If only I did this or that, [I'm told] my health would be better. [I'm told the] program in jeopardy. We already addressed this, [by getting] back up speakers. Prayer/being with God as major ministry. Hardest place is letting go of teaching—claiming myself. Not answering others' needs. [I'm told I] should develop relationships, do active work, learn. Call to be with Mom allows me to be with God in a new way I never let myself do before. Giving up teaching allows above—allows me to reclaim me, deepest wish, and second wish [is to] study. Have sense of being me, being allowed to be me (Rose Garden)—not giving up. Treadmill is not so strange any more. [Am feeling] acculturated to new planet. Purpose is just being me. Not an accomplishing purpose.

7/4/99

New way of being in world or "full circle." Back to being with God [as] in graduate school. To teaching as an expression of my own need to learn and learning and wish to contribute to the Society of Friends. SOTS—laying down a call to change Friends. Just be me. Now be me—lay down any defining of what that is. Could be defined by work with Mom, but doesn't feel like it. Not called to any other—[such as] writing. Living in more spacious, boundary-less place. Have visited before in prayer and worship.

7/31/99

I now see God prolonging SOTS ministry for as long as possible, not taking it away. I am slowly developing [ways of meeting my] needs at home. My double workload being an entrance into prayer. Allowing teaching to go on for sake of others and for me until I was ready to lay it down. I move to let go and choose life.

Mom not feeling well—weak, tired, went to doctor who rearranged her medication. Got a blood pressure monitor for home in case medication was causing pressure problems.

9/7/99

Continuation of prayer in different places. Last time taking "Sweetie" [dog] for a walk on a tired day and praying/wishing it could be joyful. Mom is having "emergency" dreams at nap time and early night. Upset sleep for her and me. Now she simply peeks in to see if we are quiet. Occasionally goes all the way downstairs before realizing it is a dream. Rarely goes through naptime.

[My] Spiritual life not one of discerning gifts in ministry or my development. Undoubtedly, [it] is, but not in the same way [now]. [It's] not about me—narrow me. [or] About Mom. Not about my identity. [It is] about me in sense of caring for self. About being with God in all of life. Not about finding meaning, purpose, direction, e.g. teaching [or being-in-doing]. Time not my own—using time to be faithful.

Spiritual life unfolding requires commitment long term, stick to it-iveness [e.g.] discerning gifts, learning skills, finding meaning and direction in practice.

But identity is an issue—You may be asked not to be who you are—in same way—nice to feel study can be there—even if there is better time [later]—not that God doesn't want me to do this. So using study piece to understand piece that doesn't use underst[anding] or study in same way. Isn't about finding meaning. May be given in sense of insight. But is more simply being; not trying/going anywhere. I can learn here, too—not trying to make self something—not in pride way—But on-going work which requires learning—skill.

10/30/99

Reflections on month

Work is hard. On one level I knew it would be. On another level, [I'd hoped] demands on my time would be lessened so things would be easier. Work is boring, yet God is present.

On a practical level, frustration is high. I am aware I'm doing many of the things I consciously decided against doing in terms of life direction, e.g. housekeeping and homemaking. Made me consider more. "I" do not create meaning, purpose, direction. Great shift in "I" emphasis. Saying this with care—not prideful. Ability to choose—circumstance given. God works through what we create—leads us there. Also there is a place beyond what I do to live into meaning, purpose, direction. When old pathway is going, one is left with closeness to God in a way deeper than [the] old path could provide. Thomas Merton's story of lay brothers.

12/2/99

Don't want to have to justify and explain my life.

Carrie Knaefler died. Mom's friend who had Alzheimer's. Three years in bed. Many years using a wheelchair and being incapacitated before that. Brought mourning for Mom's illness. Pregrieving her death. All losses—my health, new letting go, old letting go. Also brought extraordinary gift of God's love in Raj's [Carrie's caregiver] comment on the day of Carrie's death—urging her to open her eyes. Also telling her she loved her. She thought Carrie special for the way she lived into her illness. [Raj] felt privileged to care for her. Her expression of love was manifestation of God's love for all diminished ones, i.e. all of us.

1/3/2000

I see surrender of [trying to] make [the] world do what you want. Singing carols [at church] Mom became the cookie lady. I cooked lots. She went for fellowship. Cookies were a great success. She found she could sing. She wanted to give some to friends, so I baked again— simple. She helped. Last two batches cooling on the table when I went to get our turkey. [They were] gone when I got back. She couldn't remember where [she'd put them]. I searched but could not find them. She said, are you going to search all of your life? Let them go. Hard because that was a hard morning for me and raised questions of how much extra I should do. I felt so terrible.

I realize my vision of the day probably needs changing. I used to work half time and be quiet half time. Really press to get something done. Now I have to work in afternoon too. So if I work all morning at that pace, I am exhausted. So must not work if no immediate task is there. No reading project. Haven't been able to do any significant reading in months, anyway.

Mom did go to church on her own even though I had explained twice it was my day for meeting. She said later she didn't know what "meeting" meant. Mom is worrying about things being stolen, e.g. an artifact. I can't leave Mom alone now—don't know what she might do. Scream. Mom doesn't understand. Others see [mine] as a very limited schedule. I used to see it that way too . . . husband sees wife at home as not doing much.

1/31/00

Not much time to reflect his month. Haven't felt well. Doctor's appointment coming. Little time to prepare for program. Did [Mom's] income tax information. Have brochures, lectures, new ideas. Problems at home—phone off the hook all day, although Mom

[is] doing well. We did birthday and Valentines Day [cards to send] for grandchildren. [I] Feel at ease, comfortable.

I have done nothing about work/job. Am not able to do anything practical. But after May, [there will be] no work for SOTS. Many times [I] wonder if I could work any way. But I think, who knows what will come. Maybe I won't be living and won't need it. Don't want to stick head in sand.

Things I can't do. Keep up with the mail quickly. Talk on the phone or in person and therefore help people with projects or catch up with friends. Very hard to do program.

I am not to die

1. I am not sure with the way I feel. Maybe it is the road to my death more immediately. Put one step in front of the other.
2. It is a way to live with more limitation. Has to do with my health more than my mother. This is my way into prayer.
3. I do participate in my mother's decline. Each lost article impinges on me. It's not necessary that I need to hunt—often I do. Sometimes not—my decision. Now I try to make it possible [for her] to do more in life than she would alone. It is OK if life is not exciting.
4. What I hang on to of old way of life? How much is meant to go? Old pattern was fragile because of my health, financial concerns. I felt it was what my life was meant to be.
5. This calls on skills I have not developed—a way to new relationship with God. Way to be with God—not struggle.

Leaving [the] Spiritual Nurture program is not just [about] Mom, not just [about my own] health, but an independent move in another direction from effecting change in Society of Friends to living my gifts for glory of God. For me to be with God. To seeing something beyond even these deepest calls, leadings, doings.

I keep intentional prayer time. I do obligatory work with SOTS—classes, students, etc. I do [a] little spiritual life conversation work—once a week. I have agreed to two teaching assignments with other ministries for next year to carry on in areas of interest. Have reading on tap for years ahead. No time.

Leading is still in prayer. Different kinds. Being with God. Don't know what that means in regard to [SOTS] program. Keep a big toe in. Something may unfold. Can't take on a big program now. Question of time and financial need. If/when Mom were not living, I could do no Quaker ministry I know of because there is no liveable pay. I would need to work. Part-time is probably all I could manage, if that, because of health issues.

Areas of leadings, unrelated interest—work with long term care places about what is really necessary to keep a person going. Animal protection. *[Following underline was Sonnie's.]*

_____

I do not feel a need to find more of me, more of meaning, insight, direction, purpose. I do not feel a need to share. This is a great burden we put on ourselves. Process of self-growth, individualization. A chance to be. Sleep if tired,

The journal ends with the comma following "Sleep if tired." And so she did. Sonnie died at the Princeton Hospital at 1:00 am on April 4, 2000 from "mixed mullerian" cancer at the age of 57. Although Sonnie had been suffering from and seeking help with the symptoms of the disease for at least a year prior, a diagnosis of cancer had eluded Sonnie and her doctors until just three weeks before her death. CN

Epilogue

Sonnie's ministry continued to be manifest through the way she lived her final few weeks. This account was written January 11, 2005 by her sister Cindy.

In the fall of 1999, Sonnie sought the advice of her doctor concerning symptoms of what would not be diagnosed as cancer until just three weeks before her death on April 4, 2000. Her symptoms were apparently dismissed at the time, for whatever reasons. Sonnie once again sought her doctor's advice in February of 2000, as her symptoms were advancing. This time, her doctor suggested she likely had diverticulitis.

Sonnie trusted this doctor and was a very compliant and cooperative patient. She had, for example, been following with complete dedication (as she did all things) a prescribed routine of walking several miles every day, regardless of the weather and even in the face of periodic criticism from well-meaning others. It was perhaps because of having lived most of her life with various debilitating health problems that she tried more than anyone I've ever known to take good care of herself. Only a few days later, as her symptoms worsened, she again sought her doctor's advice. This time her own doctor was away and she was seen by another. He said she should be admitted immediately to the hospital.

From my home in Toronto, I spoke with Sonnie in the hospital that evening. They suspected cancer, she said. She was sounding realistic about the seriousness of the situation, but was hoping for a "miracle." I told her I loved her. I don't think I'd ever said that out loud to her before. It made her cry. The following day, my husband Ed, without a second thought, left home and his job and went to Princeton to help.

Sonnie was able to come home from the hospital for a couple of days between tests that first week, long enough to discuss with Ed all things related to my mother (who was in the early stages of dementia)—household finances, her insurance, estate and so forth. By the end of that first week plans were made for Sonnie's transfer to St. Peters, a teaching hospital in New Brunswick where she could receive a more sophisticated diagnostic work up and treatment plan.

On the eve of her transfer I, too, headed for Princeton. With Ed and Mom, I went directly to the hospital following my arrival. I was startled to see the toll already taken by the pain etched in Sonnie's face. She greeted me with a word of thanks for having left my office to be with her, to which I replied that of course my preference was to be with her. Without missing a beat, she said, that all things considered, her own preference would be to be in my office. Her continued humour was remarkable.

On this evening before her transfer to New Brunswick, she wanted me to wash and set her hair! She had held off having her pain medication, so that she could be clear headed enough to get to the bathroom where she gave me approximately two minutes (the most she could endure) to accomplish this task. We alerted the nurse to have her pain injection ready as soon as Sonnie made it back into bed. I relate this small activity because it was the first in what was to become delicate teamwork between Sonnie and me, Ed, and the medical staff, twenty-four hours a day, for the next two weeks. It was also an early example of how Sonnie would remain direct and assertive concerning how she wanted her care handled.

I accompanied Sonnie in her transfer by ambulance to the other hospital. I never left her side again until she was gone. I think somehow I felt that if I stayed with her, I could keep her "safe." I was about to learn that not only was this not the case, but sometimes the best we can do is to just stay beside someone who is on a difficult journey and be brave enough (as she might have said) to remain at the "foot of the cross."

Before she was taken into surgery, Sonnie asked me (should she not survive the procedure) to tell our mother how much she appreciated everything she had done for her and how sorry she was that she wouldn't be able to, in turn, care for her.

Following the surgery the surgeon informed me he had never seen such advanced cancer. When the medical team informed her that her diagnosis and prognosis were very bad, she calmly asked all the appropriate questions about palliative care and what might be the most she could expect from treatment that could be provided back in the cancer ward of the Princeton hospital. After they left the room, Sonnie spoke to me in a strong voice. She asked me to tell people after she was gone how much she had loved them and that she knew God to be with her. She was at peace with dying; wasn't afraid of dying (only afraid of the pain—and for good reason). She asked me to tell her students, "consultees" and friends that they had provided great meaning to her life.

I struggled with what felt sometimes paradoxical that she was at peace with dying, if that was God's will, while at the same time she was adamant that no stone be left unturned to try to save her life for as long as possible. She was willing to undergo anything that might allow her to keep living against all the odds.

Sonnie was transferred back to the cancer ward in the Princeton hospital. Upon arrival, she continued to approach her life positively and assertively. She informed the care coordinator, for example, of what she wanted to eat and at what time. Because she wanted breakfast long before the hospital served it, Ed would prepare and bring over from my mother's house exactly what Sonnie wanted, when she wanted it.

Every ounce of energy Sonnie could muster went into prayer (and handling the pain), except as required for some aspect of her care. She requested that no one visit her, except Mom, Barb and Ed, which was hard on many people, some of whom reportedly felt that it was "selfish" of her not to allow them to express good wishes for her recovery in person or possibly to say good-bye.

Sonnie didn't talk much with me either, for that matter. On one of those rare occasions, she said if her life was about to end that, in retrospect, the path God had created for her in recent months was "really quite lovely."

She had also requested, and Ed had delivered fresh from the local Mennonite market, a slice of Sonnie's favourite chocolate chip cheesecake. On what was to be the last day she ate anything, she asked for some of that treasured dessert. However, someone had taken it from the communal fridge and she had to be denied this small pleasure. I was devastated by this symbolic loss and raged against the "unfairness" of it all. She, of course, took it in stride.

Sonnie would sometimes achieve relief from pain and ease her breathing by sitting up in a recliner chair. But now the staff were no longer allowing this as they felt she was just too sick to get out of bed. So I'd decided to try to "replicate" a recliner chair for Son while she stayed in bed, but needed someone else to help me. I asked numerous staff, who declined. Finally, I approached a secretary who was willing to take part. Together, we managed to pivot Sonnie in the bed and this wonderful person sat on the floor to become Sonnie's "footrest." I became Sonnie's "backrest." At least this final wish was made possible.

The network of love and support in the larger family that felt so fragile in the 1980s testified to its importance and the tender love with which its members held one another as we faced the impermanence of life. My young daughter, Kathryn Nowina, summed it up in a letter to Sonnie dated April 3, 2000:

> There are probably a million things I would like to share with you, but there are only a few that are really important. I wish that I could be there with you to hold your hand. I'm sorry we never had a chance to get to know one another better. Time and distance can be so hard for a family, but it makes me truly appreciate our time spent together. Perhaps we'll have that chance another time, in another life. This letter is by no means a goodbye, but a "see you later." I promise to do my best to take care of your mom and sisters, you have set a fine example.
>
> I want you to know how much I love you. I will miss you terribly and think of you often. I hope you find peace and happiness wherever you go. I wish you could have seen me grow up, but I am confident that you still will. Thank you for all the love and support you have given our family. I hope you have felt the same love you have given. Forever and always you will be in my heart.
>
> P.S. Imagine the biggest hug possible and pretend it's from me.[70]

On the day before Sonnie died, she declined precious ice chips with a barely whispered "no, thank you" . . . even then, so gentle and courteous. Those were the last words she spoke.

On the morning of Sonnie's last day, just three weeks from the day she'd sought advice on the unexplained "bloating," our mother came to her bedside. Sonnie was distraught with pain and difficulty breathing. Our mother, with remarkable composure, stroked Sonnie's forehead without saying anything. Within a few moments, Sonnie became quieted. It was a miraculous sight. Sonnie died that night.

Part Two

Selected Writings
of Sandra L. Cronk

Learning to Listen

INSIDE QUAKER SILENCE

Quakers are sometimes called the Trappists of the Protestant world. The Society of Friends shares with this famous Catholic monastic order a commitment to a life of silent worship and quiet listening to God. But unlike the Trappists, the Quakers grew out of the English radical reformation. In keeping with that tradition Friends have always emphasized faithful living in the everyday world of family, work, and community. The Quaker understanding of quiet listening to God does not involve leaving this everyday world but provides a firm foundation for life in it.

Today people from many different Christian traditions are interested in incorporating a deeper inward foundation for their own lives. They ask questions about what happens in the silence and how to listen to God. I would like to invite you inside the Quaker practice of silence to give you a glimpse of the process of quiet listening and to share a few thoughts about the way God works in the silence to form and transform our lives.

Silence has no merit of and by itself. It is significant only as an occasion to encounter God. Of course, we meet God in many ways in our lives. The problem is that we are often too busy to realize that the encounter is occuring. Demands on our time and attention are heavy. Day to day living in the twentieth century is a time-consuming process: the car inspections, the health care forms, the plumbing repairs. Beyond these ordinary tasks there are the special activities we undertake as the central focus of our lives: caring for the children, working at our jobs, being committed church members. These are the activities we enjoy the most, but even they are sometimes draining to the point of depletion. When do we have a chance to drink at the well of living water? Can we hear the Word of life? In the gospel we read that when Jesus was about to be born, the inn was so crowded Mary and Joseph were forced to go to a nearby stable. Our lives are often so crowded with activities that there is no room for Christ to be born in our midst. There needs to be an empty and receptive place for Christ to enter. Periods of quiet provide such spaces in our lives.

omit

Unpublished manuscript, "Learning to Listen, Inside Quaker Silence" with handwritten notes. Sandra L. Cronk papers, Pendle Hill Archives, Friends Historical Library, Swarthmore College. Used by permission.

Renewal Among Unprogrammed Friends in America

BY SANDRA CRONK

This article was first published in Friends Quarterly, *Vol. 24 #4 (Oct. 1986) pp. 163-70, and is used by permission. Here, Sonnie spells out more fully the hopeful signs of renewal that she wrote about in her journal.*

"The Spirit of God has been moving powerfully in our midst." These words are repeated frequently by Friends in many parts of the unprogrammed Quaker community in the United States today. In the last half dozen years renewal has touched many levels of Quaker life. I would like to describe three of the areas where this quickening of the spiritual life is felt by Friends: new forms of teaching ministry, revitalization of the work of vocal ministers and elders, and expanded uses of silence as a way of listening to God.

To understand the excitement Friends feel about the new teaching ministry emerging throughout the Society, it is important to know something of the impoverishment in Quaker life which has resulted in part from the lack of such educational work in the past few decades. Traditionally, the main carriers of spiritual education work were the ministers and elders. Both of these forms of ministry have changed radically in recent years. There are historical reasons for this change. One result of the era of Quaker divisions in America was that the liberal branch of Friends became wary of the authoritarian functioning of elders and the inhibiting effect of recorded ministers. These offices were abolished in the hope that the functions would be taken over by a wider-based group of Friends in each meeting, thus leading to more participation in both kinds of ministry. In a few cases this wish has been realized. But all too frequently a job given to all is a job done by none. With no elders to nurture ministers, the gift of vocal ministry began to suffer. In particular, teaching ministry in meeting for worship almost disappeared. In addition, vocal prayer and prophetic call to community and personal accountability began to wither. Soon whole generations of Friends arose who had very little exposure to the deeper intellectual and spiritual foundations of Quaker faith and life.

Paradoxically, the problem was exacerbated by the special consideration many birthright members gave to the large numbers of convinced Friends who joined from other Christian traditions. Sometimes these newcomers felt manipulated and hurt by the heavy-handed approach to Christian faith used in their former churches. In an effort to spare further injury, Friends often gave these new members very little in-depth explanation of their new faith.

Thus it happened that Friends, old and new, did not understand Quaker worship, decision-making and testimonies as profoundly as they might have under other circumstances. Out of a sense of need, Friends began to ask for ways to fill this void and find out what Quakerism was all about.

In response to this yearning have come a variety of fine study programs and the development of a new form of travelling minister whose central concern is teaching. The oldest in the recent outpouring of educational programs, and therefore the one which has had the opportunity for the most impact, is Philadelphia Yearly Meeting's Quaker Studies Program, known as QSP. This program has a year-long curriculum which includes study of the Bible, Christian Thought, and Quakerism. Along with these study components is a strong spiritual life emphasis. Each year includes several retreats on various spiritual disciplines (journaling, devotional reading, listening in prayer and worship, etc.). Participants have the opportunity to be part of a "spiritual friendship," i.e. an on-going relationship with another person in QSP which has as its focus the chance to talk together about some of the deeper questions of life and faith we often don't speak about in everyday conversations with friends and acquaintances.

QSP has become a model for similar study programs in many local and Yearly Meeting communities across North America. Each of these programs has its own unique format depending upon local interests and needs. But all the programs have the same two intertwined threads: a serious commitment to understanding Quakerism and the Judeo-Christian heritage from which we come and a desire to move beyond intellectual knowledge alone to a transforming relationship with God.

For the last several years the Earlham School of Religion and the Quaker Hill Conference Center in Richmond, Indiana, have sponsored a series of annual Consultations on topics of vital importance to Friends from all branches of American Quakerism: eldering, discernment, ministry, accountability. These gatherings have opened up forgotten and neglected areas of meeting life in dynamic ways.

During these same years there has been an increasing number of Friends who feel led to travel among meetings, by invitation, offering an educational ministry at First-day schools, forums, week-end conferences, retreats, and workshops. These Friends usually have the sponsorship or encouragement of their local meeting, yearly meeting committees, or Quaker organizations. The New Foundation Fellowship has been especially active in promoting this form of travelling ministry. It has many workers in North America and abroad sharing the message of George Fox. Their proclamation of the early Quaker belief that Christ has come to teach his people himself has been a quickening influence for many Friends. All of these travelling Friends, taken together, offer an astonishing breadth of subject matter: Bible study, worship, prayer, spiritual disciplines, Quaker faith and testimonies, etc.

As a result of these studies (and studies is a poor word because it does not capture the deep inward motivation and spiritual life concern of these ministering Friends), many Quakers are finding ways to answer their deep religious yearning. Quaker faith has taken on new meaning, purpose, vitality, and excitement. Forgotten elements of our tradition suddenly speak forcefully to our needs today: e.g. ways of listening to God, community patterns of accountability, and understandings of God's peaceable kingdom.

These studies have also brought new appreciation of the larger Christian heritage. In this century it was common to look only at the ways Friends were discontinuous with that Christian heritage. Now

Friends are discovering that while we have a distinctive understanding of Christian faith and life, we are firmly rooted in this heritage. To cut ourselves off from it is to cut ourselves off from sources of past experience, challenge and renewal available through scripture and the history of the Christian tradition.

A second major area of renewal among unprogrammed Friends is the revitalization of the work of ministers and elders. It is more accurate perhaps to speak of seeds of revitalization than of mature plants bearing fruit. The movement is so new. Nevertheless, significant developments are influencing both vocal ministry and eldering.

Two developments have paved the way for a deeper understanding of vocal ministry. First is the recognition that Quaker faith has content. Friends have something to say about God's work in our lives; about Christ as the inward teacher, empowerer and mediator; about listening to this inward teacher and being gathered into a community of God's people which, in turn, is called to live a faithful witness in the world.

But Quaker ministry is not a matter of talking about an abstract system of belief. Rather it grows from a life of listening to and obeying the Inward Christ who directs and guides our lives. The second major development is the recognition that there are ways to practice and hone the skill of listening. In the classical era of Quakerism two modes of "practice" were of particular significance: (1) a "partner" or "apprenticeship" system for ministers and (2) regular attendance at the meetings of ministers and elders.

Travelling ministers journeyed in pairs. Young ministers could grow in their ministry by becoming a travelling partner or, as it were, an apprentice to a public Friend who was more mature in the religious life. This system allowed the younger Friend to visit many meetings for worship, participate in worship opportunities with families in their homes, and in general accompany the "mature" minister in his or her labors. In this way the younger person learned by observation and immersion in a life of ministry how to discern what God would have said to those gathered on each worship occasion, how to speak in large groups, and how to minister to individuals in need.

Another major way of maturing in the gift of ministry was by attendance at the meetings of ministers and elders. These were sessions for planning the work done by ministers. But they were much more than this. They were opportunities to enter the deep quiet together, to be fed by the Source of Life, and to learn how to recognize the movement of the Spirit in a gathered worshipping group. Out of these experiences of worship and testing of discernment ministers could learn to distinguish those messages which were led by the Spirit from those that were only intellectually insightful. They learned how to articulate the prayer which God sometimes poured forth in their midst. In short, these gatherings were schools of the Spirit from which ministry could grow.

Today Friends are practicing both these forms of nurture again. We are fortunate in having a few ministers who feel led to help those Friends new to ministry to mature in the work. They provide opportunity for such Friends to accompany them in their travels. Pendle Hill has offered a fine service to the Quaker community by having classes in ministry that are organized on this pattern. In addition, some committees of worship and ministry or ministry and counsel (as committees of elders and overseers are called in the USA) understand that, along with their function as program planners and problem-solvers, they must also be schools of the Spirit. Their meetings are becoming occasions of deep worship where all the participants can experience the work of the Spirit and learn to live a Spirit-led life.

Rediscovering the work of vocal ministry has brought with it the rediscovery of the work of elders. Friends see that it is not possible to revive the role of the vocal minister without also paying attention to the role of elder. Eldering was and is a companion ministry to that of the vocal minister. It is unfortunate that among liberal unprogrammed Friends in the United States the designation "elder" has disappeared. The term itself often conjures up an image of a rigid Friend who has only negative things to say to others about their ministry and way of life. Happily, Friends are realizing that this picture is only a caricature of the real work of elders which is spiritual nurture. Elders give help and guidance to ministers. By extension they give spiritual nurture to all members of their meeting and have oversight over the spiritual life of the meeting as a whole. The office of elder is also one of the primary structures for practicing personal and community accountability in the meeting.

Traditionally eldering ministers were chosen because they were wise in the spiritual life. They knew how the Holy Spirit worked in the lives of both individuals and meetings, forming and transforming them, leading them to greater depth of communion and service. With a clear seeing eye, they were often able to help Friends see what God was calling forth in their lives. Many ministers reported that the encouragement of an elder was a key to their next step in faithful ministry. On occasion, rightly ordered admonition warned meetings of spiritual and moral dangers they did not see.

The elders had a unique spiritual nurture role in worship as well, although that role was not usually one of vocal ministry. Elders were often gifted with the art of "centering" during worship. By prayerful attention to the one who was calling the meeting into worship, they were able to bring a whole group of worshippers to a deeper place where all could experience the movement of God in their midst.

Today among unprogrammed Friends there is great interest in this ministry of spiritual nurture or eldering. Many Friends are giving serious attention to learning to perceive how God works in our lives, both in meeting for worship and in everyday situations. These Friends would like to find ways in which we can perceive God's transforming and leading work more clearly and respond to it more faithfully.

There is a growing literature about spiritual nurture in the larger Christian church. Some church groups have formal programs in various aspects of this ministry. Monastic communities, for example, have had long experience in spiritual formation (their term for spiritual nurture). Some of the best material on the ways in which God continues to create and form us throughout our lives comes from these communities. Consequently many Quakers who are led into this ministry of spiritual nurture or eldering make use of these resources. Many also use opportunities within their meeting. e.g. partnership or spiritual friendship with a more experienced eldering Friend, and participation in ministry and counsel committees or newly formed "spiritual nurture" groups where there is opportunity for deep worship and sharing learnings about this ministry.

These developments in vocal ministry and spiritual nurture/eldering are so recent that it is not yet possible to predict how they will shape the life in our meetings. Many Friends hope that we will see the fruits in a deepened meeting life and not just in personal religious experience.

Silence: Inward Place of Listening and Transformation

The special consideration Friends are giving to listening to the Spirit as the essential foundation of all forms of ministry is part of a larger awareness of all Quaker life being grounded in an experiential, lived relationship with God. Our decisions about our lives do not just come from a rational exploration of the best alternatives in a given situation but from a deep listening to the leading of God. Friends are realizing that listening goes deeper than we often imagine. For our lives are not just a series of Spirit-guided actions, although God is calling forth actions, to be sure. But our lives have meaning as an integrated whole, centered in God. The Inward Christ is forming and transforming our whole beings so that we are able to live in closer communion and faithfulness.

The yearning to be able to say "yes" to God and cooperate with the work of the Spirit has brought many Friends to a deeper appreciation of the role of silence as an avenue for more careful listening and an opportunity for undergoing some of the struggle and surrender which are part of that deeper transformation experience.

We have long recognized that meeting for worship provides these opportunities. Today many Friends are seeking to follow this same method of worship in quiet days, week-end retreats, hermitage-visits, etc. In short, people are seeking extended times of quiet for deeper listening. Many have the same inner need which George Fox had during those intense periods of searching in his early life. He would go alone into the countryside, carrying only his bible, and seeking to hear the Word, Christ, speak in the silence. For contemporary Friends, these silent days may be occasions of inward wrestling, times of rest and refreshment, or periods for making decisions and seeing commitments more clearly.

Among American Friends there are growing demands for facilities for these quiet times. Pendle Hill, the Quaker center for study and contemplation in Pennsylvania which has always offered group retreats as part of its programs has recently been experimenting with hermitage facilities for individual use. The demand for these facilities among Pendle Hill's resident students keeps the hermitage filled on a regular basis. Many Friends look to Catholic and Protestant retreat centers or to monastic communities to find additional places for retreats. Some meetings have regular quiet days for members in their meeting-houses or in Friends' homes.

Group silent retreats are increasing in number along with personal retreats. One of the most significant developments in this field is a new model for group silent retreats which comes out of the Quaker structure of communal listening to God, i.e. the meeting for worship. For years Friends have used and appreciated the traditional Catholic and Anglican pattern for silent retreats. There it is common to have a retreat leader give a series of talks on the spiritual life. The retreatants then ponder the words in the silence, allowing the outward words to help open their inward ears to hear what the Spirit is saying to each person. This pattern is very helpful and still much loved.

The new pattern understands that discernment for Friends is primarily a communal listening process. Consequently, the retreat is seen as an extended meeting for worship. There are two or three times of formal unprogrammed worship each day. But even the time not spent in these formal gatherings is still seen as worship. The advantage of this longer time in worship is that the group can listen more deeply and allow the Spirit an uninterrupted period to work. An hour of worship once a week is sometimes just too short.

In this new pattern for silent retreats there is a facilitator who has done advance arranging and oversees practical details during the gathering. But there is no retreat leader other than the Spirit. No one gives prepared vocal meditations. During the unstructured time participants may do various kinds of quiet activities, which allows the process of unwinding, rest, and centering to occur. People may walk in the countryside, gaze out of a window at a neighboring farm or wood, sketch the landscape, knit, read, or just "be." Participants take turns preparing and serving meals. The simple act of eating together often becomes one of the most profound experiences of worship.

Vocal ministry may arise during any occasion the group is gathered. This ministry is just as appropriate as people sit quietly together after a meal as during the times formally designated worship. First-time participants are often astonished at the quality of communal listening and the mutual caring and encouragement which takes place among those gathered by God in the silence.

Friends find that unexpected levels of transformation and discernment occur when they take the process of listening to Christ seriously and devote regular time to prayerful waiting on the Inward Teacher in corporate worship, personal prayer, and retreats of all kinds.

Conclusion

"The Spirit is moving powerfully in our midst." But the test of renewal is not increased religious knowledge or even deepened personal spiritual experience. The test is faithful living. If the new knowledge and deepened inward life many Friends are finding are not translated into love and service, the renewal will not deserve the name. By their fruits ye shall know them.

We have intimations that bearing fruit may require much more from us than we now fully envisage. The most difficult parts of renewal are still ahead of us. We have not yet recognized all the places where we cling to our own strength instead of to God. We have yet to face the challenge to our individualistic notions of religious life and have not accepted the centrality of mutual accountability in our meetings. We have not recognized fully the challenge to our comfortable ways of living demanded by our testimonies on peace and social justice. The renewal is just beginning.

Learning to Listen (Part One)

BY SANDRA CRONK

Reprinted from Festival Quarterly, *Winter 1987, pp. 7–10.*
Copyright held by Good Books (www.GoodBooks.com). Reprinted
by permission. All rights reserved.

For many generations Quakers, like Mennonites, were noted for their close-knit, plain communities, separated from many of the structures of the larger society. In this century Friends have faced assimilation into the larger culture. We have had to struggle with the meaning of faithfulness as our communities have become more open to both the needs and opportunities of our world.

Super-Parents, Super-Professionals, Super-Church Members

One of the most unexpected dilemmas we have had to confront as the result of this cultural change is busyness. To live in the twentieth century, at least in most areas of North America, is to be overwhelmed with the demands on one's time and energy.

Commitment to the Friends Meeting today is often measured by the amount of time we put into a plethora of worthwhile committees, projects, boards, and programs. To do well in virtually any contemporary profession requires so much of our time, we wonder if there is any room left for the rest of our lives. To compound the situation we are bombarded from morning to night with a flow of words through newspapers, billboards, radio, and television. This barrage powerfully shapes our assumptions and expectations.

Our lives are lived against a constant backdrop of exterior and interior noise. In this psychic clutter, we have to sort out the important from the unimportant, the divine leading from the culturally-expected activity. As the world demands more and more from us, we judge our success as human beings by our ability to cope with this multiplicity of requirements.

Paradoxically, it is the most caring and committed Friends who are often the most over-extended and exhausted. These sensitive people react to the demands by trying to be super-Moms or super-Dads, super-professionals and super-church members. All the while they have a nagging sense that something is wrong. In the midst of all this fine activity, they feel as though they have lost themselves.

Very often our society treats our discontent with this busy, over-extended life as though it were a psychological problem. If we cannot cope, there must be something wrong with us. Our culture provides many psychological fixes to relieve the dilemma. There is a proliferation of psychological self-help movements. Radio talk show experts on the problems of daily living abound. Many people escape into a world of expressive individualism, remaining content with getting in touch with their inner feelings and experience but finding no answer to their problem.

Friends have had their share of this kind of response—and found it wanting. We are now ready to acknowledge that the difficulty we face is not just psychological. It is spiritual and theological. Instead of God being the center of our lives, our activity is the center. We recognize the need to start anew. But how do we do that?

A Quiet Place

Surprisingly, we are discovering that our tradition, which we had been rapidly abandoning, has a great deal to say on just this point. Quakerism has, at its heart, that quiet place where we listen to God. Through listening, our lives form a strong spiritual center and a clarity about our direction and purpose.

The most well-known Quaker practice is the unprogrammed or silent meeting for worship. This form of worship has no planned program of music, sermons, or scripture readings. Instead the worshipers enter with quiet prayerfulness into Christ's presence. The silence is merely the outward form of our listening to God's still, small voice in our midst. Vocal messages and prayer may come out of the silence as God leads worshipers within the group to speak.

Friends in my part of the Quaker world still have this form of unprogrammed worship. But contemporary Friends are discovering that a meeting for worship once or twice a week is not enough. We need a deeper quiet and listening that permeates our whole way of being. We need to live a life that quiets down enough to be able to hear that still, small voice. An otherwise hectic life, with one or two hours of silent worship a week, is hardly conducive to distinguishing God's call to faithfulness from all the cultural and self-imposed expectations.

In an attempt to reflect more deeply on this dilemma of busyness, we Friends have been looking back into our heritage to see what earlier generations might have to teach us. The first thing we have learned is that Quakerism was not just adherence to a few distinctive forms such as the silent worship. Rather the worship was but one expression of a *whole culture* devoted to listening to God.

I can remember some of that traditional culture myself. As a young person I lived on the outskirts of a Wilburite community of Friends. (The Wilburites are the Old Order Quakers, to use the parlance of the Amish and Mennonite tradition.) Whenever I visited in that community I recognized that life was lived in a manner that honored faithful response to God's leadings. The ability to recognize and respond to these leadings grew out of a quiet center of listening and permeated the whole culture.

A Silent 'Opportunity'

When one visited in the homes of conservative Friends, the conversation might lapse from the usual give-and-take into a period of silence. No one filled in the silent space with small talk as we are apt to do in our culture. People looked forward to that point in a conversation when everyone became aware that we were gathered in the presence of the One who was our Shepherd and our Guide. Those precious times of quiet would bring our subsequent conversation and our relationships with one another to an entirely new depth.

I remember on one occasion visiting an old Quaker farmhouse. The family happily showed me the big bell outside the kitchen door. Usually they rang the bell to call the laborers in the field at mealtime. But that was not the function of the bell that was mentioned to me first. Instead the family said, "We ring the bell when the travelling minister comes for an 'opportunity.'"

An "opportunity" is an old Quaker practice of having an occasion of silent worship and spiritual conversation with an individual, family, or small gathering. It was a mode of spiritual nurture often undertaken by travelling ministers who were led by God to do this visiting not only in their home meetings, but often among members of far-flung meetings. "Opportunities" became occasions to step back briefly from the workaday world to hear what God might be saying about one's life-direction, problems, burdens, hurts, and fears. It was a time to let Christ be one's true shepherd, rather than just talking about Christ as the center of one's life.

The traditional Quaker communities also honored the practice of "retirement," setting aside time, now and again, from the immediate demands of daily life to hear Christ, the Word of God, who is so easily drowned out by all our human words.

In today's language, I suppose we might talk about times of retreat instead of "retirement." But retreat has the connotation of a formal occasion that requires special arrangements and facilities. Times of "retirement" did not require anything special, not even a travelling minister. One could take a quiet hour or a quiet afternoon for reflection or just "being" in the presence of the Spirit.

One Weary Applicant

Because my own Quaker community still kept many of the old forms of quiet worship, I had not realized how far we had drifted into the fast-paced, activity-centered style of living until several years ago when I first applied to teach at the Quaker study center where I now live. The interview process was an amazing feat of endurance. I had to speak with everyone living at the center; the dean and the teachers, the cooks, the maintenance and housekeeping people and the office staff. Since we are all part of one community, all have the right to help decide on applications from those who would like to join in that community.

On one level the interview process was a fine testimony to community life. But the net result of this demanding process was a frazzled applicant. I could hardly think straight after explaining to thirty different people my philosophy on education, my understanding of Quakerism, and my views on life in a religious community.

Just when I thought I had finished the last of the conversations, the dean came by to say there were Friends from a Wilburite community on campus. They wanted to interview me too. I struggled to gather what little strength remained and walked across campus, reviewing in my mind what I could say about teaching and Quaker community life to these visiting Friends.

But when I reached the visitors, something strange happened. After a pleasant introduction all around, they said nothing. They asked no questions. I was beginning to wonder if I should launch into my own ideas on Friends' schools and Quaker theology when I realized what was occurring. We were in the midst of an opportunity.

These Friends did not want to know what I thought on various erudite subjects of theology or educational philosophy. They wanted to wait upon the Lord. They wanted to know if I could listen to God. After all, philosophies change; experience broadens and deepens. Those were not the central issues for these Friends. The heart of the matter was living a life in a listening relationship with God and being obedient to God's leadings.

That opportunity was a breath of fresh air. It was a time to recuperate from the demands of the interview process. More importantly, it allowed me to remember who I was and whose I was. My rush of activity and my rehearsal of my own views began to recede from the center of my mind. Now I could listen to the true Center.

In the quietness I came face to face with the realization that persistent busyness is the result of an exaggerated sense of pride in human knowledge, activity and skill. We live in an era when human beings consider themselves masters of the world. We have at our disposal such tremendous knowledge and power: military might, technological power, economic and political power, even the subtle power of psychological and religious insight.

We are so caught up in our knowledge that we have not been able to use it wisely. Militarily we have come to the brink of nuclear holocaust. Our technology, while bringing many advances, has also raped and polluted our earth. Our economic and political might, while preserving many fine values, has also participated in a system which systematically helps impoverish the Third World. Madison Avenue uses the knowledge of the human psyche to create a culture of illusory wants and materialistic desires. Somehow we have used the very gifts God gave us to distort and warp our world.

At the very heart of the problem has been the way we put our human powers and wishes at the center of our lives. Our activity then becomes a way to destroy rather than to redeem. It happens on an international scale and in our own personal lives. We have forgotten how to listen to God.

Climbing a Spiritual Pyramid?

We create the same problem in our spiritual lives. We often act as though the religious life were a pyramid to climb. We "advance" by mastering techniques of prayer and meditation. We increase our activity in the church or in our professional work, thinking it is a sign of our mastery of God's way of love and caring. But, in fact, we succumb to the temptation to put ourselves in charge of our own salvation.

When we stop the excessive doing and over-extended busyness, we enter again that quiet place where we can hear God's voice. It is an act of repentance. There we learn that we are not being called to be masters of our world. We are being called by One who would master us. Our master came as a Suffering Servant and calls us to follow the same path. Only then will our own activity have its proper direction, purpose, and pace.

The Holy Spirit has been moving powerfully, bringing similar understandings in many Quaker communities in the last few years. We are being called back to a life truly centered in Christ. As we have tried to respond to this call, we have increasingly recognized the role of quiet listening as the heart of faithful community life. Opening ourselves to our history and heritage has been of enormous help in this process. Our communities have not imitated the forms of earlier generations; we have been drawn to the same Divine Source.

Community Listening

We have also learned something important about the place of community in the process of listening. Listening is not simply an individual spiritual discipline. Most people do not have the power to live apart from the busy, activity-oriented world by themselves. We find we must be part of a committed meeting-community which provides alternative structures of living and gives support and encouragement to its members to live in and through those alternative structures.

Moreover, in our experience the individual spiritual disciplines alone are not sufficient. Simply adding a quiet time periodically to our personal busy schedules is not adequate by itself. That only makes the quiet time another activity to add to an already over-burdened schedule. Such a discipline does not challenge the basic structure of an over-crowded, hectic life. It is this structure which needs to be challenged.

In recent years Friends Meetings are again making a commitment to a life of listening, quiet, and reflection. We use some wonderful, time-honored practices and some new forms as well. For example, meetings and small groups have the traditional meeting for worship and newer modes such as worship-sharing groups, quiet days, and silent retreat weekends. Many Friends are once again undertaking spiritual nurture work as travelling ministers, and the number of opportunities is growing rapidly.

Not all forms of listening need to be done in groups. Our communities give encouragement to those who plan personal times of retirement: a daily quiet time, a retreat day each month, a hermitage weekend a couple times a year.

Of course, these are not the only ways to listen to God. Other religious groups may develop other forms that are particularly appropriate for their circumstances and their members. Whatever the forms, we believe that a corporate commitment to a life of quiet listening and renewed discipleship is a powerful prophetic challenge to our world which has lost itself in its own human demands and busyness. In that quiet place we can again receive God's Word of chastisement, forgiveness, healing, and direction. Our lives, our activities, and our words can go forth, grounded in the Word, Christ, answering that of God in everyone.

Learning to Listen (Part Two)

BY SANDRA CRONK

Reprinted from Festival Quarterly, *Winter 1988, pp. 14–16.*
Copyright held by Good Books (www.GoodBooks.com). Reprinted
by permission. All rights reserved.

Quakers are sometimes called the Trappists of the Protestant world. The Society of Friends shares with this Catholic monastic order a commitment to a life of silent worship and quiet listening to God. But unlike the Trappists, the Quakers grew out of the English radical reformation. In keeping with that tradition, Friends have always emphasized faithful living in the everyday world of family, work and community. The Quaker understanding of quiet listening to God does not entail leaving the everyday world but providing a foundation for faithful living in it.

Making a Place of Christ

Silence has no merit of and by itself. It is significant only as an occasion to encounter God. Of course, we meet God in many ways in our lives. The problem is that we are often too busy to realize that the encounter is occurring. In the gospel we read that when Jesus was about to be born, the inn was so crowded that Mary and Joseph were forced to go to a nearby stable. Our lives are often so crowded with activities that there is no room for Christ to be born in our midst. Periods of silence provide an empty and receptive place for Christ to enter.

It is not always easy to shift our attention to God, even when we have a time of quiet. Almost everyone who has practiced quiet prayer or attended a silent retreat recognizes the need for a process that Friends call "centering."

In our worship there is no planned program of music, sermons or scripture readings. Instead the worshippers are expected to enter Christ's presence with quiet prayerfulness. But each time we begin an unprogrammed meeting, we can actually hear the lack of inward quiet. There is coughing, shuffling of feet and shifting of position on the benches or chairs. If you asked people what was happening at this point in the worship, they would say that their minds were awhirl. They might be thinking about what to fix for Sunday dinner or making mental "to do" lists on the back of invisible envelopes. They might be wondering if they should hold a particular problem up to God or try to let go of it in their minds, while doing neither. In short, they could not hear anything from God because their minds were filled with themselves.

Centering is the process of getting below this level of whirling thoughts in order to hear God. There are two primary methods of centering. Some Friends use a discipline to focus their thoughts. They might silently repeat a short prayer, a passage from scripture or a verse from a favorite hymn. They might hold a single word in their minds, such as "Jesus" or "love." They might hold a visual image in their minds, such as the cross.

The great majority of Friends, however, use no focusing discipline. They simply wait in faithfulness, knowing that Christ will be in their midst. In a while they find that they have slipped below their own spinning words and can hear a deeper Word. They are centered in Christ.

An awareness of the need for centering, whether through a discipline or waiting in quiet trust, helps to give one the patience needed for any time of quiet listening. Without this awareness, one is tempted to give up during the first five minutes, when one hears one's own thoughts and not God's.

Openness to God

When we become centered in the Living Word, real listening can begin. We are now open to receive whatever God wishes to bring to us: comfort, chastisement, healing, direction. To describe all that might happen when we are centered in the silence is impossible. God's ways are infinite.

On one occasion we might come face to face with all that has separated us from God. We suddenly see our own brokenness and unfaithfulness. Often in our lives we try to cover our hurt and pain, our anger and fear. Sometimes we succeed so well that a problem, while not being healed, gets pushed out of sight. We are glad to have it seem to disappear. When it is pushed away, however, it pops out in our attitudes and behavior in ways that alienate us from God and from one another. In silence difficult questions and hard truths about ourselves can come out into the open again. This is sometimes unpleasant, but it is God's way of beginning the path toward healing. There in the quiet, before God, we can acknowledge our brokenness and our failures. In silence too we can discover God's mercy and love. We can receive forgiveness for ourselves and the power to forgive those who have hurt us.

On another occasion silence may draw us into God's presence to drink the Living Water. We are not aware of ourselves as much as we are of God. This experience of presence may be so overpowering that we feel as though the veil between eternity and time had been withdrawn for a period. Our response is simply to be and to let our love, praise and thanksgiving flow in gratitude. Never again will it be possible for us to live or act as though God were merely a theoretical idea we could discuss and then dismiss from our lives. Our lives are transformed.

Our meeting with God is part of a covenantal relationship. God's everlasting love and mercy call forth fidelity from us; our listening to God involves obeying the call to faithful living. In silence we may hear God's call to faithfulness in very specific ways. We may receive a leading to write to a long-forgotten friend, act on an issue of concern in our local congregation or look at the previously-ignored problem of pollution of a local lake.

Listening Together

Listening and obedience form the core of Quaker faith. In quiet listening, both individuals and the community are formed and transformed by God. Because so much material about the spiritual life today is written from a purely individualistic perspective, some people in the radical reformation tradition fear that an emphasis on a quiet listening will undercut the beliefs that God works in and through the church and that faithfulness is measured by our daily living rather than by inward experience. The Quaker tradition also stresses the disciplined community and faithful living. Our experience is that silence does not compete with these understandings but complements them. This happens in two ways.

First, listening in the Quaker heritage is a corporate process. There are times for personal reflection, and we treasure them. But the heart of our life is listening together, when the whole community comes before God in unprogrammed worship. We are formed into a people of God by our willingness to listen and respond to the Word. When we are faithful, our life together is a witness to the new order and new creation which Christ is bringing to birth in the world. Quaker testimonies on peace, race relations and simplicity result from this corporate listening.

Second, even times of personal reflection, prayer and retreat have a community dimension. A Catholic sister studying at Pendle Hill (the Quaker study and retreat center where I work) spoke simply and yet movingly about this. She had scheduled a number of quiet days during her time on campus. She said that in the silence she was with her own religious community more fully than when she was with them in person. She explained that when she was in the convent washing dishes or preparing her teaching lessons, she was too busy to reflect on the meaning of the relationships which were so important to her. She could not ponder what each sister needed or what gifts each was bringing to the community. In her quiet time she had the space to reflect on each community member and on the community as a whole. She returned to her community a more faithful and thoughtful member because of her quiet reflection.

Faithfulness

The experience of this Catholic sister is similar to that of Friends, not only in its emphasis on community but in its stress on faithfulness. It is not possible to measure the success of a time of quiet listening by the feelings we experience in silence. In fact, the search for peak experiences can be a subtle snare. The religious life is not a matter of accumulating wonderful spiritual experiences. Rather, it is a matter of the fidelity of our relationship with God. The building of this relationship often involves very difficult experiences. Sometimes the strengthening of this relationship involves no special experience of God at all. We may come into the quiet and face what seems only emptiness and nothingness. Paradoxically, this does not always mean that something has gone wrong with us or our listening. It may mean that something has gone right. For the awareness of our own emptiness may mark a significant shift in our relationship with God.

I remember a weekend retreat with a Quaker group at an old Friends meetinghouse in Lancaster County, Pennsylvania. I arrived on Friday after work, a bit worn out from getting ready to take the two and a half days away from my usual routine. But I had high hopes for the weekend. I had made a resolution to be more serious about my prayer life. In addition, there were a number of questions in my life awaiting serious reflection. I needed to hear what God had to say about these questions and about those areas in which I knew I had not been faithful. So I came looking forward to a renewed clarity about my life and an experience of closeness to God.

It felt wonderful to relax into the quiet on Friday evening. Being tired, I decided to go to bed early, dreaming of what a special day Saturday would be.

When I got up the next morning, I thought, "Now I'm going to devote the day to listening to God." After the morning meal I sat down for the long-awaited time of prayer. I sat . . . and sat. I sat a while longer. For the life of me, I could not think of one profound thought about God or about my life. "I must try to be more focused," I thought to myself. So I tried a technique for focusing my mind. No result! "Perhaps I need to be more open and not think of anything." No luck! Nothing worked.

Where was God after I had made this resolution to be more serious about prayer? I began to think this whole process was a waste of time. I must not be a very spiritual person; I was not able to have a very profound prayer life. I wished I had brought my correspondence with me. At least I could be writing letters rather than sitting here with nothing happening.

With God's grace, I did not give in to the temptation to fill the empty space that loomed in front of me with my own activity. I stayed on in what seemed only emptiness and darkness . . . .

And strangely, in that emptiness, when I felt as though nothing were happening, the real work of God began. There was no special feeling connected with it. There was simply a deep knowing that began to emerge in the darkness. I realized that it was only in this empty place when I had come to the end of myself, my own efforts to think wonderful thoughts and my attempts to conjure up the presence of God, that God could finally begin to speak to me. Perhaps it is more accurate to say that only then could I begin to listen.

Letting Go of Self

Friends talk of the stripping away of the ego-centered self as a crucifixion. It is the heart of our lives with God. All of us must let go of self to let God become the true center of our lives.

In our spiritual journey we often act as though we were in control. We believe we are the center of ourselves. We seek comforting experiences from God to give our lives meaning and direction. Sometimes our search for God hides an idolatry. To live in this way is to assume, however subtly, that we are the source of our own salvation. Mercifully, God grants us many favors even when we have mixed priorities and motivations. But at some point a fundamental shift must take place. We must confront our idols, particularly the idol we have made of ourselves. In the silence there is little we can use to support our false notions. All the idols fall away into nothingness. In the emptiness our false self dies and we receive the gift of true self in Christ. We move from asking God to enter our lives to a realization that ultimately it is God who asks us to enter the Divine Life: "In him we live and move and have our being" (Acts 17:28).

In the silence we encounter the Living God. There we are molded and transformed. We are called to enter and live faithfully in God's order. We died to our own lives and receive new life in Christ: ". . . it is no longer I who live, but Christ who lives in me . . ." (Galatians 2:20).

Finding a Usable Past

BY SANDRA CRONK

*Sonnie's vision of what the Religious Society of Friends could
become was firmly rooted in our tradition. She did not cling
to tradition for the sake of sentiment or antiquarianism, but
because she found in the past faithful examples of listening to
God, and living in faithful community under the leadership of
Christ. The following article appeared in the fall 1989* Festival
Quarterly.

Contemporary Friends are in search of a "usable past," a vision of
our Quaker heritage which will help us understand God's call
to faithfulness in the present. The fact that we are looking for such a
vision indicates that we do not always find the past very helpful to us
today.

Seeking Support From the Past

A large part of our ambivalence about the past comes from the pre-
conceptions we bring with us when we look at it and thereby measure
its usefulness to us now.

We would like the past to support one particular view of Quaker
life. Some Friends look to the past in support of their view that the
heart of Quaker faith is found in the inward spiritual life. These
Friends look for images of prayer, worship and the use of silence and
meditation. Other Friends are eager to see what early Quaker testimonies about prison reform, the abolition of slavery, simple living and
peacemaking have to say to a contemporary Quakerism built around
a life of involvement in a needy world. Still other Quakers see the
heart of Quakerism in its classical church-communities of discipline

and accountability. They look for help from the past in the building of corporate structures of obedience in our contemporary, overly individualistic, lives.

It is easy to reject, or simply not see, the part of the past which does not support our particular view of Quakerism. We can make use of our views of the past in the struggle to make our view of Quakerism become the dominant one today. For example, we may dismiss those interested in the inward life as having become part of today's individualistic value system, abandoning traditional understandings of church-community. Or we may dismiss the traditional communities characterized by plain dress and plain speech as irrelevant to a Quakerism actively involved with the needs of the larger world.

The Radical Voice of the Past

A remarkable development has occurred recently. Through new historical and theological work,[71] we have gained insights which unsettle our previous assumptions about the past and make us hear God's call to faithfulness in deeper ways. We find that the past is speaking to us with a radical voice.

"Radical" has two definitions in the dictionary. It can mean being related to the root or origin—what is fundamental. It also means being marked by a considerable departure from the usual or traditional.

When the word "radical" is applied to the past, these two definitions seem at first glance to be contradictory. How can going back to the origin mean overturning tradition? We are accustomed to thinking that roots and tradition are the same. Yet Friends are learning that when we hear the radical voice of the past it can take us back to what is fundamental and, in the process, overturn our views of tradition. Even more disconcertingly, it can overturn all our categories of contemporary Quaker life.

The Apocalyptic Root of Friends

The particular root of the Society of Friends which has had such a profound effect on our communities of late has been the apocalyptic framework of the early Quaker movement in England. The Book of Revelation (which we hardly read today) was one of the favorite books of the Bible for the early Friends. I understand that scholars of the early Anabaptist movements are finding similar apocalyptic roots in that heritage as well.

Many Friends greeted these historical findings with non-comprehension at first. The word "apocalyptic" brings to mind images of people waiting on a hillside for the end of the world or of the not entirely convincing parallels which some interpreters see between symbols in the Book of Revelation and specific events in our own era. But a dismissal of all apocalyptic themes dismisses Jesus' ministry, which centered on the coming kingdom as a real event in our lives.

It took some time for Friends to be able to understand that the apocalyptic emphasis in Quaker thought was a prophetic protest against an unfaithful world, turned away from God and rushing headlong toward death and destruction. This apocalyptic faith was also a witness to God's power to inaugurate the promised kingdom. In today's world, which hovers on the brink of nuclear holocaust and environmental decay, the apocalyptic language of early Friends takes on fresh meaning.

The Imminence of God's Order

Friends' apocalyptic views were not of the type that predicted the end of the world on such and such a day. Neither did they encourage Friends to sit quietly waiting for the rapture or to take up arms in a struggle to compel the kingdom into existence. Rather, Friends lived with a sense of the imminent in-breaking of God's order. They experienced God's power transforming their own personal lives. They believed that this transforming power was also at work in the larger social, political and economic orders. The old, unjust, ungodly structures were facing God's judgment and, found wanting, would soon be swept away. God's order was coming to birth. The Day of the Lord was at hand.

Friends felt that their communities were already participating in this new order. They worshipped in a different manner. They dressed differently from those around them. They spoke differently. They bought and sold their goods in a different way. Every area of life was transformed.

These different patterns of life became known as religious testimonies. In later generations both Friends and non-Friends saw the testimonies as outward marks of a "peculiar people," a community separated from the world. But in the first generation the testimonies were much more than this.

The Testimony of Worship

A few examples will make the role of the testimonies clear. Friends' belief that Christ had come and was inaugurating God's order revolutionized their mode of worship. The Quakers' silent, or unprogrammed, worship no doubt seemed odd to many people around them, even as it does to many today, because it eschewed the usual forms of the worship service: sermons, Bible readings, hymns, responsive readings and outward celebration of the sacraments, or ordinances. But Friends understood this silence as an opportunity for inward listening to Christ. Christ had come to teach his people himself, they said. Christ would lead them in speaking and praying. Planned sermons and prayers were not necessary and could even get in the way of immediate listening to Christ.

Friends did not celebrate an outward communion. They understood that Jesus had asked his disciples to celebrate communion in remembrance of him, till he had come again. But Christ was come, Friends believed. There was no need to have a special celebration to remember One who was already present. Friends' mode of worship reflected their belief that they were living in God's new order.

Testimonies Against Class

Through the active process of listening to the Living Christ, Friends felt called into new relationships with other people as well. Seventeenth century England was a highly class-conscious society. Friends were particularly concerned about the spiritual consequences that arose out of the pride and arrogance engendered by this social system (at least for those on top of the hierarchical pyramid). In the eyes of Friends, such people usurped the authority which can rest only with God. Therefore, Friends refused to participate in the existing social structure. They felt called to a new way of living whose patterns were expressed in such testimonies as plain dress, plain speech and set prices.

Wealthy aristocrats in the 17th century donned elaborate attire: lace cuffs and collars, fancy hats and so on. Friends, in response, wore very simple clothing (which in later generations was standardized and called plain dress). They refused to greet others by removing their hats and bowing. Indeed, this refusal was one way newly converted Quakers could be detected as such by old acquaintances. Friends even kept their hats on in meeting for worship, removing them only before the Lord—that is, in prayer.

Testimonies of Speech and Commerce

Speech also became a way of reflecting an alternative set of values. Seventeenth century English, like most European languages today, used two forms of address. The second person plural pronouns "ye" and "you" were used both to address more than one person and to give honor to any social superior. The second person singular "thou" and "thee" were used to address one person, a close family member (such as a brother or sister) or a social inferior. Friends refused to use "ye" and "you" as forms of social honor (although they did continue to use them as plural forms of address). Instead, they addressed all individuals alike with "thou" and "thee."

This "plain speech," as it came to be called, was a prophetic critique of the arrogant airs assumed by those in power. The testimony often brought forth great anger from those who felt slighted by its use. To say "thee" or "thy" to a magistrate might result in imprisonment. But Friends persevered. Their speech was another witness to the fact that they lived in God's order, where all people were recognized as sisters and brothers.

Friends' testimony on the buying and selling of goods became another sign of Christ's transforming work. In the 1600s, bargaining between buyer and seller was common. But Friends insisted on setting a fair price and refused to bargain. The practice of bargaining, they said, was a way for buyer and seller to try to take advantage of one another, each wanting to receive the best price at the expense of the other. Living in God's new order transformed the patterns of economic life.

The Lamb's War

These testimonies were manifestations of personal faithfulness to kingdom values, But they were also spiritual weapons in the struggle between God's order and the world's order. Using an image from the Book of Revelation, Friends called the struggle "The Lamb's War." The phrase referred to the war between Christ, the Lamb, and the forces of evil, unfaithfulness and destruction. This struggle takes place within each of us as we are called to surrender to Christ. But it also extends beyond our personal lives. Christ is struggling with unjust social, economic and political orders. Indeed, the whole cosmos is struggling to be reborn. As followers of Christ, we are called to enter this struggle on the side of the Lamb.

The startling juxtaposition of the images of war and lamb point to the paradox of Christ's redemptive work. The Lamb is engaged in a very strange kind of war and uses very strange weapons. Christ gives up the use of carnal weapons, such as the sword and the gun. The weapons of the Lamb are sacrificial love, servanthood, mercy, justice and the call to righteousness. As followers of Christ, these are the weapons we must use.

Through their speech, dress and business practices, Friends saw themselves as taking part in spiritual warfare. By these testimonies they were challenging the unrighteous structures and attitudes of the society around them. Friends hoped that the witness in their lives, speech and apparel would answer the witness which they were sure was already being spoken through the Word, Christ, in the hearts of those around them.

Thus these testimonies were not simply signs that Friends were a peculiar people who had decided to be a separated community through adherence to a series of minor scruples. Together these testimonies overturned patterns of behavior in virtually every basic area of human life. They expressed Friends' commitment to live faithfully in God's order, and, at the same time, they were the methods used to challenge the existing order and call it to righteousness.

New Dimensions for Quakers Today

Understanding the apocalyptic framework of early Friends has opened new dimensions of contemporary Quaker experience. We see more clearly that our present world must choose between life and death, God and unfaithfulness. The Day of the Lord is at hand for us. As followers of Christ we must see how Christ is calling us to live in God's order. What patterns of our lives must be changed?

This apocalyptic view has also made us realize that we had seen our faith in unintegrated bits and pieces, rather than as a whole. For example, it is no longer possible to define the very important emphasis Quakers have put on silent listening to Christ as devoting attention to the inward spiritual life alone. The inward dimension is clearly present and very significant. But listening to Christ is also the way in which the church is able to discern the patterns of living which give shape to community life and become its prophetic witness in the world. Listening in worship is a testimony to Christ's presence leading His people.

The apocalyptic experience has reshaped the way we understand community life as well. Friends have tended to see the plain dress and plain speech of classical Quaker communities as having little relevance to any larger witness in the world. Now we see that the very pattern of community life was not only relevant but in itself the means of carrying on the Lamb's War. Consequently, to build patterns of faithful, disciplined church community is not to opt out of active witness in the world. Rather, it is a primary way in which the church may witness. The heart of the church's testimony is its prophetic participation in God's order.

Limits to Imitating the Past

The recent historical insights have also made it clearer to us that it is not possible to participate in God's order simply by imitating the patterns of church life in the past. When society changes we need to discern God's will afresh.

For example, the English language no longer uses two forms of address, "ye" and "thou." It uses "you" as the form of address to all persons. Thus, the language as a whole has adopted the opposite pattern from the Quaker one (that is, the use of "thou"). Therefore, Friends need to reflect again to see if God wishes them to continue their use of "thee" and "thy."

Many Friends have decided that they are not called to continue using this part of traditional plain speech. Some Friends continue to use "thee" and "thy" in everyday speech. They believe that the Quaker solution to the status problem in English grammar is the better one and that God calls them to use it today. This is not the place to comment on the decisions of various groups of Friends. The point is simply that imitation of the past, by itself, is not an adequate guide for faithfulness. Rather, it is necessary to listen to God's call in our lives today. How is God's order to be expressed now? What witness is required of us? This does not mean that kingdom values are relative. It only means that they must be expressed in ways that relate them to a particular time and place.

Implications for Social Activism

The apocalyptic stance provides strong support for active witness in the world. On the other hand, it also brings powerful challenges to the kind of social activism which has become the measure of much contemporary religious life. Early Friends understood that God is bringing the kingdom to birth. We are not only witnesses to that birth, but midwives for others, as they may be for us.

This is radically different from the implicit understanding which lies behind a good deal of our recent efforts at social change. We act as though the coming of God's order depended on us. *If* we can get Congress, the President, the Soviet Union, the local town council or the church to do this, then we will have a more peaceful, just and merciful world. Sometimes we give the impression that nothing will happen unless we make it happen. This attitude is a subtle form of idolatry and disbelief in God. It leads to enormous levels of frustration and to burnout, as we realize that our efforts are not capable of producing the kingdom.

But the early Friends did not work on an If-Then basis. (If we do this, then God's order will come.) They worked *because* the seed of the kingdom had taken root in their lives. *Therefore*, they lived in a new way. Every area of living reflected their participation in the birth of God's order. Their witness did not depend on their own strength to keep up campaigns, programs and projects, although many fine projects emerged out of this new life. The root of their witness was in God's strength. Its first expression was in the transformed pattern of daily life, not in a campaign of social change. This new pattern of living itself became a profound witness to the larger world.

Community Life *and* Social Involvement

The apocalyptic hope allowed Friends to be engaged in the world but not be of the world. It allowed them to develop their faithful community life and still be actively involved in the needs of the larger society. So often in our later history, Friends acted as though we had to make a choice in arenas of faithfulness. We could retain God's patterns in our own communities or we could be active in the world. But we believed we could not do both without compromise on one side or the other.

For early Friends these were not two choices but two sides of the same witness. The apocalyptic hope helps us reclaim a more balanced vision of the church, in place of our partial and one-sided views.

Friends have been searching for a usable past to help us be faithful in the present. The vision God has given us at this moment in our history is not at all what we expected. It does not comfortably support all our existing views of Quaker life. Instead, this vision has had a radical effect. It has overturned many of our views of tradition, but it has also allowed us to reclaim a deeper understanding of our past. It has given us a perspective by which to evaluate contemporary religious practices.

We have been called back to our root, Christ. We find ourselves led not to imitate any particular cultural pattern which emerges from the past, but to listen again to Christ, who is calling us to enter God's kingdom. This kingdom is coming to birth in our midst right now. We pray that we may be enabled to listen and respond faithfully to Christ's call day by day.

Substituting Activities for Community?

BY SANDRA CRONK

At a time when many of us are tempted to chart our faithfulness by the number of church committees we are members of, the density of our calendars, the variety of retreats and conferences we attend, Sandra Cronk, a Quaker "prophet," wonders if we have mortgaged something essential. Her Quaker references seem to have Mennonite parallels, at least for those of us who are dutiful attendees of a myriad of church events. Have we, she asks, substituted activities for community?

A 'Meeting' Friend or a 'Conference' Friend?

I didn't understand the question when my friend first asked it of me. She said, "Are you a 'meeting Friend' or a 'conference Friend'?" But she jolted me into a serious reflection on the ways in which the Society of Friends today lives out its understanding of the meeting community. My friend is from a very traditional branch of Quakers which has preserved the classic Quaker understanding of the "meeting" or the "church-community." In our heritage, the fullness of God's redemptive work through Christ is understood to come to completeness as one participates in the church-community. Through that body, Christ's redemptive healing and call to faithfulness take concrete shape and form.

On a personal level, our wounded places need healing; our sorrow needs comfort; our joy needs sharing; our shallow and insensitive places need to deepen into compassion; our despair needs hope. In short, we are called to become disciples of Christ.

But Christ's transforming work generally does not take place in us overnight (although there may, of course, be critical moments of decision-making or important breakthrough experiences). We do not wake up one morning completely loving and faithful people. We have to learn how to love. We need practice giving love. Strange to say, we also have to practice receiving love. Often we build high barriers around ourselves as we try not to let anyone into the depth of ourselves, lest we be hurt, embarrassed or challenged. But the same barriers prevent God's redeeming work from taking effect in our daily lives.

It is precisely our willingness to be part of a community of faith which listens to God's will and provides mutual support and accountability that allows Christ's transforming power to re-mold our lives.

My friend's phrase—"meeting Friend"—designated one who believed in, and lived out, this understanding of Christian life through day to day commitment to the life of the local meeting. Her question was whether I had made such a commitment. But the question went further. She was suggesting that another understanding was beginning to compete with this traditional view of the church-community. My friend called it being a "conference Friend."

Her newly coined phrase was apt. It put into words what I had observed but had not known how to articulate to myself. Much of the participation in our meetings these days is not at the level of shared lives. Rather it is in the form of involvement in a whole series of special activities: conferences, classes, lecture series, workshops, committees, projects and campaigns. We take all of these activities so much for granted, at least in many Friends meetings, that we rarely step back and see their effect on the quality of our church life.

Pondering my friend's question, I could see two dangers in the new pattern of meeting life. One had to do with our understanding of faithfulness. The second had to do with experiencing the reality of Christ's redemptive work in our own lives.

Social Agency or Transformed Community?

Sometimes we see our meetings as though they were not very different from businesses, political organizations or social agencies. We see our faithfulness in terms of our involvement with its task-oriented projects, programs and committees. Indeed, Friends have an excellent structure for working on a wide variety of concerns: peace and justice, education, environment, the family, worship, etc. Without a doubt, all of these areas of concern are genuine. They address needs which are often desperate. To turn away would be the height of unfaithfulness. In fact, our heavy involvement in all of these projects reflects, in part, our reaction to a time when being a "meeting Friend" may have meant being so quiet and withdrawn from the affairs of the world that we turned away from a broken world in need of caring.

Yet to live in Christ's redemptive way is not simply to solve the world's problems. We live in a culture which tends to see human society in terms of problems to solve, not people to love. Most contemporary institutions assume that our task is to manage the world through our technological, scientific or human relationship proficiencies. Paradoxically, our skills, while helpful on one level, sometimes leave us with even more estrangement from those in need, "those people over there," who are the recipients of our benevolently bestowed techniques and manipulations.

Our broken world demands not only our skills but ourselves. We must put on the mind of Christ who emptied himself to become one with us (Philippians 2). Christ's work on the cross was not a "fixing up" of the world's problems. It was a radical willingness to be "with" our broken world, to bear the pain and hurt of our world in love and forgiveness. In that love, which carried the consequences of our brokenness, God's reconciliation and redemption flowed forth into the world. My friend's question made me realize that sometimes our heavily task-oriented attitude might hide a wish to escape from the deeper commitment to following Christ's path of servanthood. Are we willing to be "with" each other in our meetings and in the larger world, trusting that God's redemptive power will be among us?

'Talking' Faith Rather Than 'Living' Faith?

The "conference" orientation may not only threaten to distort our view of God's call to faithfulness, it may also block our reception of Christ's transforming work. We often come to our meetings looking for a magical key that will unlock the secret to a deeper, more fulfilling life. We look for the wonderful speaker, the exciting idea, the new insight. It is enjoyable to go to conferences, classes and workshops to talk about the implications in our everyday lives. But often talking can become a substitute for a way of living.

In our Quaker communities we put so much emphasis on the inward life of listening to God that we are tempted to look for the immediately uplifting experience. But, in fact, we do not stay put long enough with ourselves or with each other to come to grips with the broken and unfaithful places in our lives. These places must be faced not only in our conceptual thinking but in our daily lives with each other. We need to let God work in and through our ongoing relationships.

These reflections make me wince a bit. I am a teacher at a Quaker study center. I give courses, plan conferences and am on my share of committees. Am I unwittingly participating in those patterns of contemporary life that are working toward the disintegration of the church community? After much prayer and lots of conversation within our community, I am ready to believe that there is a rightful place for special programs, classes and conferences. They give salt and spice to our diet. They may be just what is needed to meet a whole range of needs. However, our lives cannot be made up only of salt and spice. There must be solid food to provide nourishment. Christ's redemptive power must take root in us everyday.

As we try to find faithful patterns of church life in today's world, Friends have found it very helpful to recall the accounts of meeting-communities in the past. They do not provide us with a blueprint to follow. But they often give a prophetic voice that allows us a much needed perspective on the present.

Footwashing in Isaac Baily's Bedroom

My friend's question made me remember one of my favorite stories from Quaker history, the account of the footwashing at Marlborough. Footwashing, by the way, is not part of the traditional worship patterns among Friends. This story is an exception. But its meaning touches the same understandings of love, servanthood and spiritual cleansing which are found wherever footwashing is practiced as a religious ordinance or rite.

The story turns on two fundamental characteristics of Quaker life: inward listening and the peace testimony. The heart of our life through the centuries is listening inwardly to God, not just for comfort and consolation but for guidance and direction. The peace testimony is a second important theme in Quaker life. It requires a refusal to participate in war, but it is above all a testimony to God's power to overcome brokenness and bring forgiveness and wholeness in all our relationships.

This story mentions two kinds of ministers recognized in traditional Quaker communities. The first is the travelling minister, a man or woman gifted by God with teaching, exhortation and vocal prayer in the Quaker unprogrammed meeting for worship. These ministers not only helped provide vocal ministry in their home meetings, they often travelled far and wide, attending meetings for worship and visiting families or individuals for "opportunities" (i.e. times of worship and spiritual conversation).

The second form of minister was the elder, a woman or man whose gift was not that of vocal ministry but rather of nurture and guidance. The elders were mature in the religious life and wise in the ways the Lord worked within people. Their tasks were to oversee the meeting for worship and to nurture the vocal ministers and Friends in general. They often became counsellors who could give a word of guidance and support to those who were facing problems.

The story happened in Chester County, Pennsylvania, just east of Lancaster County. It was at the time of the Revolutionary War. Two Quakers lived on neighboring farms. One was Richard Barnard, an elder, who was a war tax resister. Not able to support military endeavors because of religious convictions, he refused to pay all taxes directly related to war. On more than one occasion he had various goods seized by the tax collector and sold at auction to pay his tax bill. God's call to peacemaking was very important to this man.

His next-door neighbor was Isaac Baily, a strong supporter of the Revolutionary War. Baily was known in the area as a contentious man, often involved with disputes with his acquaintances and even with his meeting. It would have been hard to find two more unlikely neighbors than these two Friends.

A stream ran between the Baily and Barnard homes. As part of a dispute about property rights and water use, Isaac Baily dammed up the waterway.

Richard Barnard tried everything conceivable to work out a satisfactory solution with his neighbor. Following the advice of Matthew 18, he had gone to talk to Isaac, but to no avail. He had taken other Friends with him to speak with Isaac. On several occasions the matter had been put to arbitration. But nothing would induce Isaac Baily to remove the dam or be reconciled to his neighbor.

The situation was a great burden to Richard Barnard. Not only was he without the use of the water, but he suffered much inward discomfort as the result of the broken relationship with Isaac. Moreover, he was an elder in his meeting; he was supposed to be a counsellor and guide to others. Yet he could not solve his own dilemma.

One day a travelling minister came to visit. Richard Barnard opened his heart to him, describing his problem. When he finished, the minister said simply, "There is more required of some than of others." Richard was struck by his response, wondering what more could be demanded of him. He had done all that seemed humanly possible to find a solution.

Richard held up the problem to God for direction and guidance. The answer that came was beyond all "techniques" of conflict resolutions. It required giving up claims of being right and going to his neighbor in humility and forgiveness. Richard felt that God was calling him to wash Isaac's feet. The idea was so strange and unusual he kept trying to push it away. But in the end, he realized he would not have a sense of being faithful to God's leading unless he was willing to surrender his will to God and be obedient.

Therefore, one morning he filled a bowl with water from the stream that divided the two men and went to Isaac Baily's house. It was so early that Isaac was still in bed. But Richard went up to his bedroom and explained that he had come to wash Isaac's feet. He described how painful this strained relationship had been for him. He was here now, following God's leading, hoping they could be reconciled. Isaac sputtered and fussed, refusing to participate. But Richard persevered and began to wash his feet.

Gradually Isaac became quiet and let Richard complete the washing. Then Isaac dressed and accompanied Richard to the door.

Later that day Richard saw Isaac take a shovel to the waterway and dig away the dam. The water flowed again between the two farms. In the afternoon Isaac and his wife came to pay the Barnards a friendly visit, the first in a number of years. Richard was very grateful for the restored relationship.

The friendship between the two men remained deep and vibrant for the remainder of their lives. Some while after the problem with the waterway, Richard Barnard broke his leg in a lumbering accident. Isaac took special care of him during his recovery. In 1801, in recognition of God's healing work in their lives, both men gave one hundred dollar contributions to the building of Marlborough Meetinghouse. And in 1803, when Friends decided to build a new schoolhouse to meet the needs of their growing community, it was located at the junction of the Barnard and Baily properties.

In this tiny corner of the world the seed of God's peaceable kingdom took root and flourished. Christ's redeeming work touched the intertwined lives of two Friends and spread out to the surrounding community.

May we, in our generation, allow Christ's redemptive love to touch our intertwined lives. May our church communities be places where we can learn to love God and each other. We so often assume, when we hear God's call for "more," that we should become busier and take on more projects. But more busyness may not be "the more" that God requires of us. Let us not be so caught up in our tasks and activities that we miss the invitation to enter God's transformed order.

Discovering and Nurturing Ministers

BY SANDRA CRONK

One of the most significant issues facing the Society of Friends today is that of leadership. How do we recognize, encourage and nurture leaders or ministers who can help our communities be faithful followers of Christ? In days gone by, Friends gave special recognition to two forms of ministry: vocal ministers and elders (or spiritual nurturers). Both women and men served as ministers and elders. These ministers arose from the membership of the local meetings. They received no professional training. They served without pay.

Because the two forms of ministry had separate functions, persons in those roles were recognized because of their gifts in their respective work. Yet on a deeper level, these ministers were chosen because they embodied a whole way of life. They lived Quaker faith. Their ministry reflected their embodiment of a way of life as much as a particular skill.

Ministers began their work in obedience to an inward call from God. For example, a young man or woman might begin speaking out of the silence of the unprogrammed meeting for worship with some frequency. If their words seemed genuinely led by the Spirit, the more mature elders and ministers would begin a process of guidance and nurture that would enable the new minister to grow in the new leadership role. The nurture would include community recognition of the call to ministry, becoming a kind of informal apprentice or junior partner to an experienced traveling minister, and participation in the regular gatherings of ministers and elders.

Thus, in generations past, calling, skill, embodiment of a way of life, and community nurture and recognition were all important elements in the raising up of leaders among Friends. Each of these elements continues to be an important factor today, although the outward forms of ministry have become much more varied.

Friends have always put great stress on the ministry of each member. While we did have special "recorded" ministers (i.e., ministers who were formally recognized by the community by having their names "recorded" in the meeting's records), speaking in the worship service was never limited to these recorded ministers. Never did these recognized ministers feel that they were doing all the ministry which needed to be undertaken in the community.

My branch of Friends has never had pastors (i.e., single ministers who took over the central leadership functions of the congregation). Thus, the varied work of the meeting has had to be divided among all the members. We believe that every Christian is called to ministry, in the broadest sense of that term. Today this emphasis on the ministry of all is so strong in my branch of Friends that meetings tend to discontinue the practice of recognizing special vocal ministers and elders. This has put even more stress on the ministry of each member.

We all must minister if the meeting is to function properly. There must be people to preach and teach. Others must visit the sick. There must be Friends to repair the meetinghouse roof after a storm and others to prepare food in cases of need. There are members who bring a peace witness to military bases and who plan conferences for diplomats. There are Friends who devote themselves to intercessory prayer. Each of these activities is ministry when guided by the Spirit.

Which Gifts?

Because our structure depends so heavily on the ministry of each member for the on-going life of the meeting, we have taken the biblical understanding of gifts very seriously.

> Now there are varieties of gifts, but the same Spirit, and there are varieties of service, but the same Lord, and there are varieties of working, but it is the same God who inspires them all in every one. To

each is given the manifestation of the Spirit for the common good. (I Corinthians 12:4–7)

Each of us has a distinctive function and gift as part of the body of Christ. All are necessary for the upbuilding of that body.

Recently Friends have become much more explicit about the process of discerning gifts. We encourage the meeting as a whole to recognize the gifts of its members, so that persons are well matched to the standing committees which carry out the work of the meeting. Furthermore, we encourage individual members to recognize their own gifts and to become part of small groups devoted to mutual discernment of gifts.

This conscious recognition of gifts has been liberating for many people, allowing them to walk more intentionally in the way God would have them go. The process has allowed people to live more fully with family and friends, to undertake specific tasks in their meetings or in service agencies, and to make decisions about their jobs and educational needs. From a community perspective, the recognition of gifts has brought forth a tremendous outpouring of service, renewed dedication and excitement about living a life of faith.

What About a Calling?

However, the identification of gifts must be done with care. The process can result in misuse, particularly in our contemporary culture which puts so much emphasis on individual fulfillment through self expression. There is a danger that the recognition of gifts may be understood simply as an identification of human skill and talent, those areas of strength where we perform well and which often give us a sense of ego gratification.

Undoubtedly many of our talents are meant by God to be used in ministry. But paradoxically, our weakest areas sometimes become the avenues of our strongest ministry precisely because it is there that we have to accept God's power rather than our own. Consequently, these are the places where ego cannot get in the way of God's service. Thus, God seems to use them fully. But we may overlook these weak areas when gift recognition is perceived as the naming of skills and talent.

Gift identification may also be misleading because it implies that if we have a gift we should use it. But there are times when we are not called to use our talent and skill. I remember a long-term Sunday School teacher in one of our meetings who needed to let go of her teaching so that a younger teacher could receive appropriate experience and so that her own proprietary grip on the Sunday School did not block her perception of God's new leading.

Gift recognition is not a sufficient basis for undertaking ministry. We need to listen to God's calling as heard in our prayerful listening and as expressed through the needs and discernment of the community. Our ultimate task is to obey God's call and not simply to express our gifts.

Moses did not (indeed, could not) sit down and identify his skills as ones that would make him a good liberation-leader. Just the opposite was the case. When God spoke to him from the burning bush, telling him that he was the one called to bring forth God's people from slavery, Moses replied, "Who am I?" He presented every argument he could think of to show that he was not gifted for the task. He did not know God's name. People would not believe his call. He was not an eloquent speaker. As Moses' questions were answered one by one, he realized that his strength was not in himself but in God alone. This is precisely the power that he had to offer his people: God's power. Paradoxically, it was ultimately by obeying God's call and relying on God's power that Moses was able to use skills and strengths he never knew he had.

Listening and responding to God's call has been a cornerstone of Friends' ministry through the generations. This process has been especially important for women. Because the larger society has not always recognized the gifts of women, many women have not been able to perceive their own gifts. It is strange but true that it is almost impossible to recognize one's gifts when no one else honors them. Quaker women have also had to deal with this problem, even though their meetings were more receptive to women in ministry than was the larger society. Thus, it was not primarily recognition of gifts, but faithfulness to God's call that allowed generations of Quaker women to take active leadership roles in such diverse ministry as preaching, prison reform and women's suffrage.

Recognition of gifts is a significant part of encouraging ministry. But gifts must be understood as part of a larger context of being called by God.

Ministry: A Profession?

We Friends have been struggling with a second cluster of issues, closely related to those of gifts and calling. These have to do with the recent introduction of the professional model of ministry and its relationship to the older model of the minister as the embodiment of a way of life. Our culture today generally considers ministry (in its narrowly defined sense) a profession or a career. Ministry has followed the pattern of medicine, law, teaching, social service work and many other fields which require extensive formal education.

For many generations, the argument against professionalization in Quaker circles has centered around the question of pay. Gospel ministry should be free, we have said. But the issue of pay has hidden a whole spectrum of other questions.

The professional model assumes that ministry is primarily a skill or body of knowledge that is offered to recipients. These skills are part of a job. But in earlier years Friends saw ministry much more as a way of being and relating. Ministers were recognized for their skills, to be sure, but they were leaders more because their whole way of being pointed toward God or conveyed God's love and caring. Their words, actions and relationships were their ministry. In this old Quaker conception, ministry is not just a matter of doing but of being.

The difference between using skills in a professional setting and entering into relationship in the traditional manner is at work in a story a European Quaker told me recently about a young man in her country who suffered from a severe case of cerebral palsy. For most of his childhood, he had lived in a fine institution devoted to residential care for people with his illness. But as an adult he chose to leave the institution in favor of life in a newly founded village whose residents included those with and without physical handicaps. All were equal in the village. The non-handicapped people chose to be there as a life commitment. They were not paid.

The parents of the young man were hurt that he decided to leave the institution which they had so carefully chosen for him because of its fine professional staff. They asked if he had not been treated well there. He responded that he had been treated very well. But he saw that when five o'clock came, the staff members went home. No matter how pleasant and concerned they were during working hours, they would not choose to spend their time off duty with him. In this village no one went home at five. There was no on duty or off duty. In the village he was not treated as simply the recipient of skilled care. In the village, he was home.

It has been my experience that those who carry out their ministry through professional work are extraordinarily dedicated. Their lives are committed to God. And non-professional ministers are not magically exempt from the need for rest and refreshment. They need to have time alone. Jesus took time away from the crowds for prayer. The question is not one of personal dedication. The difficulty is on a structural level.

There are problems with the kind of structure which compartmentalizes life into private and professional spheres. This kind of division tends to make ministry a task. It prevents a full relationship with another human being in which redemption can happen.

This critique does not mean that Friends have decided to reject all forms of professional work. Indeed, to carry out many forms of service in our contemporary social setting, some people will use the structures of professional life. However, we all need to remain clear that this pattern has disadvantages. It cannot capture all that ministry is.

What Kind of Education?

A second area which sometimes causes problems in the professional model is its emphasis on formal training and education. Friends have always had a high regard for education. It was once said that wherever there was a meetinghouse one could expect to find a schoolhouse. If anything, our devotion to education has increased today.

In a culture where the Bible is no longer taught in public schools, adults who are well educated in most subjects may be ignorant of the basic understandings of Christian faith. Friends have recently recognized that we must take on a massive educational effort to help adult members acquire a basic understanding of the Bible, church history and Quaker thought. Without these foundational levels of understanding, it is impossible to form communities of commitment. Educational programs of all kinds are proliferating now. There are year-long classes, weekend conferences, lecture series and fine publishing endeavors. All of these have helped produce a significant deepening of the spiritual life and reinvigoration of the meeting-community.

Of course, professionalization requires education beyond that which is offered to all. It implies specialized training for people who are going to undertake very particular kinds of work. Friends recognize the validity of this kind of training for diverse ministries as well. A prospective doctor needs training at a medical school. A person who plans to do peace work with diplomats should be well grounded in politics, economics and history. A person doing counseling should have extensive background in psychology. All forms of ministry and service need to grow out of an understanding of Christian thought.

The problem, then, is not with education itself, but with the attitudes and unintended by-products of the professional use of education. Our culture has an assertive orientation. Professionals assume they are the experts and have access to the appropriate skills and learning to clear up the problems in their area of expertise. Lawyers solve legal problems. Doctors cure illness. Ministers come to be seen as experts in their area of work. And experts are those with power. The recipients of their skills are in a dependent position.

This model tends to make the minister the leader by virtue of power and to disempower others in the community of faith. But ministry among Friends is meant to do exactly the opposite. It is meant to build a community of faith. It assumes that in such a community all minister to one another. A minister is thus not one with power over others, but a servant. While the professional model sometimes talks of service, it usually does not operate in a servanthood pattern.

The professional model arises out of our very human centered culture. Our larger society rates human skill and knowledge highly.

It believes that the "good life" comes through that human expertise. In our Quaker heritage (and, I am sure, in the Mennonite heritage as well) our communities are rooted in God's power. On the deepest level, we believe that God ushers in the kingdom. We do not build the kingdom through our own efforts. (Of course, as citizens of that kingdom we are called to follow God faithfully. The kingdom takes shape through our lives and actions. But God remains the one who empowers and guides.)

The difference in attitude is evident in a phrase which George Fox (one of the founders of the Quaker movement) used frequently in talking about ministry. He said that by staying faithful to God's leading (call) one could "answer that of God in everyone." Answering that of God in everyone became one of the primary ways Friends understood the nature of ministry.

The phrase may need a bit of explanation. "That of God" is the redemptive, transforming, guiding and empowering work of God in our lives. Friends believe that the Living Christ is present among us. The Light of Christ works in each person's life to show us our disobedience and unfaithfulness; it turns us again toward God in repentance. The Light reveals both our brokenness and Christ's healing power. Christ is our guide and empowerer, showing us the path of righteousness.

Of course, people do not always obey God's call. We may, and often do, turn away. God does not force our obedience. But we are called to answer faithfully that of God in our own lives. As ministers we are called to answer that of God in others. To "answer" that work of God means to respond to it, to nurture it, to call it forth, to dig up any entangling weeds which might be strangling the New Life beginning to grow. Our life, our words and our actions should direct others to see the work of God in their lives and to respond to it more fully.

The Fundamental Work of Ministers

So the fundamental work of the minister is not to fix all the problems in the world. It is to discern what God is already doing in every person and every situation to bring to birth the kingdom. The minister is a midwife, recognizing that God is the author of our salvation, yet understanding the place of faithful human response to God's call.

Consequently, for Friends in years gone by, the most important preparation for ministry was "training" in the work of discernment, i.e., learning to see the movement of the Spirit or Christ's redemptive work in our daily lives. This training did not occur in a separate school. It took place within the community. In fact, this setting was absolutely essential. For discernment arose out of the process of listening to God. Listening happened in many ways. Paramount among these were the community times of listening in the meeting for worship and meeting for business. There were also special gatherings of ministers and elders which were devoted largely to the work of worship and discernment. All of these occasions were opportunities for learning the art of listening and for testing one's discernment through the listening skills of the rest of the community.

The professional model is built on experts and human action, rather than the community and the power of God.

Learning to Perceive

The pattern of listening and obeying helps us understand the significance of the traditional Quaker expectations that ministers would embody a way of life. There has been a great deal of misunderstanding of this point. For some contemporary Quakers the old expectation makes no sense. They think it means that a minister must abide by a pious but outmoded way of life which has little to say to their problems today. But embodying a way of life did not mean following a legalistic pattern of behavior or a utopian vision of church discipline. It meant, very simply, living a life of listening and responding.

The traditional ministers learned to perceive God's call and healing work in their own lives. They became very sensitive to the movement of the Spirit in the lives of others. They paid careful attention to the way God gathered a community of faith. (They understood that communities are called and shaped just as individuals are.)

In short, it was just this ability to perceive the ways in which God's transforming power touches our lives that allowed these ministers to speak so powerfully to the condition of those they met. Our literature is full of accounts of the extraordinary gift of such sisters and brothers to say the right word or undertake the right actions to help individuals and whole communities take the next step in faithfulness. They were able to "answer that of God in others." This way of life is available to us today. But it requires the same commitment to listening and responding.

The fact that listening to God was such a central commitment for traditional Friends had profound implications for the minister's personal life and for Quaker views on preparation for ministry. To live in this on-going relationship with God meant letting one's life be molded by God. One problem with the skills oriented preparation for ministry is that it assumes that a person, at the point of decision-making, will choose to follow a Christ-like action. Therefore the training concentrates on the technical ability to undertake a certain task. But in the traditional preparation for ministry there is a recognition that a person will not automatically make a Christ-like decision unless he or she has become a ChristLike person.

Learning from Community

The traditional preparation for ministry concentrated on the deeper molding or forming carried out by God. This formation is not something that happens primarily in school (although God's work may continue in any location). It happens in a special sense as we participate in the community of faith. It happens as we discern God's will together and hold each other accountable to God's leading. It happens as we practice being channels of God's love and caring for one another. It happens as life in community brings to light our limitations, brokenness, unfaithfulness and dark places. In the Light of Truth, Christ's redemptive love begins to shape us anew. Only as we live in that redemptive love are we able to minister to the brokenness of the world.

Many of the outward forms of ministry have changed among Friends in our contemporary setting. But as we have explored the meaning of ministry and wrestled with the way to nurture ministers today, we have reaffirmed many of the basic understandings of ministry which have been important in our tradition from the beginning.

First Faithfulness

We recognize the importance of identifying the gifts of all members. However, that identification must be done in the larger context of discerning God's call to each of us. For sometimes our gifts are not manifested until we go forth in faithfulness. Moreover, our fulfillment comes in that faithfulness, not in purely individual expression of talents.

We have adopted aspects of the professional model of ministry. To relate to the needs of the larger society, some forms of ministry will be carried out through professional channels. We appreciate the emphasis on competence and quality which professional standards ensure. But there are aspects of the professional model which we do not accept as a definition of ministry. We do not accept that ministry is the job of the few who are the "experts." We are all called to ministry. We work hard to provide the basic educational tools to allow all to follow their calls to ministry.

While preparing for ministry may include the growth of skills and knowledge, a deeper development must also be taking place. Preparation for ministry is learning to discern how the Spirit is moving in our midst so that we may respond accordingly. Preparation for ministry is learning to let God mold our lives so that we become channels for God's love and caring in the world. Preparation for ministry is learning to hear the Word, Christ, so that we may have a word of life to speak to others. To be a minister is not first and foremost to take on a particular task; it is to live in faithful relationship with God so that we can "answer that of God in everyone."

This work of preparing may include formal education in a school or university setting. But primarily it involves being part of the community of faith where this work of discernment and the process of formation and transformation takes place. Friends are becoming more intentional in the recognition of this deeper preparation of ministers. We encourage meetings and small nurture groups within the meetings to take seriously the work of mutual discernment and accountability. As individuals and communities we wish to perceive and respond to the work of Christ molding us and calling us to righteousness.

Even the small steps we have taken in the direction of more faithful nurture of ministers [have] brought an amazing outpouring of new leadership and new life in our meetings. Many can testify to the extraordinary movement of the Spirit in our midst in recent years. Or perhaps we have only begun to listen once again.

Notes

1. This refers to those branches of Friends that maintain traditional waiting worship in expectant silence without a pre-planned program of invocation, hymns, sermon, prayer, and so on.
2. Unacknowledged quotations are from Sonnie's Journal, p. 18.
3. Cleveland Friends Meeting records.
4. See for example, James W. Fowler, *Stages of Faith: The Psychology of Human Development and the Quest for Meaning* (San Francisco: Harper & Row, Publishers, 1981); M. Scott Peck, *The Different Drum: Community Making and Peace* (New York: Simon & Shuster, 1987), 188–200; Ken Wilber, *A Theory of Everything: An Integral Vision for Business, Politics, Science, and Spirituality* (Boston: Shambhala, 2000), 9–12. Wilber defines the skeptical, Enlightenment stage in present-day terms as aiming for "diversity, multiculturalism, and sensitivity" while it refuses to acknowledge any interior causation, believing only in "scientific materialism," *The Theory of Everything*, 84–88, 123–25. For an explanation of the stages Quaker ministers went through in their spiritual development, as described in their journals, see Howard H. Brinton, *Quaker Journals: Varieties of Religious Experience Among Friends* (Wallingford, PA: Pendle Hill Publications, 1972), 4–5.
5. The Religious Society of Friends has a structure that generally consists of local congregations that gather once a month to consider the business of the group; these are called monthly meetings and are the basic unit of Friends' governance. Traditionally, regional groupings of monthly meetings gather four times a year as a quarterly meeting (although some newer yearly meetings do not have quarterly meetings). Larger geographical groups of quarterly meetings constitute a yearly meeting. More conservative yearly meetings tend to have a hierarchical structure with the yearly meeting making final policy decisions affecting the entire group. More liberal yearly meetings tend to view the structure as one of widening circles of discernment, with the monthly meetings being fairly autonomous. In earlier days the larger body recognized and established the smaller body. But in the 1920s groups of like-minded people were encouraged to form their own local, independent meetings. In the 1960s there was an effort to bring these into existing or newly-forming yearly

meetings. Cleveland Meeting finally decided to seek dual affiliation, joining both Ohio (Conservative) and Lake Erie yearly meetings in 1965. The break-away Community Meeting joined only Lake Erie.

6. Cronk, "Learning to Listen," *Festival Quarterly*, Winter 1987, p. 8.

7. For a good explanation of the genre of Quaker journals, see Howard Brinton, *Quaker Journals: Varieties of Religious Experience among Friends* (Walingford, Pa.: Pendle Hill, 1972).

8. Journal, p. 13.

9. Sandra Cronk, "Why I am Interested in Teaching at Pendle Hill," essay accompanying her application for a position on the staff, 1978.

10. Cronk, "Why I am Interested in Teaching at Pendle Hill," essay applying for a teaching position at Pendle Hill.

11. Early Friends eschewed pagan names for the days of the week, preferring to simply number them. First Day School is Sunday School.

12. The clerk of a Friends' meeting or committee is approximately equivalent to a presiding officer, although the connotation of the service required is somewhat different from the hierarchical executive sometimes assumed by the title "president." The clerk (or co-clerk if two Friends are sharing the job) brings the agenda, and introduces the various items of business, but is expected to be sensitive in discerning the sense of the group and to help guide it into unity.

13. Journal, 7-5-1975, p. 20.

14. Cronk, *Dark Night Journey*, 78.

15. Mennonite Phyllis Pelham Goodman, at Goodbooks, Inc., formerly involved with publishing the *Festival Quarterly*, explained "'Plain people' is most accurately used to describe what we refer to as 'Old Order' groups who do, in fact, dress plain. That would encompass the Amish, Old Order Mennonites, and Hutterites. There are several other Old Order groups such as the River Brethren (linked historically to the Brethren in Christ) and a group that is related historically to the Church of the Brethren (whose name escapes me right now). Today, Schwenkfelders, Moravians, and Shakers would not usually fall within the 'plain people' grouping." E mail, 4m/9/2007. Sonnie was interested in all these groups.

16. Sonnie's Course Description for "The Plain People," spring term, 1979.

17. The Amish response to the massacre of their school girls on October 2, 2006 exemplifies what Sonnie saw in their faith, lived out in all they did.

18. From an outline Sonnie drafted of the course she would like to offer on Religious Community. I don't know how closely the actual course

followed this early outline, but it illustrates the way she thought about the topic.

19. Attributed to David Kline, an Amish bishop in Ohio.
20. As quoted by Roger Dreisbach-Williams at Sonnie's memorial service at Princeton Meeting.
21. Sandra Cronk, "Why I am Interested in Teaching at Pendle Hill."
22. For discussion of Friends' unfortunate habit of criticizing and undermining those in leadership positions, see, for example, Paul Lacey, *On Leading and Being Led,* and *Friends and the Use of Power*; and Grundy, *Tall Poppies.* (These are all published by Pendle Hill, Wallingford, Penna.) This behavior may not be unique to Quakers.
23. PhD in History of Religions from Divinity School, University of Chicago; dissertation title: "Gelassenheit: The Rites of the Redemptive Process in the Old Order Amish and Old Order Mennonite Communities."
24. Cronk, "Why I am Interested in Teaching at Pendle Hill."
25. Cronk, "Why I am Interested in Teaching at Pendle Hill."
26. Cronk, "Renewal Among Unprogrammed Friends in America," 164.
27. According to a Mennonite web page, the Keystone Bible Institute of the Lancaster Mennonite Conference held adult studies courses at various locations during the winter months in the 1980s.
28. Cronk, *Peace Be With You: Spiritual Basis of the Friends Peace Testimony* (Philadelphia: Tract Association of Friends, n.d.), 14.
29. Cronk, *Peace Be With You,* 3.
30. Cronk, *Peace Be With You,* 3.
31. Cronk, *Peace Be With You,* 16.
32. Cronk, *Peace Be With You,* 17.
33. Cronk, *Peace Be With You,* 16.
34. Connie McPeak Green.
35. Journal, p. 74.
36. Sonnie seemed to use both terms to describe those she companioned. Both words seem to deliberately avoid the vocabulary of spiritual direction/guidance with which Sonnie was later to feel more comfortable.
37. Letter from Sally Palmer to Margaret Cronk, April 14, 2000.
38. William Moreman, in his review in *Weavings* (July/August 1992), of Sonnie's later book, *Dark Night Journey: Inward Re-Patterning Toward a Life Centered in God.*
39. Cronk, *Dark Night Journey,* p. 10.
40. Peter Ivory, in the Woodbrooke logbook, 1985.

41. Annette Wallis, in the Woodbrooke logbook, 1985.

42. Cronk, "Renewal among Unprogrammed Friends in America," p. 163.

43. Cronk, "Renewal among Unprogrammed Friends in America," p. 170.

44. Letter to M. Grundy, 8/22/1997.

45. Editor's note, *Festival Quarterly*, Winter 1988, p. 14. *Festival Quarterly* was a Mennonite magazine of arts, literature, and theology for a general audience, published from 1972 to 1996.

46. Her article on "ordnung" is in the Global Anabaptist Mennonite Encyclopedia Online at http://www.gameo.org/index.asp?content= http://www.gameo.org/encyclopedia/contents/T39ME.html

47. Letter from Sonnie to Ronald T. Pinheiro, 9m/11/1989.

48. Letter from Sonnie to Ron Pinheiro, 9m/11/1989.

49. For an example of her impact on others, see Alfred C. Krass, "Sandra Cronk as a Spiritual Guide," *Friends Journal*, Vol. 46, no. 10 (Oct. 2000), 18–21.

50. Letter from Sonnie to Larry J. Peacock, Methodist minister who had been a Pendle Hill student the year before, and his wife Anne, dated 12/26/1985. Used with permission.

51. Moreman, in his review in *Weavings* of Sonnie's book, *Dark Night Journey*.

52. Kathryn Damiano's undated draft proposal.

53. See Charlotte Lyman Fardelmann, *Nudged by the Spirit* (Wallingford, Penna.: Pendle Hill Publications, 2001), for a description of the Lyman Fund, and for Kathryn's funding, 66–67ff.

54. Open letter to Kathryn Damiano, 2/15/1999.

55. Kathryn's label for a year of stress, wrangling, and disarray within the SOTS board and of tension among the core teachers.

56. Letter from Sonnie to the Board, 2/15/1999; emphases in the original.

57. Letter from Sonnie to Sr. Kathleen, dated Sept. 9, 1999, used with permission.

58. E mail from Linda Chidsey, April 29, 2006.

59. Letter to Sonnie from Allison Randall, dated April 3, 2000.

60. The "Middle Way" founded by Kaspar Schwenckfeld (1489–1561) in Silesia, sought loving community rather than arguments over external symbols. Both Catholics and Lutherans proclaimed him a heretic, and he spent much of his life in hiding. Some 200 followers eventually migrated to Pennsylvania in the 1720s.

61. The Amish were followers of Jacob Ammann, a late 17th c. Swiss Mennonite bishop who insisted on a strict literalism in interpreting their confession of faith. Like the Mennonites in general, they stress the importance of community and oppose hierarchy.

62. With roots in the teaching and practice of Jan Hus (d. 1415) in Bohemia, the Moravians stress a simple life of community, where Christian living is the hallmark of their faith. Cruelly persecuted, in 1722 a remnant was invited to live in Saxony on the land of Count Zinzendorf, who joined their community. An extraordinary unifying transformation in 1727 revived the group with evangelical fervor—not to convert people to the Moravian Church as much as to stir up their devotion to Christ as Savior. In the 1740s Moravians settled several communities in Pennsylvania.

63. This date appears to be incorrect; perhaps she meant 10-1-1977?

64. This might perhaps be more correctly dated 10-2-1977?

65. Job Scott (1751–93) was a quietist Friend who traveled widely in the ministry.

66. Dyck Vermilye was Dean at Pendle Hill.

67. We have been unable to discover what book on vocations Sonnie was reading.

68. Sonnie may be referring to the withering of schools for free slaves in the south, started and supported initially by Friends, but when other interests came along and racism became more overt, the effort waned.

69. "Oversight" is a traditional Quaker term for corporate care for an individual or project that calls forth accountability on the part of that which is being overseen.

70. Letter to Sonnie from Kathryn Nowina, April 3, 2000, and used with permission.

71. More information about the apocalyptic experience of early Friends can be found in Douglas Gwyn's book *The Apocalypse of the Word: The Life and Message of George Fox (1624–1691)*, Richmond, Indiana: Friends United Meeting Press, 1986.

Publications by Sandra Lee Cronk

Books and Monographs

These are all still in print and can be ordered from QuakerBooks, 1-800-966-4556.

Dark Night Journey: Inward Re-Patterning Toward a Life Centered in God. Wallingford, PA: Pendle Hill Publications, 1991.

Gospel Order: A Quaker Understanding of Faithful Church Community. Pendle Hill Pamphlet #297, Wallingford, PA: Pendle Hill Publications, 1991.

Peace Be With You: Spiritual Basis of the Friends Peace Testimony. Philadelphia: Friends Tract Association, 1983.

Articles and Papers

"Spiritual Nurture Ministry Among Friends," *Quakers in Pastoral Care and Counseling, 1993 Conference Report: "Spiritual Integrity."* Richmond Indiana: Earlham School of Religion, 1993.

"Ordnung," entry in *Mennonite Encyclopedia*, Vol. V, Scottdale, PA: Herald Press, 1990. [Volume V includes updates on materials in the first four volumes plus nearly 1,000 new articles.]

Festival Quarterly [Mennonite arts, literature, and theology for a general audience. Illustrated. Published quarterly from 1972 to 1996. Address: 3513 Old Philadelphia Pike, Intercourse, PA, 17534]. Five-part series:

"Finding a Usable Past" (Fall 1989)
"Discovering and Nurturing Ministers" (Winter/Spring 1989)
"Substituting Activities for Community?" (Summer 1988)
"Learning to Listen," part 2 (Winter 1988)
"Learning to Listen" (Winter 1987)

"Work in Anabaptist/Mennonite Thought and Experience." Distributed by the Mennonite Central Committee, Canada, as part of the collection of papers from their Colloquium Work, held at the Mennonite Brethren Bible College, Winnipeg, Manitoba, June 1988. Reprinted in *Old Order Notes* (May, 1988).

"Renewal Among Unprogrammed Friends in America," *Friends Quarterly* 24:4 (October 1986). [Succeeds the *Friends' Examiner* (1867–1946), published 1947 to date in Great Britain, now by Headley Brothers Ltd., Ashford, Kent.]

"Comments," forming part of the Quaker Theological Discussion Group cluster of papers on atonement, *Quaker Religious Thought* (Spring 1986). [Published 1959 to present. Sponsored by the Quaker Theological Discussion Group.]

"Gelassenheit: The Rites of the Redemptive Process in Old Order Amish and Old Order Mennonite Communities," *Mennonite Quarterly Review* (January 1981): 5–44.

"Old Order Amish and Old Order Mennonites: Loving Community Based on the Power of Powerlessness," *Quaker Witness* (Spring 1977): 3–6. Reprinted in *Old Order Notes* No. 4 (Spring 1981): 9–15.

Book Reviews

"The Mennonite Encyclopedia V: A Record of Paradigm Shifts" (a review), in *Mennonite Historical Bulletin* LII: 3 (July 1991): 1–4.

Review of *Elizabeth Fry: A Biography*. By June Rose. In *Quaker History* (Fall 1983).

About the Editor

Martha Paxson Grundy is a prolific Quaker author. Her writings include *Resistance and Obedience to God: Memoirs of David Ferris (1709-1779)*; *The Evolution of a Quaker Community: Middletown Meeting, Bucks County, Pennsylvania, 1750-1850*; *Tall Poppies: Supporting Gifts of Ministry and Eldering in the Monthly Meeting*, and contributions to numerous Quaker publications. She received her PhD in American history at Case Western Reserve University. Marty is a member and has served as clerk of Cleveland Monthly Meeting, Lake Erie Yearly Meeting, and FGC's Traveling Ministries Committee. She has participated in national and international Quaker organizations.